PLANNING, POLITICS AND CITY MAKING: A CASE STUDY OF KING'S CROSS

BY PETER BISHOP AND LESLEY WILLIAMS

RIBA Publishing

© RIBA Enterprises 2016

Published by RIBA Publishing, 66 Portland Place, London, W1B 1AD

ISBN 978-1-85946-635-3

The rights of Peter Bishop and Lesley Williams to be identified as the Authors of this Work have been asserted in accordance with the Copyright, Designs and Patents Act 1988 sections 77 and 78.

All rights reserved. No part of this publication may be reproduced, stored in a retrieval system, or transmitted, in any form or by any means, electronic, mechanical, photocopying, recording or otherwise, without prior permission of the copyright owner.

British Library Cataloguing-in-Publication Data
A catalogue record for this book is available from the British Library.

Commissioning Editor: Fay Gibbons
Project Manager: Michèle Woodger
Copy editor: Sally Mavin
Designed by Richard Krzyzak
Printed and bound by CPI Anthony Rowe
Cover image: CGI Showing Granary Square, Anderson-Terzic Partnership

While every effort has been made to check the accuracy and quality of the information given in this publication, neither the Author nor the Publisher accept any responsibility for the subsequent use of this information, for any errors or omissions that it may contain, or for any misunderstandings arising from it.

www.ribaenterprises.com

ABOUT THE AUTHORS

Peter Bishop

Peter trained in town planning at The University of Manchester and has spent his entire career working in London. Over the past 25 years he has been a planning director in four different Central London boroughs and has worked on major projects including Canary Wharf and the development of the BBC's campus at White City. Between 2001 and 2006 he was director of environment at the London Borough of Camden, where he was responsible for the negotiations with Argent on the King's Cross development.

In 2007 he was appointed as the first director of Design for London, the Mayor of London's architecture and design studio. He is currently professor of urban design at the Bartlett School of Architecture at University College London and a director at Allies and Morrison. He is a visiting professor at the School of Architecture, Design and the Built Environment at Nottingham Trent University, and an honorary fellow of both University College London and the Royal Institute of British Architects (RIBA).

Lesley Williams

Lesley trained in environmental sciences and later in town planning at the Bartlett School of Architecture. She has worked for the Civic Trust, CAG Consultants and the Environment Trust. For the past 15 years, as a freelance consultant, she has specialised in the design and facilitation of stakeholder involvement processes, consensus building and partnership development. She currently works as a writer and sculptor.

The authors' previous book, The Temporary City, explored the drivers behind pop-ups and urban strategies for temporary uses and was published by Routledge in 2012.

ACKNOWLEDGEMENTS AND LIST OF INTERVIEWEES

We would like to thank our interviewees for their time, insights and contributions. Job titles were correct for 2000–06 unless otherwise stated.

Argent
Roger Madelin CBE – chief executive officer
David Partridge – deputy chief executive officer
Robert Evans – director of planning
André Gibbs – senior project officer
Peter Freeman – non-executive director
Anne Hughes – King's Cross Recruit, centre director (current)
Anna Strongman – senior projects director (current)

Camden
Bob West – head of King's Cross team
Richard Kirby – principal planning case officer, King's Cross team
David Reidy – London Borough of Camden sites team manager (current)
Frances Wheat – principal planner, development control (current)
Asha Paul – head of committee services
Cllr (Dame) Jane Roberts – leader of Camden council (to 2005)
Cllr Heather Johnson – chair of development control subcommittee (2005–06)
Cllr John Thane – executive member for environment
Cllr Theo Blackwell – executive member for regeneration
Cllr Jake Sumner – member, development control subcommittee
Cllr Sue Vincent – vice chair, development control subcommittee
Cllr Mike Greene – executive member for environment (2006–10)
Cllr Raj Chada – leader of Camden council (2005–06)
Janet Sutherland – principal housing officer
Alison Lowton – borough solicitor

London and Continental Railways
Stephen Jordan – managing director
David Joy – chief executive (current)
Roger Mann – director of property Hyperion/Exel

Consultants
Dr Demetri Porphyrios – architect and masterplanner, Porphyrios Associates
Bob Allies OBE – architect and masterplanner, Allies and Morrison
Graham Morrison OBE – architect and masterplanner, Allies and Morrison
Robert Gordon Clark – executive chairman, London Communications Agency
John McAslan CBE – partner, John McAslan + Partners
Robert Townshend – principal, Townshend Landscape Architects

Other participants
Paddy Pugh – principal officer, English Heritage
Michael Edwards – King's Cross Railway Lands Group
Colin Wilson – senior planner, Greater London Authority
David Lunts – executive director, Homes and Community Agency
Michael Hurn CBE – senior civil servant, Department for Communities and Local Government
Steve Hitchins – leader, Islington council

Sir Stuart Lipton – chief executive officer, Rosehaugh Stanhope Developments
Camilla Ween – senior transport planner, Transport for London

Contributors to Chapter 2
Peter Rees – professor of Places & City Planning in the Bartlett Faculty of the Built Environment
Pat Hayes – director of environment and planning, London Borough of Ealing
Rosemarie Macqueen MBE – strategic director of built environment, City of Westminster (2007–14)
Sir Stuart Lipton – developer, Lipton Rogers Developments (previously Rosehaugh Stanhope and Chelsfield)
Alan Leibowitz – joint managing director, Dorrington Properties
Adrian Penfold OBE – head of planning, British Land
Cllr Daniel Moylan – Conservative councillor at Royal Borough of Kensington and Chelsea
Lorraine Hart – director, Community Land Use
Sir Robin Wales – leader (1995–2002) and Mayor of London Borough of Newham since 2002
Dominic Ellison – chief executive officer, Hackney Co-operative Developments CIC

Particular thanks are due to Argent's Roger Madelin for the huge amount of time he spent helping to piece the story together, and for his generosity and openness. Also to Robert Evans for his total recall of events. We are grateful to Argent for accepting the objectivity of this book and for the immense trust and openness it has shown over its contents.

We would also like to thank Demetri Porphyrios, Bob Allies and Graham Morrison for their insights. Bob Allies and Graham Morrison also provided generous support in helping us assemble and redraw images for the book. Thanks, too, to John Sturrock for his generosity in allowing us to use his photographs, and Alex Ford (Allies and Morrison) and Isaac Amin (Argent) for their considerable help with the images.

Our reviewers, through RIBA Publishing, Duncan Bowie (University of Westminster), Colin Haylock (Haylock Planning and Design) and Peter James Heath (Atkins Masterplanning) provided invaluable insights on an early draft of this book.

Peter Bishop and Lesley Williams

CONTENTS

Kings Cross transport infrastructure timeline	**viii**
Political and planning timeline	**x**

1	**Introduction**	**1**
2	**The planning and development process**	**7**
	The UK planning system	9
	The role of planners	11
	The role of politicians	12
	The development sector	14
	Community involvement and the mistrust of planning	15
3	**History and development context**	**17**
	The history of the King's Cross area	18
	First regeneration proposals	26
	The King's Cross partnership	31
	Rail infrastructure	33
	Completing the site assembly	38
	Selecting a development partner	39
	Conclusions	41
4	**Establishing the framework for negotiations**	**43**
	Camden: the place and its politics	44
	Engaging councillors	47
	Preparing for the negotiations	50
	The negotiating teams	51
	The negotiating process	52
	Negotiating tactics	56
	Establishing the policy framework	63
	Deciding the nature of the planning application	65
	The bottom line	67
	Conclusions	69
5	**The masterplan**	**71**
	The role of the masterplan	72
	The masterplanning team	73
	Site context	74
	Early discussions	76
	The first masterplan	77
	Developing the masterplan	81
	Refinement of the masterplan	86
	Linking the plan to the wider area	94
	Conclusions	101

6	**The middle game**	**105**
	The break-up of Argent's partnership with St George	106
	Housing	107
	Management of the public realm	115
	Environmental performance	117
	Transport	119
	Other planning benefits	123
	Calculating the value of the section 106 agreement	127
	Reflections on the negotiation process	129
	Conclusions	131
7	**Community consultation**	**133**
	Pre-application consultations	134
	Consultations on the original planning applications	139
	Consultations on the revised planning applications	140
	King's Cross Railway Lands Group	143
	Conclusions	149
8	**The decision**	**151**
	Camden's officer-councillor interface	152
	The development control subcommittee	154
	The decision	160
	Rebuilding political support	164
	The judicial review	165
	Islington's decision on the 'Triangle' site	166
	Conclusions	167
9	**Building King's Cross Central**	**169**
	The land valuation and transfer	170
	The first phases of development	173
	Variations to the planning consent	176
	Adoption of the public realm	177
	Place-making at King's Cross Central	177
	Employment and training	182
	North Central One	183
	The new King's Cross station square	185
	Impact on the surrounding areas	187
	Conclusions	188
10	**Conclusions**	**189**
	Evaluating the success of the King's Cross Development	190
	Lessons from the King's Cross Development	193
	Implications of recent changes to planning and funding regimes	200
	Postscript	202
11	**Appendices**	**203**
	Appendix 1: Summary of the section 106 agreement	204
	Appendix 2: Development data and financial information	206
	Notes	**209**
	List of acronyms	**220**
	Index	**221**
	Image credits	**226**

KING'S CROSS CENTRAL AND ASSOCIATED TRANSPORT INFRASTRUCTURE

TRANSPORT INFRASTRUCTURE		PLANNING PROCESS
Privatisation of British Rail, but King's Cross lands retained by government	1993	
CTRL Act confirms St Pancras as Eurostar terminus LCR appointed as CTRL developers and operators	1996	Establishment of King's Cross Partnership (KXP) under SRB
	2000	Argent St George appointed as developer
Works start on King's Cross St Pancras underground interchange	March 2000	Camden Unitary Development Plan (UDP) adopted, identifying the area for redevelopment
	July 2001	Argent St George publishes Principles for a Human City
	October 2001	Camden publish King's Cross: Towards and Integrated City including key objectives. This is endorsed by the Leader of Islington Council
	December 2001	Camden publishes for consultation, a deposit draft of a revision to Chapter 13 of the UDP Argent St George publish Parameters for Regeneration identifying 18 parameters for regeneration
	June 2002	Draft London Plan published, identifying King's Cross as an 'Opportunity Area' and recognising the importance of its development for London as a 'Global City' Camden publishes King's Cross – Camden's Vision
	July 2002	Inspector endorses Camden's UDP Chapter 13
	Sept 2002	Argent St George publish for consultation A Framework for Regeneration
LCR ask government for additional £1 billion for CTRL	May 2003	Camden's UDP Chapter 13 adopted
	June 2003	Argent St George publish Framework Findings, an analysis of responses to the consultations
	December 2003	Joint Camden and Islington Planning and Development Brief for King's Cross published
Government funds for fit-out of underground concourse for Thameslink frozen	February 2004	London Plan adopted
	May 2004	Argent St George submit three planning applications and eight heritage applications for the site Camden publishes revised deposit draft of UDP
	November 2004	Argent buys out St George's interest
London wins bid for 2012 Olympics at Stratford. Works recommence on underground infrastructure	June 2005	
	September 2005	Argent submits three revised planning applications

	March 2006	Camden resolves to grant planning permission
	November 2006	Section 106 agreement approved by Camden
	December 2006	Camden signs section 106 agreement and issues consents
	February 2007	KXRLG apply for judicial review
	May 2007	Judicial review hearing. Dismissed
	June 2007	Enabling works commence on site
	July 2007	Islington refuse planning permission for the 'Triangle' site
CTRL terminus at St Pancras opened	November 2007	
	July 2008	Argent's appeal against Islington's refusal of planning permission upheld by secretary of state
	October 2008	'Credit Crunch' in full swing; nevertheless, University of the Arts London (UAL) succeeds in borrowing funds to complete King's Cross deal
New platforms for the domestic rail services from Kent King's Cross St Pancras underground interchange completed	2009	
	2010	Property market recovery starts
	September 2011	Boulevard opens
St Pancras Hotel reopened	October 2011	UAL opens
King's Cross station concourse opened	July 2012	Granary Square completed First affordable housing completed Caravan opened in The Granary
	2013	Great Northern Hotel opens
	January 2013	Google buy long lease on site on Boulevard
	November 2013	First office building complete at One Pancras Square
Completion of new underground concourse for King's Cross station Completion of new public square in front of King's Cross station	2014	Construction of final office building on Pancras Square begins
	Summer 2014	Camden's new offices at King's Cross complete
	2015	Lewis Cubitt Park opened

POLITICAL AND PLANNING TIMELINE

		2000	2001	2002	2003
Political events	GLA	GLA created (May 2000); Ken Livingstone mayor (Independent)			
	Islington	Labour	Liberal Democrat		
	Camden	Labour; Leader: Jane Roberts (2000–03) / Raj Chadah (May 2004–06); Executive Leader (Environment): John Thane (May 2000–06)			

		2000	2001	2002	2003
Planning events	Infrastructure			Construction commences on CTRL stage 2	
	Planning applications	Argent appointed	Draft UDP consultation	UDP inquiry	UDP approved
	Key documents	Principles For A Human City	Camden Objectives towards an Integrated City; Argent publishes parameters	Camden King's Cross Vision	Framework For Regeneration
	Negotiations	First formal meeting; Visit to Brindley Place; Camden agrees budget for negotiations	First meeting with mayor Ken Livingstone	Camden and Islington leaders agree to cooperate	Camden executives agree objectives

Key
Camden document
Argent document

	2004	2005	2006	2007	2008	2009
	Ken Livingstone mayor (Labour)				Boris Johnson (Conservative) (May 2008–16)	
			Lib Dem / Conservative coalition Leader: Keith Moffat (2006–10) Executive Leader (Environment): Mike Greene (Conservative) (May 2006–10)			

2004	2005	2006	2007	2008	2009
Suspension of government funding on interchanges	Funding restored		St Pancras opens for Eurostar Trains	Thameslink station reopens	
First planning application (May); Argent and St George split; London Plan approved	Revised planning application (September)	Planning approved	Section 106 approved; Judicial review; Islington refuses 'Triangle' application	Work starts on Phase 1 of King's Cross development	
Draft Camden planning brief	Draft Camden planning brief; Joint Camden Islington brief; Application				
English Heritage raises no objections	Camden Town appeal; CTRL appeal	GLA / mayor raise no objections (February); Rebriefing of new council			

1. INTRODUCTION

Physicists have calculated that dark energy and dark matter constitute 95.1 per cent of the known Universe.[1] They cannot be observed, but their existence can be deduced through their effect on the 4.9 per cent of the Universe that we can see and measure.[2] There is a striking analogy here with the cities and places that we inhabit. They are physical and material; we can see them, use them, walk through and live in them. We can debate their qualities and theorise about them. We can deduce that they came into existence through, and are held in place by, other forces. However, these forces are usually invisible and are very difficult to measure. The dark energy that lies beneath the surface of our cities, creating, adapting, destroying and renewing them, is in the broadest sense, politics; the individuals, communities and organisations that work together (or against each other) to shape the places in which we live and work. This book aims to explore this world and to throw some light on the unseen forces that drive urban change, through a detailed analysis of the way in which one development – King's Cross – was achieved.

The King's Cross scheme is one of the largest and most complex developments taking place in Britain today. It covers 27 hectares of land to the rear of King's Cross station at the northern edge of Central London (Figure 1.1), and is being developed by the King's Cross Central Limited Partnership (KCCP). The planning negotiations, which started in 2000 and took six years, were probably some of the most exhaustive debates ever over a development. During this period, over 30,000 people were consulted by Camden council and Argent. A report of over 600 pages of technical information was eventually presented to a committee at Camden council. After two evenings and 10 hours of presentations and debate, the committee approved the scheme by just two votes.

There is extensive architectural and planning literature analysing the design and function of new buildings and places. However, the process through which development proposals are actually fashioned is largely undocumented and poorly understood outside a small professional and technical cohort. This complex negotiation and deal-making often involves many different stakeholders with different agendas. Conventional planning theory tends to assume a logical, rational and linear decision-making process. This bears little relationship to reality. This book aims to shed some light on that reality. It offers an insight into a little understood but much maligned process that shapes the cities in which we live. It is not a book on the dry process of planning procedures and policy. It focuses on how the city is contested, how commercial negotiations are carried out,

> **The planning negotiations, which started in 2000 and took six years, were probably some of the most exhaustive debates ever over a development.**

1: INTRODUCTION

Figure 1.1: King's Cross location.

- Cultural buildings
- Green spaces
- Stations
- Railway

and how deals are made. King's Cross is now attracting considerable attention both in the UK and internationally, and there is interest in how to replicate its successes.

Many individuals have contributed to this book and some of the key players have generously opened up their files and records so that different perspectives on the negotiations could be examined. The authors were given access to information on the negotiation strategies, financial calculations and bottom line assessments of the council and the developer. This allowed us to explore, in retrospect, what each side believed the opposing parties were doing and how they adjusted their strategies accordingly. It is very unusual for this to happen and we would like to record our thanks to all the individuals and organisations concerned (a full list of acknowledgements is given on p.v). The King's Cross development was a colossal project, and a team effort undertaken by many individuals. Consequently, we only refer to individuals by name where they are quoted directly, or where their involvement was personal and distinct from that of their organisations.

Writing the book has presented a number of challenges. It is based on interviews with 40 individuals and they have approved their separate contributions. As far as possible we have also tried to verify these through paper records and personal diaries. Despite every attempt to check for accuracy, in view of the complexity of the process and the number of different perspectives represented, errors may remain, for which we take full responsibility and apologise. As is inevitable with events that took place over a decade ago, memories fade and there were also differences in the way in which the parties involved recalled and interpreted the events. Where this has occurred we have endeavoured to provide a perspective by setting out the different views.

The book was also written with the benefit of both hindsight and a wider perspective than was available at the time. Negotiations are, by their nature, complicated and often muddled. It is quite normal for parties to take different interpretations of events away from the same meeting. As in any set of events, it is common for relatively trivial events to dominate attention or derail a process. Consequently, the issues may appear clearer now than was apparent at the time. This book does not pretend to provide a comprehensive assessment of all the arguments put forward by all the stakeholders at different junctures. We have, however, sought to identify and analyse the key issues.

Development on this scale is always contentious. There was opposition to the scheme from some in the surrounding communities, which found focus through the King's Cross Railway Lands Group (KXRLG). Theirs was an

> **Negotiations are, by their nature, complicated and often muddled. It is quite normal for parties to take different interpretations of events away from the same meeting.**

1: INTRODUCTION

important voice in the debate. Unfortunately, some of the prominent members of this group were not willing to be interviewed for this book, but we would like to thank Michael Edwards for providing us with background information on the campaign and its objectives.

While we have sought to present a balanced and objective view on the King's Cross development, it must be stated clearly that Peter Bishop, one of the authors, was director of environment at Camden council and a key protagonist in negotiations from 2000 to 2006. Some bias is therefore unavoidable. Where possible, his co-author sought to challenge his account of events, but as she had no involvement in the project, assessing objectivity was not always straightforward. Peter Bishop's involvement in the project ceased when he left Camden council at the end of 2006, and Chapter 8, on events since the granting of planning approval, is based entirely on interviews.

The scope and structure of the book also presented challenges. The development of King's Cross was dependent upon a number of key rail infrastructure projects. While we wanted to avoid excessive detail on these, it was necessary to provide sufficient background to place the development of the railway lands in context, particularly where these projects impacted on the scheme. Similarly, it has been necessary to provide sufficient background on the UK planning system to enable those unfamiliar with it to follow the narrative, but without disturbing the flow or inducing sleep. Where possible, such background is provided as boxed text, which the informed reader can avoid. The majority of events in the book took place between 2000, when Argent was appointed as the King's Cross developer, and the end of 2006 when planning permission was granted for the scheme. However, the negotiations are more easily understood with some knowledge of the history of the site, the area and Camden council, the local authority. We cover those aspects of history that had a significant bearing on development proposals, those which set the context for Camden council's planning and social inclusion policies at the time, and those which influenced the attitudes and beliefs of the key councillors who would make the decision on the planning application.

As far as possible, we have structured the book chronologically, but there are exceptions to this. Although the evolution of the physical masterplan and the consultation processes with local communities took place throughout the period of negotiation, both justified separate treatment in order to provide clear analysis and evaluation. To clarify this complex process, we have provided timelines at the beginning of this book.

It is too early to judge the success of the King's Cross development, which is still under construction at the time of writing. Future generations will do this in due course.

**Peter Bishop and Lesley Williams,
January 2016**

2. THE PLANNING AND DEVELOPMENT PROCESS

Planning may proclaim to be a technical process, but in practice this is rarely the case. The British planning system is based on a set of broad policy frameworks within which development consents are negotiated. It involves people and powerful interest groups with different agendas and tends in reality to be subjective, unstructured and intuitive. But sometimes it can find bespoke solutions that are considerably better than rigidly applied zoning codes or land use allocation plans.

It is a common misconception that new urban areas owe their existence to individual agents, whether the planner, the architect or the developer. In a democracy, power is diffused between multiple stakeholders – landowners, government bodies, politicians, technical experts, community and interest groups, individuals and development companies. Planners, architects and their clients have to be able to navigate this complexity, and if possible, broker agreements. Figure 2.1 was produced by Design for London[1] to illustrate the number of different stakeholders that might be involved in the design and construction of one piece of new open space in London. It is not meant to be easy to understand. It is complex, but occasionally if one can find a path through this complexity, put the right people together and understand how different agendas can be reconciled, change can happen. And sometimes this can be beneficial.

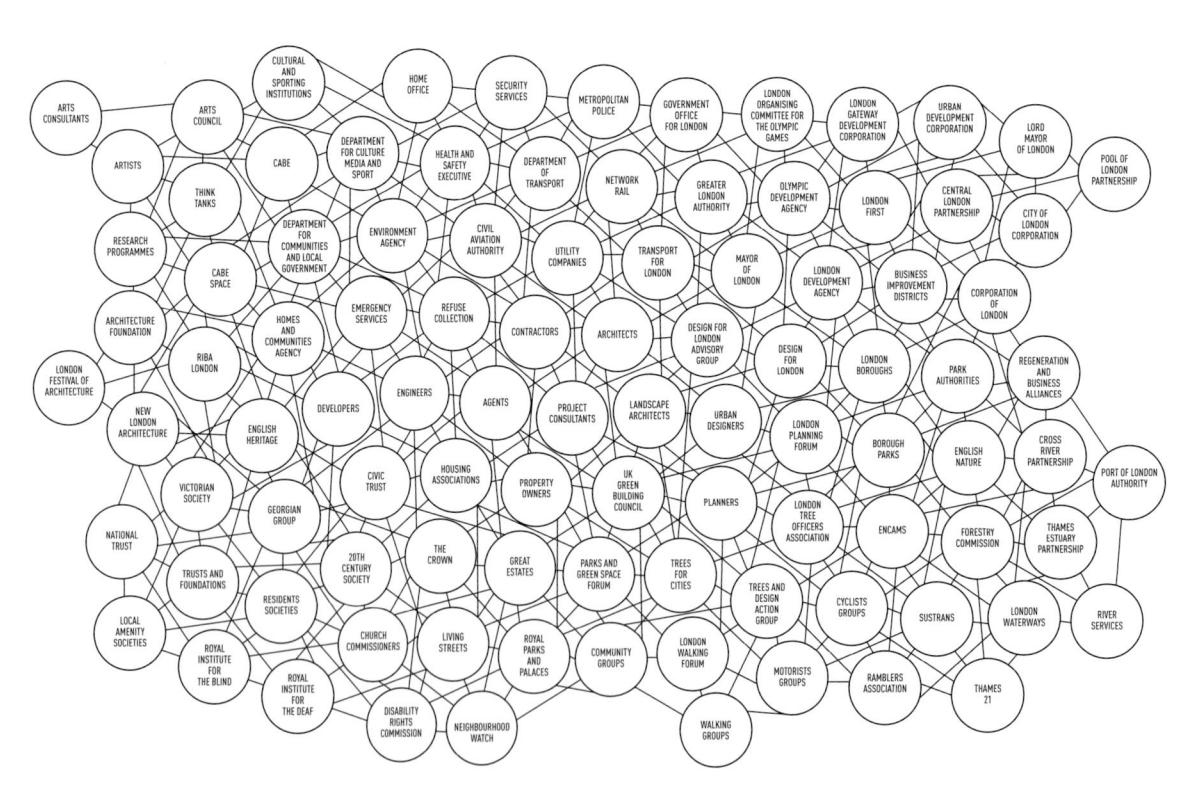

Figure 2.1: The complex stakeholder networks involved in the design of one open space in London.

Planning is not just about control and regulation; it is about brokering agreements and making deals.

THE UK PLANNING SYSTEM

The criteria for deciding whether or not to give consent to a development proposal are pretty clear. Broadly, there are two questions that need to be addressed. First, does it comply with the policies set out in the approved local plan (the Local Development Framework) and second, would it harm the character and amenity of its immediate neighbourhood or the wider area? Subject to these two basic questions, there is a presumption in planning law that planning consent should be granted unless there are clear grounds to the contrary. Although economic viability will almost certainly be raised in the course of negotiations, the question of whether the developer is going to make a large profit should not come into the question.

While the criteria for determining a planning application may seem straightforward, their interpretation and application are not. The British planning system is long established, much reformed and, because consent can bestow a huge increase to the value of the land, is highly contested (for a brief summary of the English planning system, see textbox on pp.10-11). The system dates from the 1940s[2] as a response to the economic conditions in the immediate aftermath of the war. It was designed to manage competing social and economic needs within a small, congested, but essentially pluralistic island. Effectively, the Planning Act removed – basically nationalised – many of the rights of the landowner concerning how they might use and develop their land. The process of consenting development, and therefore restoring development rights back to the landowner, was vested in elected politicians and planning professionals. These decision-making powers are constrained by the law. Decisions have to be reasonable and based on an agreed plan that itself has been subject to public scrutiny.

The system's fundamental purpose is to manage competing social, economic and environmental interests. This puts planning into an inherently political arena. Under the British planning system, notwithstanding what is said in a statutory plan, each application has to be considered on its own merits, in other words, negotiated. This is different from many other planning systems in the world where planning and land use zoning can be quite specific. It can produce very good bespoke developments when it works, and delays and frustrations when it does not. The safeguard in the system is the right of a developer to appeal to an independent inspectorate. In significant schemes this will result in a public inquiry where all aspects can be considered, often with protagonists represented by expert witnesses and senior lawyers. While recognising the value that such public scrutiny can bring, the quasi-judicial

> **The British planning system is long established, much reformed and, because consent can bestow a huge increase to the value of the land, is highly contested.**

THE ENGLISH PLANNING SYSTEM[3]

National government
Secretary of state for communities and local government: The secretary of state (SoS) oversees the planning system and sets national legislation and planning policy. The SoS also oversees the appeals process and occasionally 'calls in' major applications for public inquiry (see textbox on planning appeals, p.57). The National Planning Policy Framework (March 2012) consolidated all previous policy documents, guidance and circulars, and provides national planning policies for England covering the economic, social and environmental aspects of development. Prior to this, government policy was set out in thematic planning policy documents and guidance notes. These policies must be taken into account in preparing local plans and are a 'material consideration' in deciding planning applications.

Regional government
The mayor and Greater London Authority: In London, the mayor is responsible for producing a strategic plan for the capital (the London Plan). Local plans in London need to be in 'general conformity' with the London Plan, which guides decisions on planning applications by London borough councils and the mayor. The mayor is consulted on major developments and has powers to direct refusal.[4]

Local government
The London boroughs are responsible for most planning matters – preparing local plans, and determining planning applications. They are known as the Local Planning Authority (LPA).

- Elected councillors: In London, councillors are elected locally every four years. The controlling party is that with the most elected councillors. They set council policy and make most key decisions. Some councillors will sit on the planning or development control committee (which makes decisions on planning applications). All councillors have a role to play in representing the views and aspirations of residents in plan-making and when planning applications affecting their ward are considered.

- Officers: Local planning authorities appoint planning officers to assist with the operation of the planning system. Most minor and uncontroversial planning applications (around 90 per cent) are decided through delegated decision-taking powers to officers. Larger and more controversial developments are decided by a development control subcommittee, guided by officers' recommendations.

- Local plans: Any planning application must be determined in line with the development plan (the LDF and the London Plan). Local plans set out a policy framework for the future development of the area, engaging with their communities in doing so. They address needs and opportunities in relation to housing, the local economy, community facilities and infrastructure. The local plan is examined by an independent inspector whose role is to assess whether the plan has been prepared in line with the relevant legal requirements.[5] Most local plans are effectively policy documents with accompanying illustrative maps.

- Planning permission: Once the local planning authority has received a planning application, it will publicise the proposal so that people have a chance to express their views. The formal consultation period is normally 21 days. Comments will be taken into account, which are relevant to the proposal and 'material' to planning. 'Material' considerations, in broad terms should relate to the use and development of land. Each application is considered on its merits. A local planning authority has up to 13 weeks to consider major development, such as

- Community benefits through planning obligations: Most development has an impact on infrastructure, such as roads, schools and open spaces. It is accepted that developments should contribute towards the mitigation of its impact through a charge based on the size and type of proposal. At the time of the King's Cross development, planning obligations were secured under section 106 of the Town and Country Planning Act 1990 (as amended). A developer may be required to enter into an obligation to, for example, provide affordable housing or provide additional funding for services. Any planning obligation must be directly related to the development and be fair and reasonable (see textbox, below, on CIL and section 106 agreements).

large housing or business sites, although an extension of time may be agreed between the developer and the LPA.

nature of the proceedings has pushed local planning into a defensive position, entrenched behind rafts of policies that are often obscure and occasionally conflicting. Because the whole system is subject to precedent, it can be over legalistic and err on the side of excessive caution. Consequently, resources are often drained away from the creative planning of new places and neighbourhoods into a target-based, process-driven, regulatory system.

THE ROLE OF PLANNERS

Successive governments have criticised planning as a brake on economic growth and as a convenient scapegoat for lack of investment in housing and infrastructure. In 2011 the prime minister, David Cameron, described planners as 'enemies of enterprise'.[6] Policies to roll back regulatory control have therefore been a consistent theme of government. The four years that the Heathrow Terminal 5 planning

SECTION 106 AGREEMENT AND THE COMMUNITY INFRASTRUCTURE LEVY (CIL)

Many planning consents include a set of separately negotiated legal obligations under section 106 of the Town and Country Planning Act 1990, commonly known as a section 106 agreement. It can cover the provision of anything that is required to offset any wider (negative) implications of a development. It is commonly used to secure affordable housing, new schools, health clinics, open space and the infrastructure necessary to support the development (including contributions to upgrade public transport). There are clear tests regarding eligibility; any demand has to be reasonable and related to the development. Although the value of the 'planning benefits' negotiated should only relate to those that are strictly necessary, inevitably the value of the section 106 agreement is seen by some as a measure of negotiating prowess.

The system is now in transition to the CIL, which came into force on 6 April 2010 through the Community Infrastructure Levy Regulations 2010. The CIL aims to provide a more clear-cut, if less flexible approach relating the size of the developer's contribution directly to the development's square footage.[7]

inquiry took (with a further two years awaiting a ministerial decision), are often cited as an example of the suffocating nature of the planning system. This is of course true but often these delays arise from genuinely different points of view that in a democracy require proper consideration.

Despite its shortcomings the British planning system is one of the fairest and least corrupt in the world. Where skilfully handled it is capable of bringing a high degree of subtlety to urban development through the negotiation of bespoke solutions that respond to complex and contested issues. Here some notable 'enemies of enterprise' give their own perspectives on the system.

Peter Rees, director of planning at the City of London (1987–2014). Major developments included Broadgate, St Mary Axe (the Gherkin), and 20 Fenchurch Street (the Walkie Talkie). Professor of city planning at The Bartlett School of Planning, University College London.
'Planning in the City of London after "Big Bang"[8] was like steering a chariot in a race. Planning has limited influence and can only nudge the inevitable. But without planning, developers would not employ architects. It is only the right combination of planner, architect and developer that will produce a good scheme.'

Rosemarie MacQueen, strategic director of built environment, City of Westminster (2007-14). Responsible for setting the planning and environmental policies in London's West End. Oversaw the preservation of 11,000 listed buildings, the redesign of Leicester Square, and the regeneration of Victoria.

'Planning concerns itself with people and how they make their way in the world. It maintains a constantly adjusting balance, preserves that which is good and eliminates that which can be harmful. It is a misunderstanding to talk about conservation preserving things in aspic. Aspic is flexible; like cities it stretches, it absorbs and can have many outlines whilst keeping a recognisable shape.'

Pat Hayes, director of environment and planning at the London Borough of Ealing. Major projects include the regeneration of Ealing town centre, Old Oak Common and Park Royal.
'The planner is the intermediary between the developer, the politician and the community. You have to work with what the developer puts in front of you, and the planner is there to mould and improve this, to add value (in the broadest sense) and to allow the city to continue to evolve.'

THE ROLE OF POLITICIANS

Councillors, the elected representatives of their communities, are ultimately the decision-makers in planning. They have responsibility for granting planning consent or refusal, but have to operate within national and regional planning policy guidance. Most major authorities are organised along party political lines and decision-making takes place through a cabinet style system of senior portfolio holders from the controlling political party. Operational decisions around, for example, licensing or planning applications are usually devolved to subcommittees.

The local councillor is in daily contact with

> **By and large, though, the role attracts some extraordinarily selfless individuals who genuinely believe in serving their communities.**

his or her electorate. Responding effectively to local issues is a key to political survival where electoral turnout is usually low and a safe seat might have a majority of just a hundred votes. Being a councillor can be a rather thankless and poorly remunerated task. The role attracts the politically ambitious who see their local council as a stepping-stone to higher office, as well as community campaigners, who may have a single political agenda. Sometimes it attracts mavericks and the deranged.

By and large, though, the role attracts some extraordinarily selfless individuals who genuinely believe in serving their communities. The system is democratic, representative and ultimately accountable and the work of local councillors is often overlooked. To voluntarily take on the responsibility for managing a local council and be able to get to grips with a whole range of technical issues is remarkable. Most metropolitan authorities and London boroughs have a turnover that would place them in the FTSE 100 if they were private enterprises. Three of these individuals explain why they do it.

Daniel Moylan, Conservative councillor at Royal Borough of Kensington and Chelsea, deputy chairman of Transport for London (2008–12). Championed the improvements to Exhibition Road and Kensington High Street. Chaired the mayor of London's Design Advisory Panel.

'Planning negotiations are completely different from commercial business discussions. They are essentially asymmetrical, the planning authority starts with its hand open, its policy framework is public knowledge, a developer's intentions and bottom lines are confidential. However tempting it might be to extract the maximum benefits from a developer, this is not the role of planning. Planning is there to represent the needs of the community and ensure that any harmful impacts from a development are ameliorated.'

Steve Hitchins, leader of Islington council (2000–06), now chair of the Camden and Islington Primary Care Trust.

'In the private sector profit is the driving ambition. If you don't achieve this you don't survive. There is no such driver in the public sector. The objectives are broader and more complex. A politician's task is to find the balance between competing interests and clearly spell out priorities. When considering strategies to address tracts of neglected inner city land there will always be different opinions. The voices of people opposed to development need to be heard but there is a difference between constructive opposition and a protest movement.'

Sir Robin Wales, leader (1995–2002) and mayor of London Borough of Newham since 2002. During his leadership he championed the regeneration of Stratford around the London

Olympics, and the Royal Docks.

'If you put in good transport along with development land, then things will happen, but the central question is always, "who should benefit"? Canary Wharf, for example, may have been a commercial success, but has not transformed the lives of local people. Regeneration is not just about physical development, it is about changing people's lives, in particular getting them into long term sustainable jobs. It is up to the local authority to champion this and develop programmes to bring benefits to some of the poorer and most disadvantaged.'[9]

THE DEVELOPMENT SECTOR

There is a common public image of developers as wealthy and venal, triggering gentrification, displacing communities and riding roughshod over democratic debate. Although this might well apply to some in the industry, as in all generalisations it is inaccurate. Developers are the instrument of change in cities. They channel investment, renewing and remodelling obsolete infrastructure, neighbourhoods and buildings. They create new places, housing, workplaces and public spaces. A city without development is static or dying, as London nearly found out in the property crash of 2008–09. Developers come in all sorts of guises from the lone operator, often like a Broadway impresario, to large corporate concerns, independent and quoted on the stock market. There are bad developers that aim to maximise short-term returns regardless of long-term consequences, and there are the good developers who are instrumental in shaping the city for the better. Here are personal perspectives from some of the good developers operating in London today.

Adrian Penfold, head of planning at British Land. Major London developments include Regent's Place; the Leadenhall Building (Cheesegrater); refurbishment and extensions to Broadgate.

'There is a lot of chaos around the way the world works, the challenge is how to minimise it. You have to be optimistic and dogged. The Leadenhall Building took us 15 years. If we had known this in 2000, would we have started it?

You purchase a building as an asset with an income stream. To develop it, you first obtain vacant possession. This means that you no longer have an income stream, only overheads. After investing up front in the process of obtaining planning, you then demolish the building, so you no longer have an asset. You are now horribly exposed, but you don't have any choice but to continue. You plough more and more money into the construction. If you can control costs, avoid recessions and find an occupier, then – and only then – do you make a return.'

> **Planners and politicians are seen as increasingly remote and communities are less willing to accept a series of solutions imposed for the public good.**

Alan Leibowitz, joint managing director, Dorrington Properties, a development and property investment company with a portfolio of over £1.6 billion, comprising offices, commercial and residential properties in London and the south-east.

'Development as a business is completely misunderstood by the public; it is not about the camel-coated, Rolls Royce-driving speculator any more. Most development is by large publicly-quoted companies, often funded through pension funds. It is complex, difficult and risky. The risks cannot be underplayed. It is great in the good times, but given the length of time that it takes to build anything, you inevitably end up having to battle it through the bad times as well. But while developers are masters at spotting the deal, honing the negotiation, maximising potential and running the process, they are, with few exceptions, programmed to over-build, cram down costs and focus purely on the bottom-line to the detriment of the quality of masterplanning, urban design and architecture. Developers, and indeed many architects, are generally ill-prepared for an understanding of what really makes for good design, and the evidence for this is in the huge number of mediocre schemes all around us. This is as much a failure of the planning system as it is of the development industry.'

Sir Stuart Lipton, developer, Lipton Rogers Developments (previously Rosehaugh Stanhope and Chelsfield). Major schemes include Broadgate, Chiswick Park, Paternoster Square, the Commonwealth Institute and the Royal Opera House.

'The development of London's great estates, by architects like Nash and Cubitt, with their mix of uses, streets, squares and public buildings is still one of the most successful urban models ever devised. We know how to create great places, but the central question is whether the country as a whole has the will to do things properly. The decline in planning has resulted in the loss of many of the individuals that used to make our cities better places in which to live and work.'

COMMUNITY INVOLVEMENT AND THE MISTRUST OF PLANNING

Today's society is considerably more pluralistic and fragmented than when the planning acts were formulated in the 1940s. Planners and politicians are seen as increasingly remote and communities are less willing to accept a series of solutions imposed for the public good. From the 1960s, opposition to excesses of road building, property speculation and the wholesale clearance of neighbourhoods led to an increasing demand for democratic debate on the future of neighbourhoods and their communities. Public consultation has become a statutory requirement within mainstream planning, and successive governments have taken action to strengthen citizens' rights within the system. Wider consultation does, however, sit uncomfortably with the desire to speed up the decision-making process.

The growth of public involvement has coincided with a significant reduction in the power of local authorities as fiscal control has become tighter and ever more centralised. The technical nature of the planning system has also increased to the point where it is difficult for the public to understand it, let alone participate in its workings. Local plans tend to be long, technical and often dull policy documents, of little obvious relevance to the communities that they are meant to serve.

Although the system is flexible and open to interpretation and debate, the organisations that administer the process, local planning authorities, have often lost the confidence of their citizens. The fragmentation of political consensus has led to the emergence of an important third voice in the process. Well-organised communities can play a vital role in challenging and enriching the debate. At one end of the spectrum are NIMBYs,[10] simply seeking to protect their interests; at the other end are articulate and skilful individuals and organisations that have had a fundamental influence on their immediate and wider communities. Here are the views of two of them.

Lorraine Hart, director, Community Land Use, an organisation that supports community-led development and regeneration.
'Communities have little sympathy for developers' problems about scheme viability and risk. Their view is often that developer risks are hedged by the fact that even if they have not got a scheme approved they've got the land to sit on as an asset. If they get planning consent they do not even have to take the risks associated with building it – they can still make money by selling it on with uplifted value from getting a planning consent. Communities' view of development is that it can risk their homes, their quality of life, the character of their area and the facilities that it offers to them and their children, but there is not a level playing field in terms of the influence they can wield in the process. They have to rely on the planning authority to do that for them and their experience across many levels is that they do not often do that very well.'

Dominic Ellison, chief executive, Hackney Co-operative Developments CIC (Community Interest Company).
'Despite the best intentions of councils and communities to work in partnership there is, sadly, often a disconnect between the aspirations in policy and the reality in delivery of regeneration projects. The context is set by the need to maximise value and this can sit uncomfortably with the scale and historic fabric of local neighbourhoods. Where this happens regeneration can leave behind local people and when the economic benefits are not distributed social division can ensue.'

In the following chapters we attempt to dissect this political process and describe how it works in practice. But development is not an abstract exercise. Sites have histories and contexts and these also frame the possibilities for the future. A failure to understand context is possibly one of the most damaging mistakes a developer can make. Organisations also have histories. In the words of Alison Lowton, former borough solicitor at Camden council, 'one of the odd things about planning is that things go on long after they have happened'.[11] In the next chapter we look at the history of King's Cross.

3.
HISTORY AND DEVELOPMENT CONTEXT

PLANNING, POLITICS AND CITY MAKING

This chapter provides some historical background on the King's Cross area to set the stage for Argent's present development. It covers the area's industrial heyday and subsequent decline and then considers regeneration attempts in the 1980s (associated with the decision that King's Cross station would be the Channel Tunnel high speed rail terminus) and the community opposition that these engendered. It then considers the construction of the high speed Channel Tunnel Rail Link (CTRL) into the terminus at St Pancras, and other rail infrastructure projects that were underway at King's Cross St Pancras. It concludes with an explanation of the process through which Argent St George was selected as the developer for the King's Cross site. A timeline to clarify the historical development and complex period of overlapping infrastructure projects can be found on pp.viii-xi.

THE HISTORY OF THE KING'S CROSS AREA

Historically, what is now known as the King's Cross area was the low-lying and marshy edge of the early City of London where the dispossessed lived and worked on the fringes of society. Rocque's map of 1769 shows a smallpox

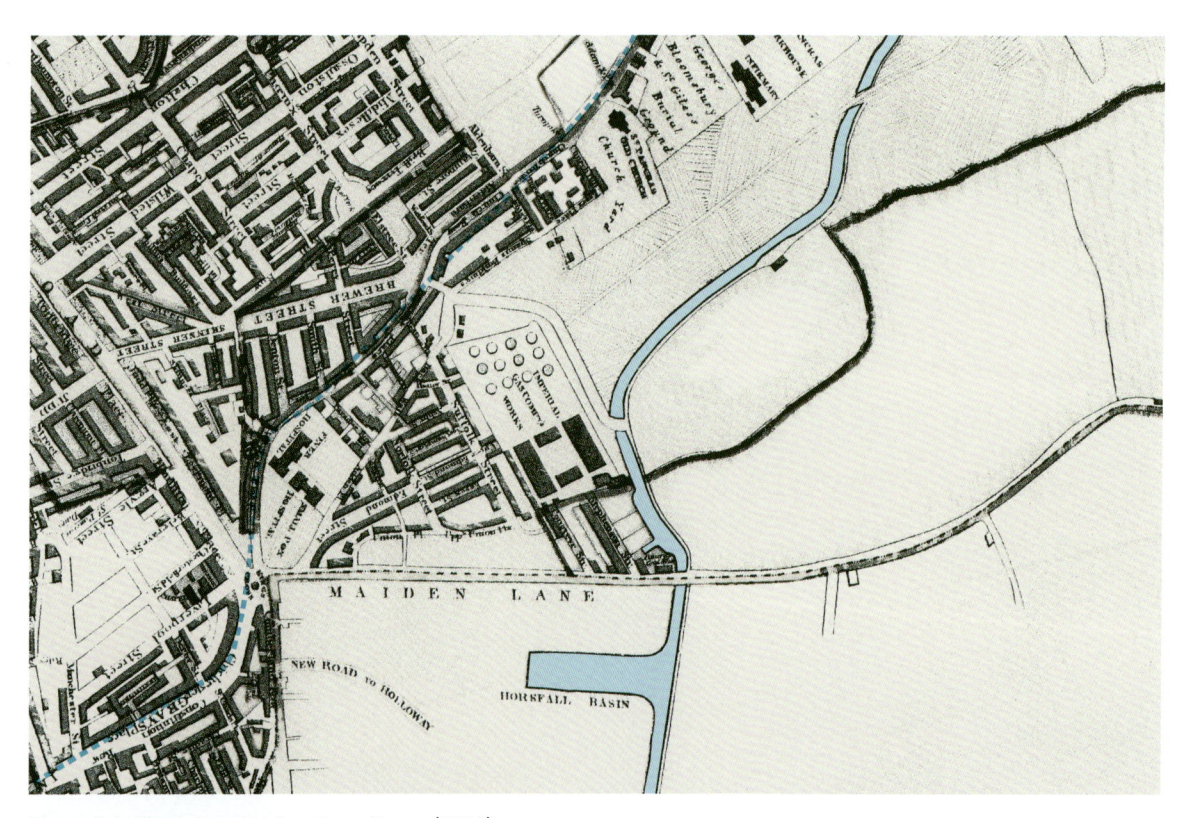

Figure 3.1: King's Cross before the railways (1834).

3: HISTORY AND DEVELOPMENT CONTEXT

hospital and later a fever hospital on the site of King's Cross station.[1] In close and unhealthy proximity to the hospital was the Great Dust Heap, a mountain of ash, bones and other rubbish picked over by scavengers from the locality. It was finally cleared in 1848 to make way for the construction of the railway.

Despite the expansion of London in the 18th century, King's Cross remained largely rural. It was the completion of Euston Road in 1756 that led to the development of the first permanent occupation of the area, low quality, two-storey terraced houses on the southern part of the King's Cross site.

The 19th-century industrial heyday

As London grew, so did the demand for food, fuel and building materials. The Regent's Canal, completed in 1820 (Figure 3.1), linked King's Cross to Birmingham and the new industries of the Midlands. It crosses the centre of the King's Cross site and remains in use today, albeit for leisure purposes. Urbanisation brought workers' tenements, a gas works supplied with coal by canal, and soon afterwards more industry and then the railways. In 1830, in a move to improve the area's poor image, a statue of King George IV was erected at the Battle Bridge crossroads (now Euston Road, York Way and Gray's Inn Road). The design was vulgar and it immediately attracted ridicule. Although it was demolished in 1842, the new name for the area, 'King's Cross', stuck.

Whereas the railways in south and east London (Charing Cross, Waterloo, Fenchurch Street and Liverpool Street) penetrated right to the edge of the city, the owners of valuable property in north and west London lobbied successfully to stop railway construction south of the Euston Road. King's Cross, Euston and later St Pancras stations were consequently confined to the poorer neighbourhoods on the northern city fringe (Figure 3.2). This did not lessen their impact; in 1866 the construction of St Pancras resulted in the demolition of 4,000 houses and displaced around 12,000 people.

The Great Northern Railway (GNR) purchased land at King's Cross for a station, goods terminus and steam locomotive depot. The present station, built in 1852 (Figure 3.3),

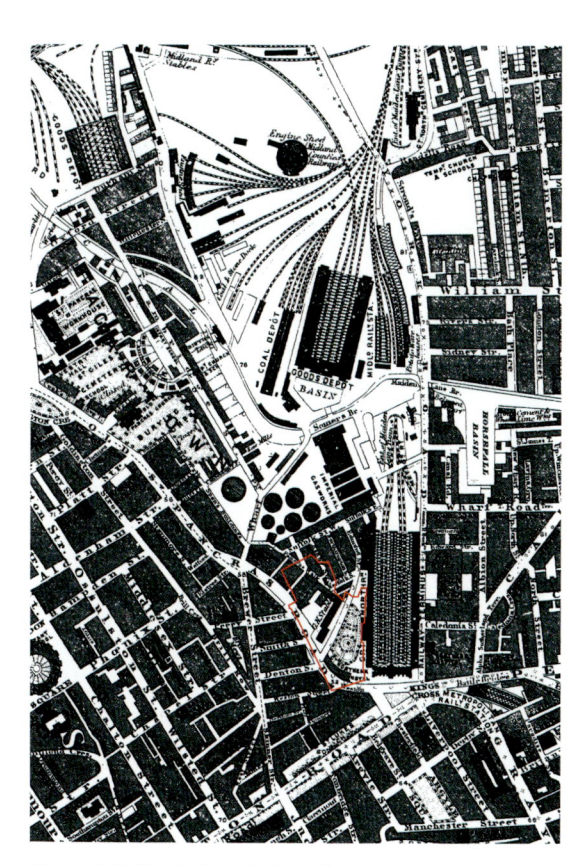

Figure 3.2: King's Cross before the construction of St Pancras station (1862).

Figure 3.3: King's Cross station and the Great Northern Hotel (c.1900).

and the Great Northern Hotel, built in 1854 (Figure 3.4), were both designed by Thomas Cubitt. King's Cross station was soon joined by that of the rival Midland Railway at St Pancras. Designed by William Barlow and built between 1866 and 1868, the single span roof (Figure 3.5) was one of the wonders of Victorian engineering. The Midland Grand Hotel (Figure 3.6), designed by George Gilbert Scott, was completed in 1876. The stations were built separately by private companies that were in competition with one another; there was no planned interchange. Indeed, looking at the stations today, it is clear that they are not only very different architecturally, but that they almost deliberately turn their backs on one another. It was only with the coming of the high speed rail links into St Pancras 125 years later that this problem was finally addressed.

As London's population increased in the 19th century, so did congestion. The Metropolitan Railway, the world's first underground railway, was completed in 1863 to address this, and linked the main line railway termini at Paddington, Euston and King's Cross. By the latter part of the 19th century, King's Cross had become a major goods transport interchange, bringing food, fuel and raw materials from the north of Britain and

Figure 3.4: The Great Northern Hotel (c.1890).

Figure 3.6: The Midland Grand Hotel, St Pancras.

Figure 3.5: The restored roof of the Barlow canopy at St Pancras station (2016).

Figure 3.7: The Granary complex and Regent's Canal (1999) depicting the gasometers and Culross Buildings (bottom right).

trans-shipping them by barge and horse and cart for distribution around London. Behind the stations a number of important buildings were constructed. These included the Granary Building (1850–52), again by Cubitt (Figure 3.7), and the Eastern coaldrops (1851) and Western coaldrops (1860s). Meanwhile, ever expanding rail traffic saw further buildings constructed, including Stanley Buildings (1864–65), to provide affordable housing for railway workers; several new gasholders (1880–1900) and the German Gymnasium (1864–65), a club and sports facility for the German Gymnastics Society.

The transport and goods depots needed low wage labour and the construction of low quality housing followed. The areas immediately around King's Cross became home to an urban underclass. To the west of King's Cross, Somers Town slipped steadily into decline and makes an appearance as a poor neighbourhood in a number of Charles Dickens' novels, including The Pickwick Papers, Bleak House and David Copperfield. In response, the Bedford Estates, south of Euston Road, erected gates to keep out the undesirables, cementing the social divide across Euston Road. This is illustrated in Charles Booth's 1898/99 map of poverty in London (Figure 3.8).[2] The lowest three categories of

3: HISTORY AND DEVELOPMENT CONTEXT

social strata in Victorian urban society were classified by Booth as: 'poor'; 'very poor, casual, chronic want'; and 'vicious, semi-criminal'. These three categories occupied most of the surrounding area.

By the beginning of the 20th century, the area was a mass of stations, sidings, railway buildings and related warehouses. The two stations were the gateway into London for commuters, visitors and immigrants, as well as for goods from the north of England and Scotland. It was busy, congested, dirty, but efficient. The adjacent neighbourhoods housed the working poor and the destitute. It was not an attractive place, but it worked (Figure 3.9). And as intended by the Duke of Bedford, it stopped firmly on Euston Road, a boundary between rich and poor that was to endure for over a century.[3]

The 20th-century decline

For the first half of the 20th century, King's Cross continued to function as an unloved but essential part of the London economy. The stations became dirtier, gloomier and seedier. The spaces around them filled with kiosks and bus stands, and the once grand railway hotels went downmarket. In the aftermath of the second world war, the nationalisation of the railways in the 1947 Transport Act meant that the land passed into public ownership. With the switch to

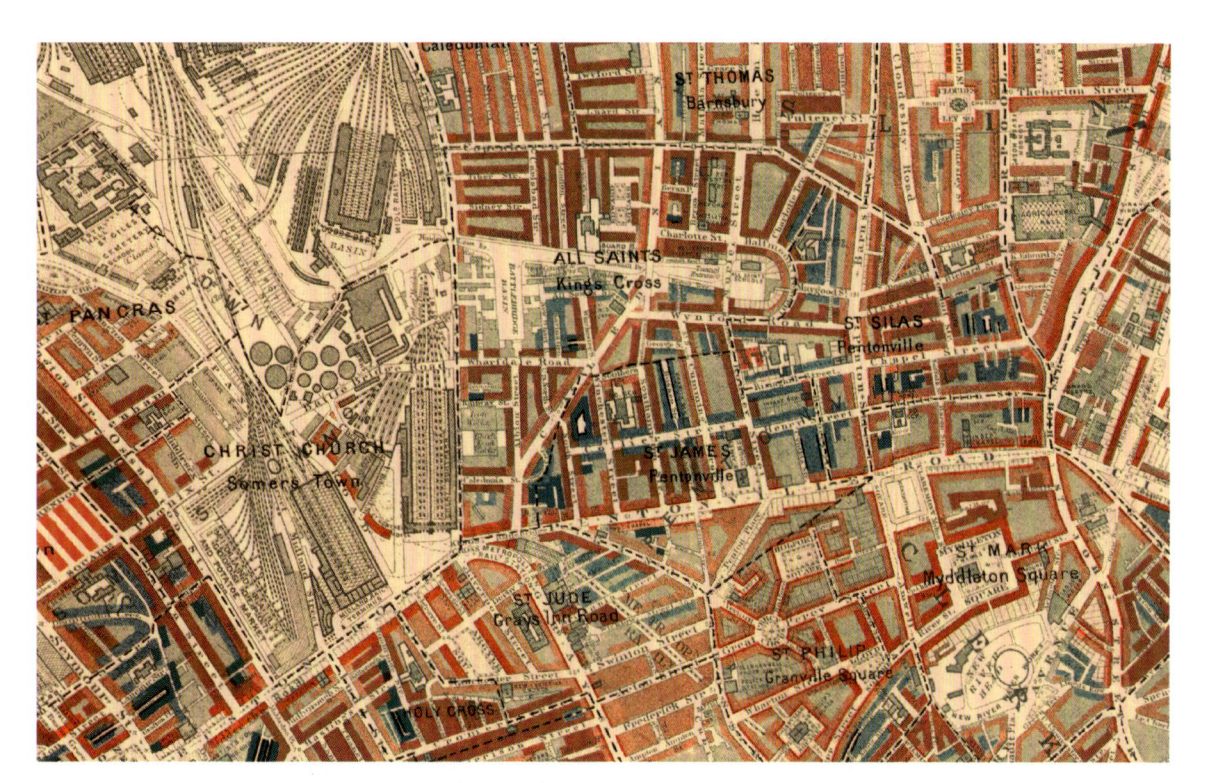

Figure 3.8: Booth's Map of Poverty in London (1898–99). The housing shaded dark blue and black was occupied by the 'vicious and semi-criminal' classes.

PLANNING, POLITICS AND CITY MAKING

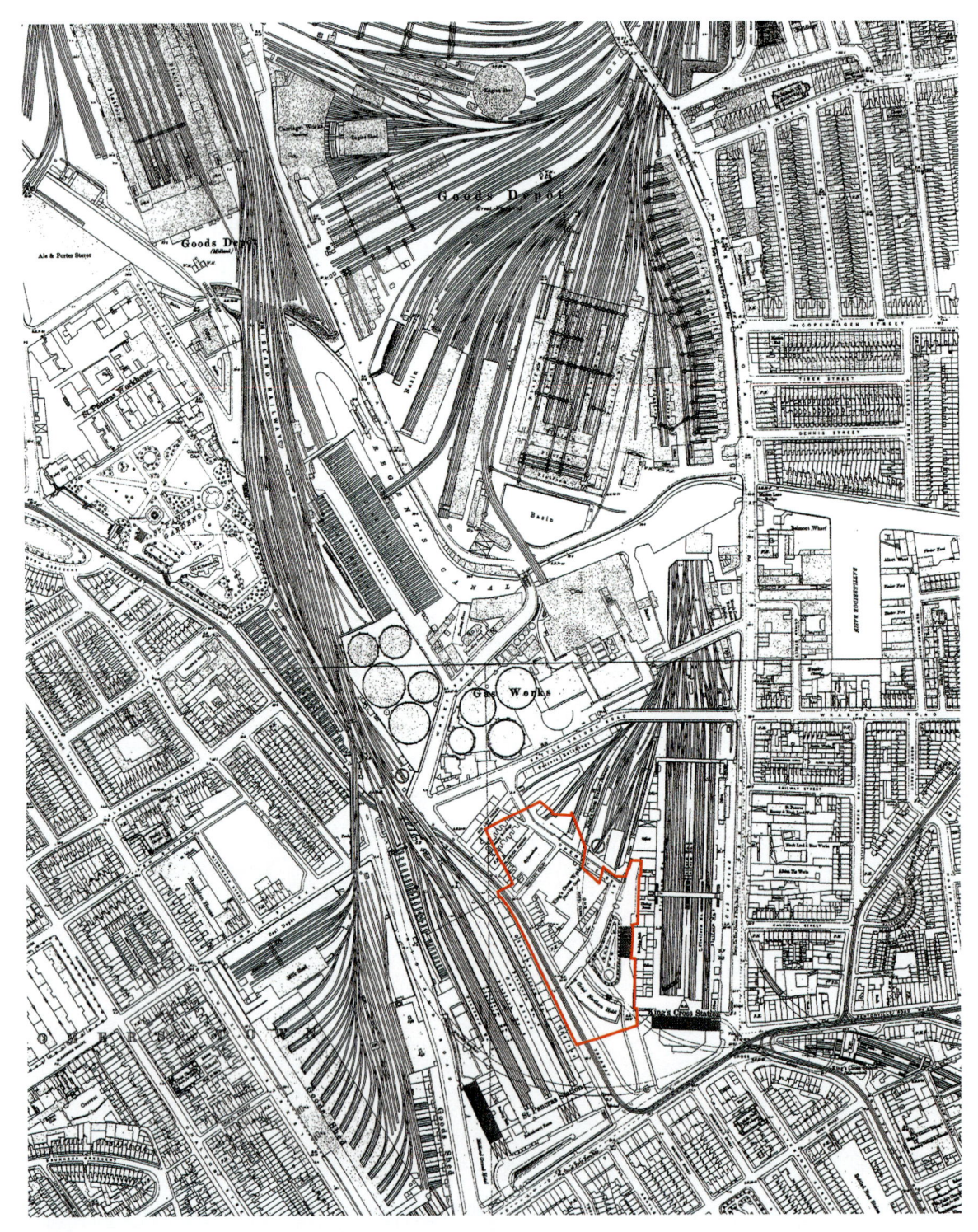

Figure 3.9: King's Cross at the height of the railway age (1894).

containerised rail freight, the King's Cross goods hub effectively became obsolete. In the southern part of the goods yard, most of the rail lines were lifted in the 1980s. The area ceased to be a busy industrial and distribution centre and land and buildings became vacant and derelict. The loss of jobs had a serious impact on local communities and social deprivation increased. By the 1980s, the area around King's Cross station was notorious for crime, prostitution and drug abuse, a reputation that further dissuaded investment. The railway lands became largely vacant, but provided cheap workspace that attracted artists and clubs and its own sub-culture.

The first signs of tentative development interest appeared in the Balfe Street area to the east of King's Cross station – an area of residential streets and eclectic 19th-century industrial buildings.[4] The area had been allowed to deteriorate by the owner, Stock Conversion and Investment Trust, in the expectation that it could be comprehensively redeveloped for offices. Residents fought the redevelopment plans, and in 1977 succeeded in getting it designated as a conservation area, thus saving it from demolition. This and subsequent campaigns[5] represented the emergence of a vocal and organised community opposition.

Conditions for change

In the post-war period there were a number of changes in the ownership of the railway lands that would have an important impact on its future development. In 1969, the British Railways (BR) Sundries Division (which managed its property assets) was hived off into a separate government owned entity, the National Freight Corporation

Figure 3.10: St Pancras gasworks in the 1950s.

(NFC), and with it went ownership of the central area of the King's Cross site (around Granary Square). The remainder of the site was retained by BR, effectively splitting up the strategic land holding. This was followed in 1982 by an employee buyout of NFC and the site passed out of public ownership into Exel logistics. Roger Mann, previously head of property at BR and NFC, transferred into Exel, became managing director of its estates division, Hyperion. The investment climate in London was changing, regional policy was being relaxed and government restrictions on office development were eased. With deregulation of the City on the horizon, the property market sensed a coming boom.

> **Several factors laid the foundations for the negotiations on King's Cross to begin in earnest.**

FIRST REGENERATION PROPOSALS

The first tentative discussions about developing King's Cross came in 1984. Hyperion was approached by Godfrey Bradman and Stuart Lipton from the company Rosehaugh Stanhope, which was building an impressive reputation as a developer in the City of London following the 13-hectare redevelopment of Broadgate, the largest office development in London until the arrival of Canary Wharf in the early 1990s. The catalyst for their approach was the government's decision to commit to the construction of the Channel Tunnel and high speed rail links from Folkestone into London. The ambitious plan in 1987 was to construct a £1 billion new terminus, beneath the existing King's Cross station.

The London Regeneration Consortium plc (LRC) was formed as a joint venture between Rosehaugh Stanhope and British Rail. The terminus beneath King's Cross station would be cross-subsidised through developing the 120 acres of goods depots and sidings north of King's Cross. Skidmore, Owings and Merrill (SOM) and Norman Foster were appointed as separate masterplanners in a star team that included Frank Gehry and David Chipperfield.

In a confidential memorandum from September 1987,[6] LRC noted that the development offered the opportunity for significant cash receipts but that speed was of the essence if the development was to hit the property market before other large schemes, Canary Wharf in particular. Camden council was broadly supportive, seeing the advantages of regeneration and new housing. The expectation was that planning approvals would be granted within six months, with development commencing soon after in the summer of 1988. This proved to be an optimistic assessment.

The plan to bring the CTRL into King's Cross was perceived as a renewed threat to the area east of the station, and some of the community groups that had opposed the Balfe Street proposals joined forces in opposition as the King's Cross Railway Lands Group (KXRLG).[7] The opposition groups rejected the findings of a House of Lords committee (September 1987) that King's Cross station should be the terminus for CTRL and maintained that St Pancras would be the better terminus. In this respect their views were ultimately vindicated (1993).

After extensive public consultation, Camden council published a Community Planning Brief in 1988. This set out requirements for housing, training facilities, open space and industrial floor space, but set no upper limits on the quantum of development. The housing envisaged was predominantly low rise family accommodation at a density of around 70–110 habitable rooms per acre (hra).[8] The LRC recognised that the community was apprehensive about the scheme,[9] but its approach to consultation was more of a marketing process than genuine engagement with the community.

3: HISTORY AND DEVELOPMENT CONTEXT

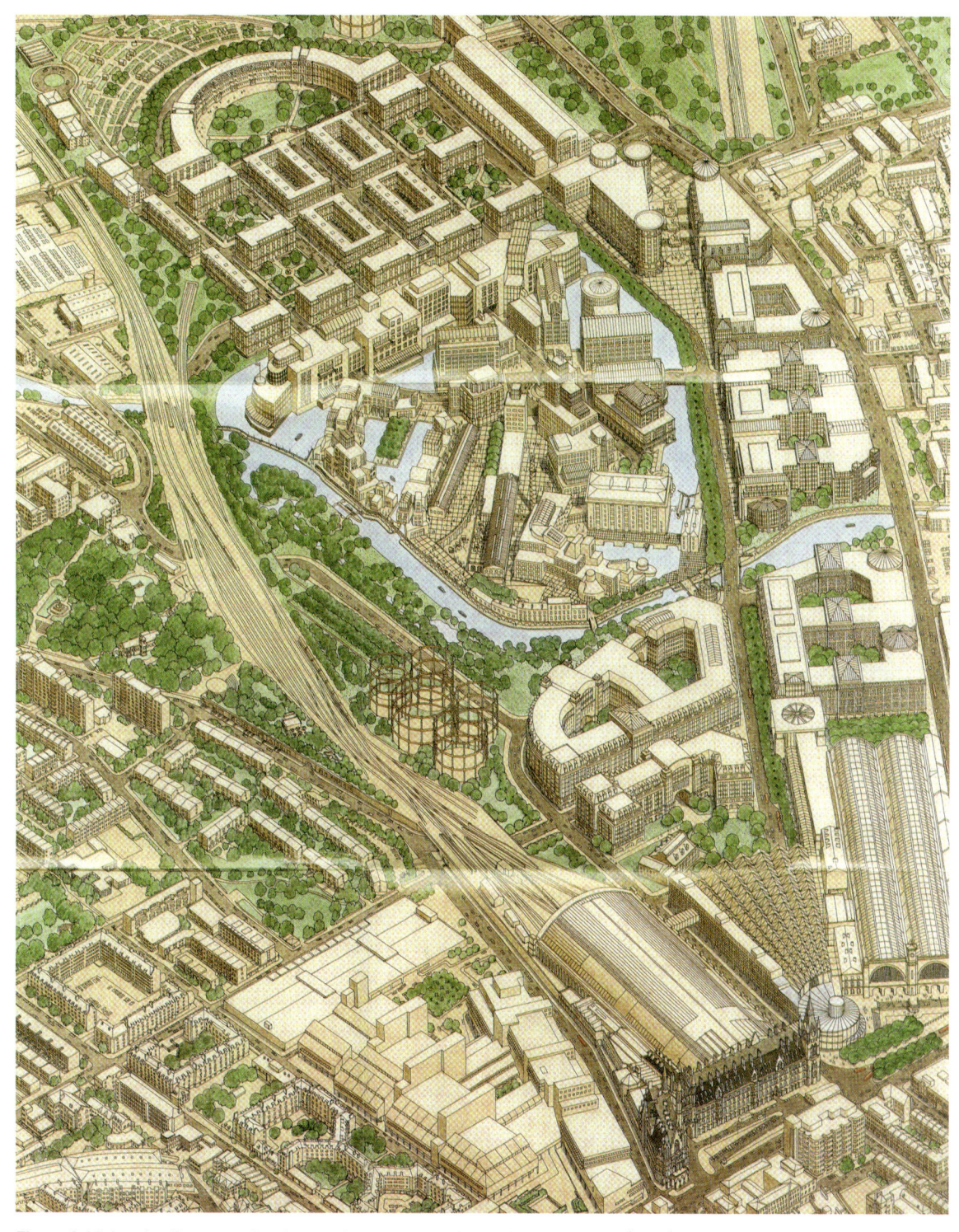

Figure 3.11: London Regeneration Consortium proposals from SOM masterplan (1989).

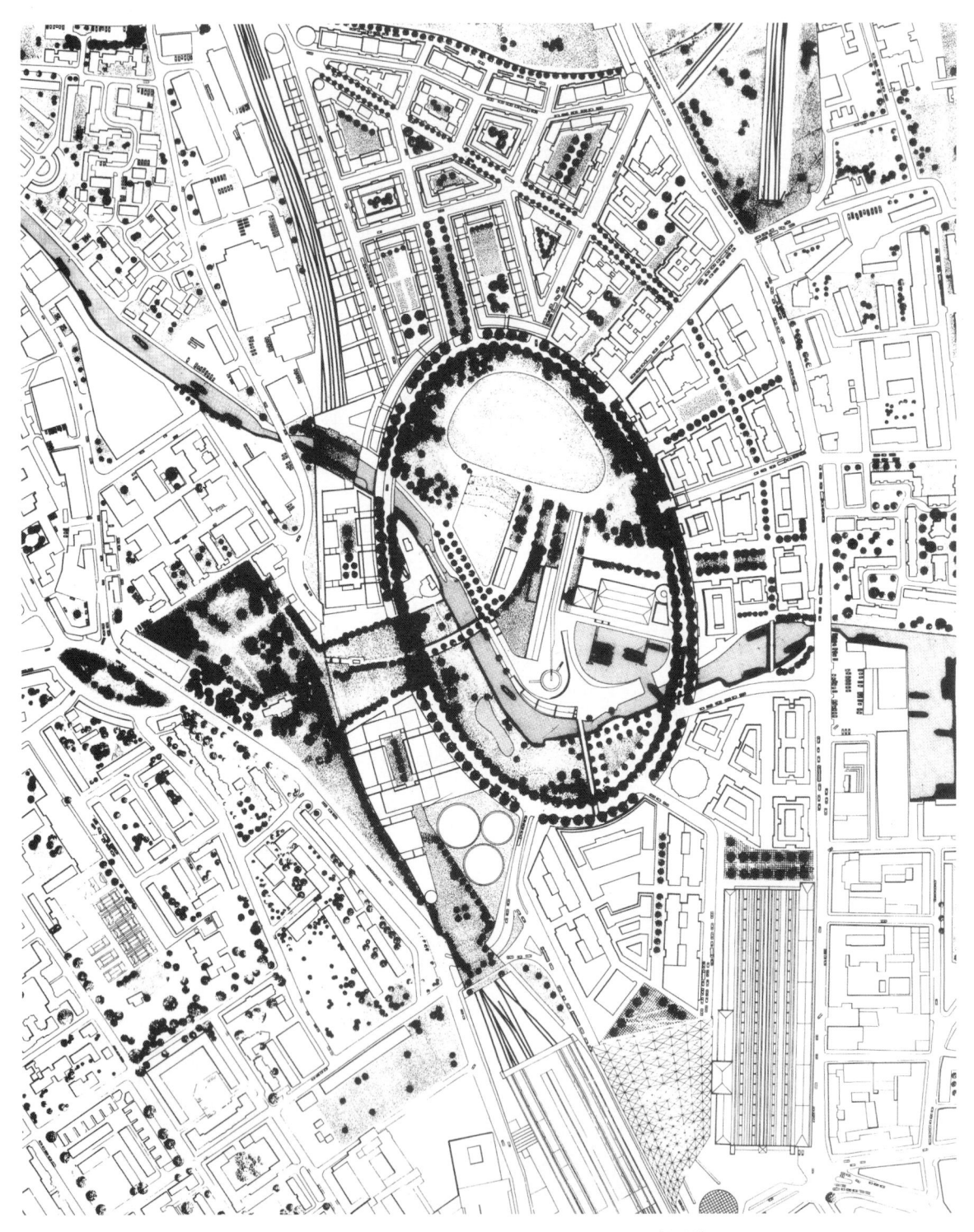

Figure 3.12: London Regeneration Consortium proposals from Foster's masterplan (1989).

A planning application was submitted by LRC in October 1989. The scheme envisaged almost 12 million square feet of development, of which nine million would be commercial and 1.7 million housing. Under the SOM masterplan, the proposal was to deck over the railway tracks (using the consortium's experience at Broadgate) and to develop large floor plate office buildings along York Way and between the two stations. The majority of housing was to be located to the north of the site within a grid of streets and squares. The centre of the site was designed around a linear park and a set of new canals that created a moated mixed-use area. Within this sat those historic buildings that were to be retained, in a plan that could best be described as 'picturesque'. The proposed building heights were four to ten storeys with no significant tall buildings (Figure 3.11).

The Foster masterplan took a different approach. It still decked over the tracks and concentrated the commercial floor space to the south, with housing to the north. Here, however, it proposed perimeter blocks on a street grid enclosing private spaces. The radical difference was an oval park in the centre of the scheme around the canal. Here the few historic buildings that were retained would be standalone museum pieces (Figure 3.12). Sir Norman Foster also proposed a new station between King's Cross and St Pancras on the site occupied by the Great Northern Hotel (Figure 3.13).

The development was structured so that the landowners would receive their existing use values plus the development uplift after LRC had taken its costs and a developer's profit. The valuation was to be based on an assessment of each land parcel once planning permission had been granted. For British Rail, this amounted to a projected profit of £155–£466 million (at 1987 prices), and with an anticipated 7 per cent rise in rents, this would increase to between £461 million and £1 billion.[10]

The scheme started to run into difficulties on a number of fronts. The station box beneath King's Cross station was a huge technical challenge and presented a considerable financial burden for the scheme. With the benefit of hindsight, it is also clear that British Rail was inexperienced in property development and this role was subservient to its railway operations remit. Although the LRC had engaged with, and achieved the support of Camden council, it had underestimated the power of the local community. In an era of radical local politics where community development projects such as the Coin Street Community Builders on London's South Bank[11] were established as workable precedents, attempts to 'sell' the LRC scheme locally did not wash. Community opposition influenced the council and delayed the process, eventually pushing it into the unstable times of the 1990s recession. For a developer, a sound working relationship with a council depends on

❝ Community opposition influenced the council and delayed the process, eventually pushing it into the unstable times of the 1990s recession. ❞

Figure 3.13: Proposals for new station concourse at King's Cross (1989).

stable internal politics. At the time, Camden was financially and politically unstable. It was in crisis and easily influenced by a determined and well networked local community. The development consortium had failed to understand this.

The London property boom, stoked by the Thatcher government's policies of deregulation, peaked towards the end of 1989, and then collapsed. The council's environment committee determined in July 1992 that it was 'minded to grant' outline planning permission if a number of significant matters could be resolved, but time was running out. Progress was halted when British Rail abandoned plans to bring the CTRL into King's Cross and in March 1993 the government announced its preference for a CTRL terminus at St Pancras.[12] This decision coincided with a major economic downturn. Many property firms were seriously exposed, and a number, including Rosehaugh Stanhope, went into receivership. The King's Cross deal collapsed. In total some £52 million had been invested in the scheme without any return.[13]

Although the LRC scheme collapsed, it left a significant legacy in terms of local community politics. KXRLG and other groups had engaged and brought forward alternative views of how King's Cross might be developed.[14] They had also developed a close and cooperative working relationship with Camden council. In the words of Michael Edwards of KXRLG, the group 'worked with sympathetic councillors and officers (with grant support from Camden) and the combined effect was – in hindsight – a fairly effective episode in consultation, if not full participation'.[15] Later, when the Argent scheme emerged, KXRLG had strong views about the site and may have hoped that these would be given the same prominence by Camden councillors and officers.

THE KING'S CROSS PARTNERSHIP

For the time being, the King's Cross site lay dormant again and was occupied by a range of low intensity temporary uses. During the 1990s a more business-oriented culture had entered government, joint public/private ventures were the preferred way forward and this culture had percolated down to local authority level. Activism through pressure groups was being replaced by more formal partnerships embracing local residents' groups and other stakeholders, including local health authorities, businesses and the police.

The government's Single Regeneration Budget (SRB) programme marked a departure from the distribution of regeneration funds based on measures of relative deprivation. Instead, funds were allocated to public/private partnerships on the basis of clear investment and regeneration objectives. In response, the King's Cross Partnership (KCP) was set up in 1996. The founding partners were the London Boroughs of Camden and Islington, and the two railway companies – Railtrack and London and Continental Railways (LCR) – were appointed as the consortium that would construct and run the new high speed rail link to the Channel Tunnel. It also included community representatives and other public sector bodies. The partnership bid received £37.5 million from the government for a seven-year programme of work starting in April 1996.

The KCP board was chaired by Sir Bob Reid, chairman of the British Railways board from 1990 until 1995. Its explicit objective was to bring forward investment programmes that would prepare the local area for the anticipated regeneration, and increase opportunities for local people. Part of its money was spent on training and education but in the absence of any specific development proposals, most of its effort was devoted to changing the image of the area through promotional material, improving housing estates, streets and open spaces, and implementing measures to combat crime. Perhaps its greatest legacy, though, was the working relationships that it helped to develop between the key organisations and institutions in the area. Crucially, the KCP provided a vehicle for dialogue between stakeholders and a sounding board through which difficult issues on King's Cross could be aired. It also built close relationships with the Government Office for London (GOL).

PLANNING, POLITICS AND CITY MAKING

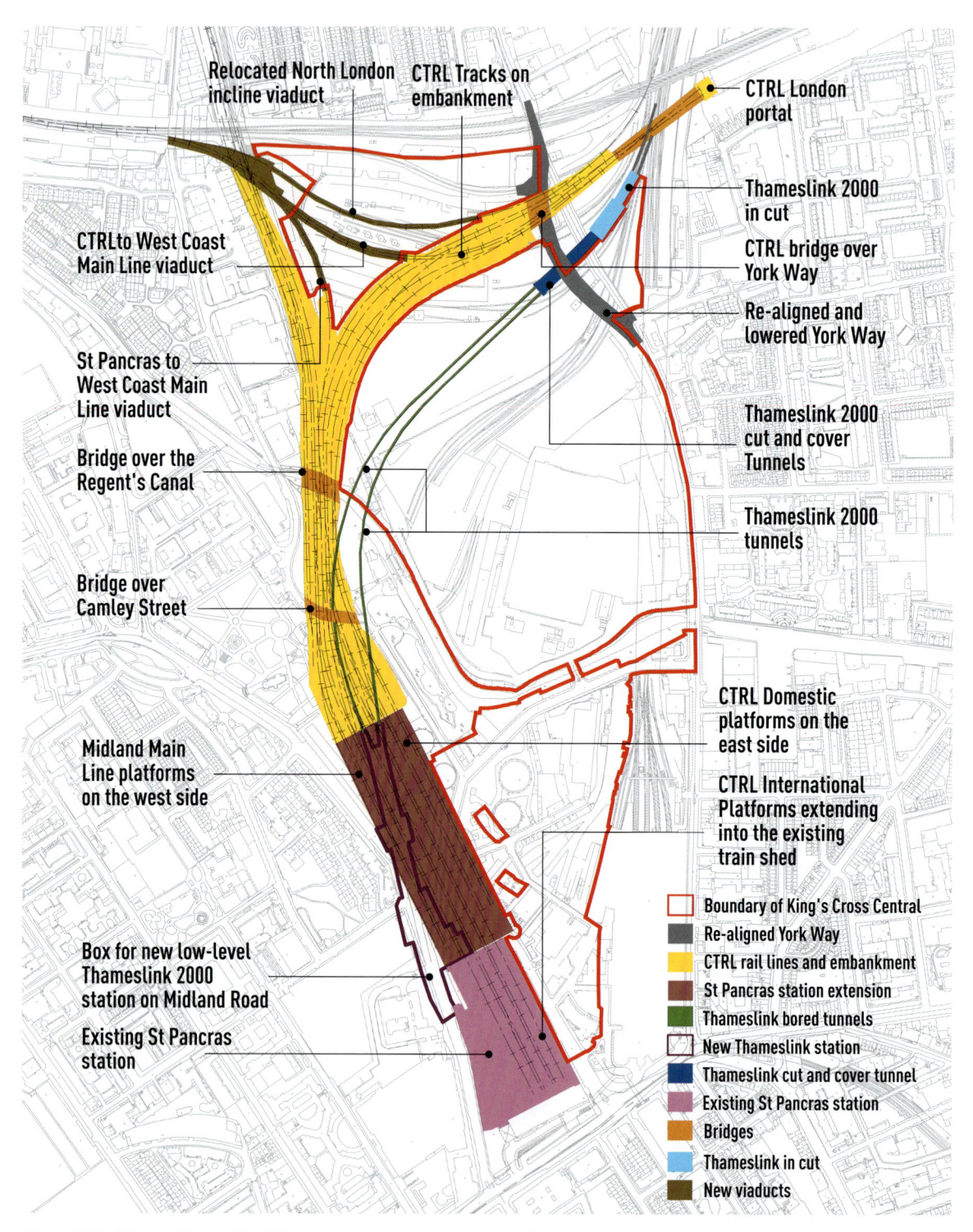

Figure 3.14: Channel Tunnel Rail Link infrastructure and site boundaries.

RAIL INFRASTRUCTURE

The development of the King's Cross railway lands was tied intricately to the construction of the CTRL into the terminus at St Pancras, and other rail infrastructure projects (see Figure 3.14).

The King's Cross underground concourses

Following a fire at King's Cross station in 1987, a decision had been taken by the government to invest £774 million in the renewal of the King's Cross underground concourse. Designed by Arup, this complex reconfiguration of the ticket halls and concourses improved safety, increased capacity and helped to create the passenger capacity needed for the increased footfall through the stations when St Pancras was eventually chosen as the terminus in central London for Eurostar trains (Figure 3.15). The works also created the additional capacity that would benefit the future development of the railway lands. It is common practice in the UK for developments to be required to pay for any transport improvements that they may necessitate. Potentially, this government funding liberated the development of the railway lands from what might have been a considerable financial burden for transport improvements.[16]

The Channel Tunnel Rail Link (CTRL)

In March 1993, after much deliberation, the government accepted the case for a high speed line through north Kent and via Stratford into St Pancras (Figure 3.16). This was duly authorised in the CTRL Act 1996. In accordance with the new orthodoxy of government policy, a public-private finance initiative meant that the risk of building and operating the new railway would be transferred to the private sector in return for future fare revenues. Part of the contract arrangement included land at King's Cross and Stratford, which the government retained after railway privatisation in 1993.[17] The government decided to use that part of the King's Cross site still in its ownership to offset some of the development costs of the CTRL. Under this arrangement, the government would recoup the pre-agreed land base values, but the development uplift would be retained by the operator.[18] The basis of the government tendering arrangement was that private finance would be raised through debt and equity to build the railway. In consequence, this expenditure would be 'off balance sheet' and would not impact on tight government spending restrictions. The government tender to construct and operate the railway was won by LCR.[19]

St Pancras station and Chambers

The CTRL would run from Stratford under the existing North London Line (now the overground) and emerge from a tunnel at the north of the King's Cross site onto an embankment leading to a new upper level terminus at St Pancras.[20] Sir Norman Foster was selected to extend and redesign St Pancras station. The Foster plan moved the existing Midland mainline platforms to the side, constructed a large extension to the rear of the station with platforms over 400 metres long to accommodate the Eurostar trains, and placed the ticketing and retail facilities beneath in the old station undercroft. Work on stage two of the CTRL works, which included St Pancras station, began in July 2001.

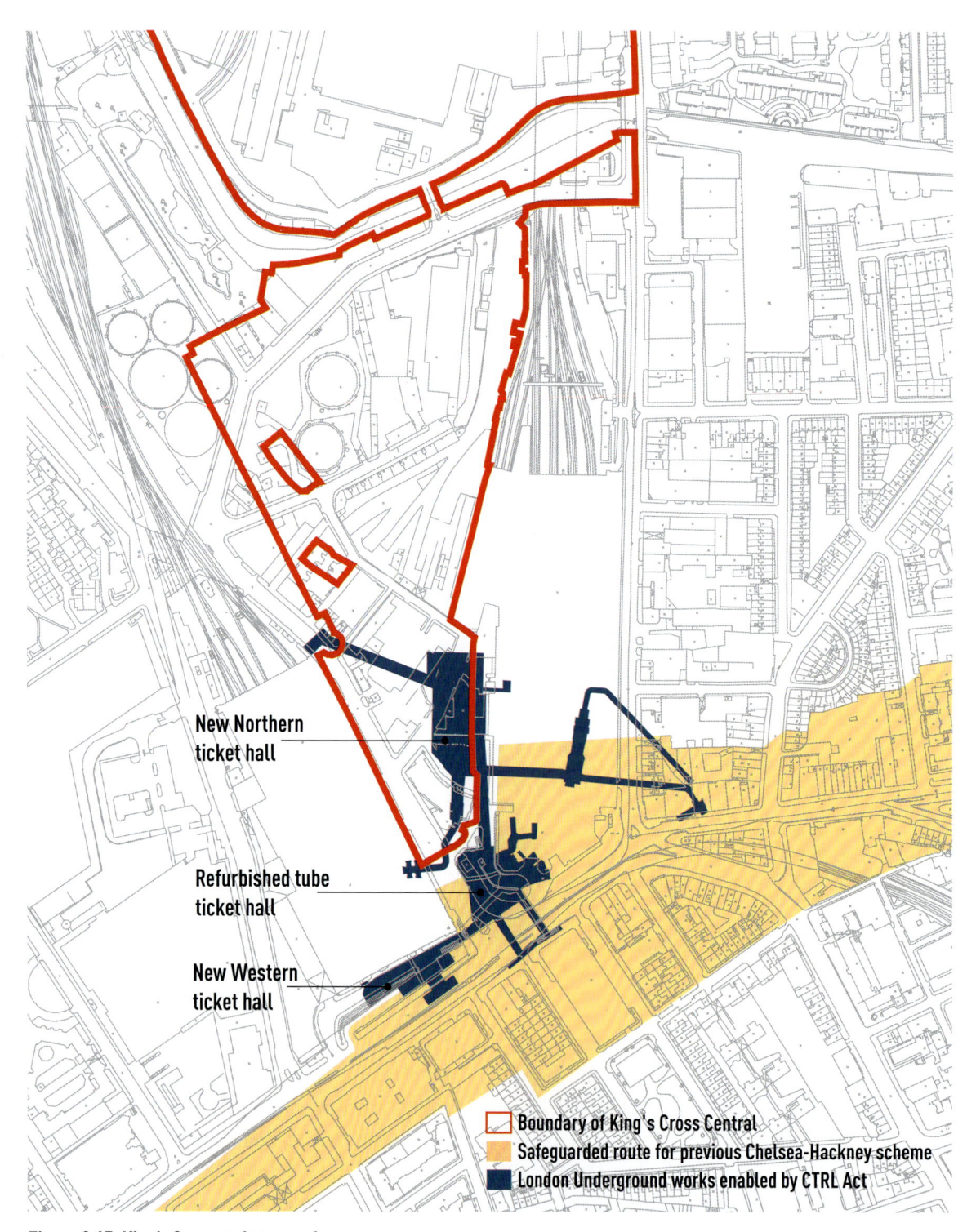

Figure 3.15: King's Cross underground concourses.

FINANCING CTRL AND THE INTERCHANGE

It was possible to calculate the construction costs of the CTRL in advance, but the unknown variable was the operating revenues. Subsequent changes in the revenue streams, due partly to the advent of cheap airfares, significantly reduced the income forecasts of Eurostar. The debt required ballooned, banks backing the consortium withdrew their support and in 2003 LCR had to go back to the government and ask for a further £1 billion. With the project in jeopardy, John Prescott, then deputy prime minister, intervened and pushed the problem back to government departments to solve. Initially, there was talk of selling the King's Cross landholdings, with Argent novated as developer. However, LCR persuaded Prescott that the land would be worth far more if held for the long-term. Without Prescott's agreement that LCR should retain the land, the development under different ownership would probably have been substantially different.

An internal deal was finally brokered between the office of the deputy prime minister and the Treasury, who agreed to guarantee the loans. The condition was that some of the shares would be handed over to the government once the railway was finished and thus LCR would effectively become a government-owned company.[21] This unlocked the problem, but put the expenditure back 'on balance sheet', a state of affairs that was contrary to government policy and for which MPs and the chancellor (Gordon Brown) in particular, were apparently unaware. When this agreement was unearthed in 2004 by a government select committee, uproar ensued and the chancellor subsequently withdrew funding from (and therefore suspended work on) the underground concourses and City Thameslink station.[22] With work on the interchange suspended indefinitely, the southern part of the King's Cross site could not be completed. This impacted on the transport assumptions underpinning the scheme and potentially on investor confidence. To compound the problem, LCR had been subcontracted to build the City Thameslink station box, but the £60 million for the fit-out was also frozen. For more than a year there was no certainty as to when the City Thameslink station would become operational. Fitting-out the underground station at a later date would have required land in King's Cross being set aside for future working areas, with all the associated blight. Intensive lobbying from LCR, Camden council and Argent failed to resolve the problem. It was only when London won the bid for the 2012 summer Olympics in June 2005 that funds were released by the Treasury and work could resume. The implication of this decision is picked up later in Chapter 9.

LCR's stations and property managing director, Stephen Jordan, came from a marketing and development rather than a railways background. As a shrewd and well-connected operator, Jordan was to play a pivotal role in the development of the railway lands. He had a detailed knowledge of the area and its opportunities, and brought a strong personal ethos of consensus-building to the development process. He actively engaged with Camden and Islington councils, English Heritage and local communities through the KCP (see p.31), and helped to build long-term relationships that were invaluable in subsequent negotiations on the development of the railway lands. He saw stations not just as transport interchanges, but as gateways that set passenger expectations. When executed well, he understood that they

Figure 3.16: King's Cross in 1999. View of the stations looking northwards.

could also be valuable property assets. A team was assembled that studied and visited stations in Europe and the United States with the objective of making St Pancras 'as good as we could make it'.[23] To 'celebrate' the experience of the railway, LCR was therefore prepared to invest considerable sums of money to restore the Victorian magnificence of the station. Foster's design restored and revealed the grandeur of the Barlow station and canopy in a spectacular fashion and St Pancras station was formally opened as the Eurostar terminal in November 2007.

Originally, St Pancras Chambers (the grand Victorian hotel in front of the station), was not included in the railway package as the government was nervous of the potential costs of refurbishing the Grade I-listed building, by now in a state of severe disrepair. After winning the contract, however, LCR insisted on its inclusion, seeing it as the vital 'front door' to its project. Control of the hotel also allowed a comprehensive restructuring of St Pancras to occur, and maintained the integrity of LCR's landholdings.

The refurbishment of the hotel presented considerable problems due to poor internal circulation and awkward room configurations.

3: HISTORY AND DEVELOPMENT CONTEXT

Figure 3.17: King's Cross in 1999. View of the stations looking southwards.

LCR mounted an open competition to find partners to carry out the refurbishment, and it was awarded to Manhattan Loft Corporation. Its proposals were to extend the hotel on the west side of the station to provide additional rooms and facilities commensurate with the requirements of a five star hotel. The upper floors, which were difficult to reuse as hotel bedrooms, were to be converted into upmarket loft apartments. The hotel plans were approved in 2005 and it opened in 2011.

To complete the interchange, the Thameslink services were to be upgraded and the cramped station on Pentonville Road moved to connect

> **As so often in the negotiation process for the development, trust between the individuals involved was crucial.**

directly into St Pancras. As a result, St Pancras and its Eurostar services would be connected directly to Gatwick and Luton airports.

Coordinating the transport projects

This substantial investment in transport infrastructure was implemented by three independent companies under separate contracts: LCR was constructing the CTRL terminus at St Pancras, Network Rail the new King's Cross Thameslink stations, and London Underground Limited (LUL) the new underground concourse. Close project liaison arrangements were put in place. However, London's successful bid for the 2012 summer Olympic games in July 2005 brought a need for more formal coordination mechanisms to ensure that the concourse at King's Cross, the central London terminus for the games, could be completed in time. This issue is picked up in Chapter 9.

COMPLETING THE SITE ASSEMBLY

With the appointment of LCR, the landholdings at King's Cross passed out of government control into private ownership (Figure 3.16 and 3.17). In order to complete the site assembly, LCR approached Exel's property wing, Hyperion, owners (as described earlier) of the central part of the site. The orthodox approach to land valuation would have been to employ large teams of surveyors to agree the relative values of the land as yet undeveloped for unspecified uses. Alternatively, the valuation could be postponed to some time in the future. LCR and Hyperion both recognised the difficulties of this. There were simply too many unknowns (particularly site preparation and decontamination costs), to come to an accurate or meaningful valuation of the two parcels of land. Yet leaving the valuation to the completion of the scheme could have caused internal rivalry, with both parties attempting to manipulate the masterplan in order to maximise the values of their respective sites.

Fortunately, Stephen Jordan of LCR and Roger Mann, director of property at Exel/Hyperion, had previously worked together in the early days of the National Freight Corporation. They left their advisers to argue respective valuations, withdrew to a wine bar and thrashed out a deal.[24] As so often in the negotiation process for the development, trust between the individuals involved was crucial. Jordan and Mann agreed to apportion profits purely in accordance with the percentage of landholdings each put into the pot, with LCR taking a 5 per cent fee as project managers. As a safeguard, the partners appointed an independent arbiter to act in the event of any dispute. He was briefed monthly but was never used. This pragmatic solution was based on a belief that ultimately the value of both of the landholdings would be maximised by getting the right scheme built.

With the land deal secure, LCR could proceed with the selection of a development partner for the King's Cross site.

SELECTING A DEVELOPMENT PARTNER

It was agreed that LCR would bear the pre-development costs and lead on the selection of a development partner. In 1999, Jones Laing LaSalle was appointed to manage a two-stage open competition. In setting the terms of the competition, LCR deliberately did not ask for a masterplan or design. It considered the development problems to be economic, and political rather than architectural. It therefore sought a partner who could demonstrate a clear process and strategy for dealing with the complex planning and development process, and one with a participatory rather than an adversarial approach. LCR also wanted commitment to a long-term partnership whereby growth in value would be realised through the development of a 'place'. The selection criteria were:

- Participatory approach and ability to work with Camden council and other stakeholders.
- The quality of the development team, and commitment from specific named individuals.
- The financial deal – not a sum, but an equation that maximised long-term values.

In seeking a joint venture, LCR did not require an up-front payment but instead offered an equity share. The landowner would provide the land and the developer would provide the cash on a 50:50 basis. This committed both parties into a process of maximising long-term values. The government also agreed to plough back the existing land value and take a return once planning permissions had been received.[25] The approach ran counter to the standard procurement model that is weighted to achieving the highest financial offer.

The competition involved a wide trawl of potential firms, leading to an initial long list of 24. This was subsequently reduced to three, one of which was Argent.

Argent

Founded in the 1980s by Peter and Michael Freeman, Argent grew rapidly as a property investment and development company.

Argent's major breakthrough came in 1993 with the acquisition of Brindleyplace, a 6.9 hectare site on the edge of Birmingham city centre, when its developer, Rosehaugh, went into receivership. Although it was still a relatively inexperienced company, Argent brought with it a fresh approach and understood the relationship between design, masterplanning and delivery in difficult and uncertain market conditions. It revised the masterplan to make the scheme more flexible; plot sizes were reduced to accommodate a variety of building sizes; circulation and access were reconfigured;

> **The competition involved a wide trawl of potential firms, leading to an initial long list of 24.**

> **The vision is to develop a distinctive London destination, sensitively combining exciting new architecture with existing listed buildings.**

and a greater emphasis was placed on the public realm. Crucially, the revised plan was capable of being implemented in a variety of different phases according to prevailing market conditions. Argent then appointed respected architects to design individual buildings within an overall development framework.[26] Brindleyplace was largely complete by 2001 and served as a useful reference point against which ideas for King's Cross could be assessed.

In 1997 Argent was effectively bought by Hermes, the manager of the British Telecom pension fund. This gave Argent immediate access to £100 million of venture capital, as well as the larger resources of a £36 billion pension fund. The long-term investment perspective of a pension fund meant that high-quality design and astute estate management were valued as methods to maximise returns.

The Argent bid for King's Cross
Initially the Argent board was not particularly interested in bidding for the King's Cross development, but agreed that its chief executive, Roger Madelin, could submit a bid if he wished. Madelin was travelling to Birmingham on the 07.15 train from Euston when he turned his attention to the bidding documents and saw that the deadline for submission was 12.00 that day. He wrote a covering letter and submission on the train, mobilised the Birmingham office to type and fax it to London, where the background documentation was assembled. It was delivered to Jones Lang LaSalle's offices with three minutes to spare. The submission was, by Madelin's own words, 'light',[27] but out of 24 initial bids it made the shortlist of three, alongside bids from Lend Lease and AMEC. At this point Argent mobilised. Recognising that the development would have a substantial residential component (where they had limited expertise), it entered a joint venture with St George, a subsidiary of the volume house builder Berkeley Homes, and formed a joint venture company, Argent St George. Both Roger Madelin and LCR's Stephen Jordan have no doubt that without teaming up with a specialist house builder, Argent would not have won the bid. Argent and St George eventually parted company in November 2004 (see Chapter 9).[28] The panel for the final interview comprised representatives from Exel and LCR.

While Lend Lease and AMEC presented detailed proposals and plans from internationally renowned architects, Argent St George's pitch was different. Its proposition was that both the site and the political context were complex, and it would therefore be inappropriate to propose even initial ideas before a comprehensive analysis of the site conditions and constraints had been undertaken. Its experience from Brindleyplace underlined the need for flexibility to deliver a development that might run over a 20-year timeframe and at least three property cycles. Argent St George presented a single sheet of paper that set out a process. Central to this was sufficient time to have an extensive dialogue with local politicians and communities in order to achieve a proposal that would be robust and implementable. It was simple, brave and convincing; Argent St George was awarded the role of development partner.

Argent St George's appointment

Initially, the decision to appoint Argent St George was not unanimous and split the panel. On paper at least, Lend Lease represented the lower risk option due to its size and experience. Four principle factors favoured Argent St George. First, the proposal was backed by an institutional investor (the British Telecom Pension Fund) and this guaranteed financial stability and continuity over the life of the project. Second, Argent's development at Brindleyplace was gaining recognition as an exemplar and offered a convincing model for King's Cross. Third, the panel was impressed by Madelin's reputation and leadership credentials and sensed that it would be able to work with him. Finally, Argent's stress on the importance of consensus building chimed with LCR's own ways of working.

In establishing the joint venture, it was agreed that the land would be valued once the scheme had secured planning permission. The land owners had to deliver vacant possession of the site (see Chapter 9) and there was to be a calculation about how much value Argent St George would add through the planning process. The arrangement was that Argent St George would get an increasing discount on the price of purchasing their 50 per cent share of the development, incentivising optimal value through planning. In March 2000, the London Communications Agency (LCA), working on behalf of Argent St George, issued a press release to announce its appointment:

'The vision is to develop a distinctive London destination, sensitively combining exciting new architecture with existing listed buildings. LCR envisages that the area will be a major new metropolitan centre, incorporating a variety of office, retail, residential and urban entertainment uses. Argent St George will be encouraged to set the development in its wider area context by relating it to the surrounding district and its local community of residents and businesses.'[29]

CONCLUSIONS

The first attempt to regenerate King's Cross failed for a number of reasons. The construction of a new terminus for the CTRL under the Grade-I listed King's Cross station was an expensive and risky engineering solution and although LRC had every right to believe that the government was fully supportive of its proposals, this was not cemented into an approved Act of Parliament.[30] Without such assurances, the risks were very high. The LRC did appreciate the volatility of the London property market, but may have underestimated the difficulties in working with a Labour-controlled council compared to the more predictable environment in the City of London. The early 1990s economic downturn was unlucky, but no one ever accurately predicts such crises.

> **Shared aspirations led to compatible working relationships and trust between landowners and partners. This relationship was to prove crucial in decision-making.**

The final lessons from the scheme concerned the internal dynamics of the partnership. The LRC scheme was capable of being built, but British Rail was unable to focus sufficiently on property matters and seize the moment. The delay proved fatal; development is all about 'timing, timing, timing'.[31]

The SOM and Foster masterplans were products of their time. Their approach to the listed buildings, demolishing some and preserving the rest as 'artefacts', now looks outdated. They did, however, act as a useful prototype against which subsequent plans could be compared.

Several factors prompted the negotiations to begin in earnest. First, the decision to terminate the railway at St Pancras removed uncertainty and risk from the development. It also resulted in the assembly of a site unencumbered by operational constraints, and in just two ownerships. The second factor was the government's provision of direct investment in the interchange, and the financial arrangements that allowed private investment to be leveraged into the project. Third, the landowners agreed a pragmatic mechanism to value their landholdings. Personal relationships and the trust engendered were significant in setting a firm foundation for the scheme.

The decision to seek a development partner (Argent) who understood delivery, aspired towards high quality and was able to work collaboratively was a decisive factor. This might appear obvious but many procurement exercises, especially in the public sector, stress financial offer and risk minimisation as main criteria in decisions. Shared aspirations led to compatible working relationships and trust between landowners and partners. This relationship was to prove crucial in decision-making.

Several other points are important to the subsequent narrative and the success of the scheme and are worth re-emphasising. LCR's insistence on taking responsibility for refurbishing St Pancras Chambers enabled a fully comprehensive project to take place. The refurbishment provided a dramatic and dignified entrance to the development and a clear statement that real change was at last happening at King's Cross. It also established its credentials with English Heritage as a sensitive steward of historic buildings, and this helped to smooth later discussions on the future of the historic buildings on the railway lands. LCR also built strong networks with local stakeholders, and passed these on to its development partner. In consequence, Argent St George inherited a high degree of goodwill with the council and the local community, and this meant that subsequent negotiations started on a positive footing.

4.
ESTABLISHING THE FRAMEWORK FOR NEGOTIATIONS

With Argent St George selected as developer for the site, Camden council had to gear up to deal with the development proposals. While the strength of Argent's bid for the role of London and Continental Railway (LCR)'s development partner was its track record and proposed development process, the absence of any specific proposals meant that there was a long way to go to a development scheme.[1] It was anticipated that the negotiation process would take years, not months, and would involve many different parties. Elected councillors needed to provide a clear policy steer for negotiations and to do this, had to be engaged and briefed. Planning officers needed to work out a strategy for the negotiation process, and ensure that an appropriate statutory policy framework was in place, and the Planning Department had to be properly resourced. Other service directorates also had to be prepared for the potential policy, service and financial implications of the development.

This chapter focuses on how these elements were put in place. In order to understand the policy context and organisational culture of Camden at the time, it is important to start with a brief history of the borough and its political power structures.

CAMDEN : THE PLACE AND ITS POLITICS

The London Borough of Camden (Figure 4.1) was created in 1965 in a comprehensive reorganisation of London government.[2] Camden combined a high business rate base in central London with liberal middle class areas in the north (Hampstead) and traditional working class areas around Euston and Camden Town. The result was one of the wealthiest left wing councils in the country. It was a confident, high tax and high spend borough, committed to high-quality service provision. Very much a Labour flagship, public support was reflected in the results of local elections that saw the Labour Party re-elected term after term.

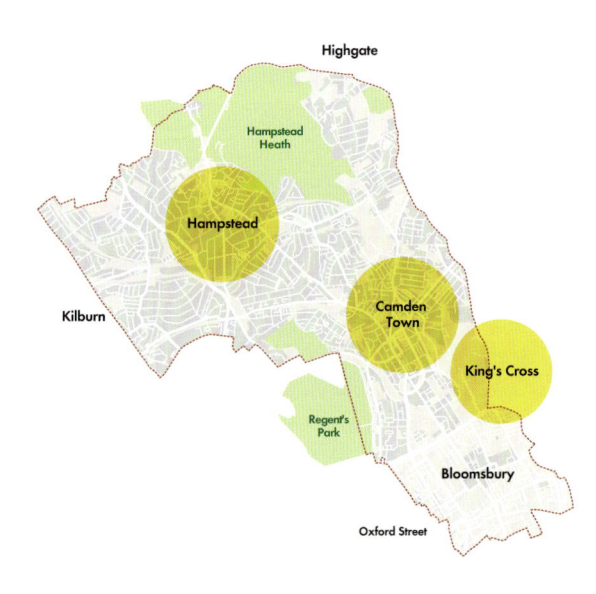

Figure 4.1: Map of Camden. Drawn by Allies and Morrison specifically for this book.

Anti-development campaigns in the 1960s and 1970s

Camden politics were marked by a series of landmark campaigns from the 1960s and 1970s, as residents and some of their politicians began first to question and then oppose large-scale redevelopment and the displacement of communities. As the tower blocks rose, so the building conservation movement gathered strength, and a number of epic planning battles took place. Opposition to a proposed urban motorway network saved Camden Lock. St Pancras station itself was saved from demolition by a high profile campaign led by Sir John Betjeman. Covent Garden was saved from comprehensive redevelopment plans in the 1970s, and plans by the British Museum to redevelop the historic area south of Great Russell Street for a new British Library were also thwarted. Other campaigns, such as the 'battle' for Tolmers Square,[3] were less successful. Due to political continuity in the council, the battle scars from this period were still apparent many years later and a deep suspicion of large scale development remained among some of the councillors.

The social equality agenda
From the 1960s onwards, the ethnicity of the borough diversified, first with large numbers of Irish and Greek immigrants and then in the 1990s with the arrival of Somalis and Bengalis. It also attracted a growing number of younger and wealthier residents, especially in the south. The result was a diverse and pluralistic borough with a deep sense of social justice, which in the words of council leader at the time, Jane Roberts, was 'edgy and contested'.[4]

Camden was also (and remains) a place of extreme contrasts. Every part of the borough has areas of affluence alongside areas of poverty. The diversity in the borough encompasses wide inequalities in household income, employment, health, disability, education, housing, crime and other indices of deprivation. These indices are put together to produce an Index of Multiple Deprivation (IMD).[5] In 2004 the IMD ranked Camden among the 21 most deprived districts in England.[6] By taking the difference between the highest and the lowest ward scores on the IMD, Camden was, in 2003, the most polarised borough in London (having a score of 33 compared to the least polarised, Richmond upon Thames at 342). The indices of deprivation also show that the St Pancras and Somers Town wards (immediately west of the King's Cross site), were in the 10 per cent most deprived areas in England in 2007.[7] The effects of this are graphically illustrated by the fact that there was a 15-year difference in male life expectancy between the richest and the poorest neighbourhoods in the borough. In some places this is just a five-minute walk.[8] As a result, a key aim for Camden's Neighbourhood Renewal Strategy (2003) was to 'reduce the inequalities that exist in the borough, generate social cohesion and create a more inclusive borough'.[9] Table 4.1 provides some baseline statistics for the borough around the start of the King's Cross negotiations.

Many of Camden's social characteristics were shared with the adjacent borough of Islington. It too combined wealthy and poor areas and had high levels of social housing. Two of its largest council estates, Bemerton and Barnsbury, adjoin King's Cross, and along with the Caledonian ward sit within the most deprived wards in the country.

The severe budget cuts imposed by the Thatcher governments in the 1980s changed the political environment. Both boroughs

Table 4.1: Statistics for Camden	
Population	193,000[10]
People employed within the borough	240,000[11]
Population from ethnic minorities	27%[12]
People living in families in receipt of all means-tested benefits	57,000[13]
Housed in some form of social rented housing	33.1%[14]
Unfit houses	11.9%[15]
Languages spoken in Camden schools	120[16]
Primary school children with English as a second language	44%[17]
Primary school children who are refugees	15%[18]
Unemployment in King's Cross ward	12%[19]
Average unemployment in Camden	6.3%[20]

went through a brief but disastrous period of opposition to the government, ran up huge debts and suffered near political and managerial breakdown. Decline set in, programmes were abandoned, staff made redundant and frontline services came close to collapse. In Islington, the ruling Labour group failed to take action to respond to the crisis. This led to the rise of a credible opposition and in 2000 the Liberal Democrats took control of the council from Labour.

By 2000, the political environment was very different. In Camden, a new generation of councillors had emerged, led by Jane Roberts, a pragmatic, centre-left politician. Roberts was a modernising leader who, unusually in local government, trusted her professional staff to get on with matters. She set out her priorities as the new leader of the council in a letter to the chief executive in 2000.[21] She was concerned over the increasing polarisation and inequality in the borough, and wanted to place social justice and quality of life at the heart of the council's agenda. She also stressed the importance of effective communication between the council and its residents, and a desire that the council should be 'thoughtful, imaginative and unafraid to experiment'. Unusually for a council leader, Roberts was also interested in urban planning, and a follow-up letter to the chief executive a few months later provided a clear commitment to the pursuit of good design.[22] Roberts was also clear that 'the authority is in the task. If there is a task to be done, you have to do it, not shirk it.' As leader of the council she was not under challenge, due partly to her consensual style of leadership, and had the respect of her fellow councillors and officers, but she did not seek to control all areas of council decision-making. Committees such as the development control subcommittee operated with a good deal of independence.

Camden's decision-making structure

Until 2000, decisions in Camden were made through committees dealing with areas, such as social services finance, planning or housing. These might have a number of subcommittees dealing with specific areas of business such as licensing or planning applications. In an attempt to modernise and streamline decision-making, the Local Government Act 2000, replaced the committee system with the leader and cabinet model. Each cabinet member held a separate portfolio, such as housing, finance, environment or education. This effectively created a two-tier structure, leaving some backbench councillors feeling excluded. Although the subcommittees conducted front line business, they were increasingly detached from policy-making, were no longer under the oversight of a senior committee chair and could operate with a great degree of independence. They came to represent a forum where backbenchers, excluded from influence by the cabinet system, could play a meaningful role in public life. As Chapter 8 demonstrates, this relative autonomy of the development control subcommittee had major implications for the King's Cross planning application. Council business also became shaped by the personalities and approaches of the individual executive portfolio holders. They developed close working relationships with their departmental chief officers, which in turn gave chief officers a high degree of managerial autonomy. Camden's particular decision-making structure for the King's Cross scheme is outlined in the box below.

ENGAGING COUNCILLORS

If officers were to have credibility at the negotiating table, they would need to have the long-term support of their local politicians. Local councillors are the democratically elected representatives of local people and their knowledge of, and links to their local area are

DECISION-MAKING STRUCTURE IN CAMDEN COUNCIL IN RELATION TO KING'S CROSS

Full council: comprising all 54 elected councillors. The ultimate decision-making body of the council from which all powers are delegated.

The executive: similar to the central government cabinet and comprising politicians with major portfolios. Chaired by the leader, it met monthly with officers from the senior management team. While it was not a decision-making body, it did set and review council policy and provided an opportunity for informal discussions on strategic issues. It was a useful forum for briefings on aspects of the King's Cross scheme, and acted as a sounding board during negotiations.

Executive member for environment: responsible for making executive decisions on planning policy, transport and environmental services, including the budget and performance of the environment directorate but with no responsibility for the operation of the development control subcommittee. Until May 2006 the post was held by councillor John Thane (Labour) and from May 2006 councillor Mike Greene (Conservative).

The development control subcommittee: one of the few public committees, and the most important in relation to the King's Cross development as it would decide the planning application. Over the course of a year, an authority like Camden will receive around 4,000 planning applications, ranging from small-scale domestic extensions to major developments. Roughly three-quarters will be approved, sometimes after negotiated changes. A large percentage of these are minor developments that are delegated to planning officers for decision. Anything of significance though, is decided by the development control subcommittee.

important. If they were to become alienated by the King's Cross scheme, the internal politics of Camden would be upset. Senior officers have to be able to manage the political interface, and failure to do this is usually perceived to be a serious and career-threatening weakness.

The King's Cross development was perceived by many local councillors as being long term, technical and divorced from the imperatives of day-to-day politics. Local politics are largely concerned with the issues affecting people's everyday lives, such as housing management, school places, street cleaning, refuse collection, crime and parking tickets. Local politicians are very responsive to such issues and a local councillor can often buck national and local voting trends through hard work and popularity. Many political campaigns have been won on a 'one vote at a time' basis and this inevitably skews the political agenda towards local, short-term micro-management. For many, King's Cross was also synonymous with drugs, crime and prostitution. While this state of affairs was not sanctioned, there was a belief among some councillors that at least the problem was containable within a part of the borough that was largely out of sight. Some feared that regeneration would merely result in displacement of the problems to Labour-held wards around Somers Town and Camden Town.

The first issue was how to engage with the planning of King's Cross without it becoming a party political issue. Since local politics are people-centred, the development had to be framed in terms of its impact on local communities. It was not about planning a distant future but about breaking the cycle of poverty and deprivation in the immediate area. Officers produced four starting propositions, all of which were intended to reframe the development into issues of political concern:

1 A child born in adjacent wards in 2001 would be 18 by the time the development was completed. They would have spent their entire childhood living next to a building site. The council therefore had a responsibility to manage the development process efficiently, and to ensure that other agencies did likewise.

2 Children entering Camden secondary schools in 2001 would be finishing their education when the first jobs in King's Cross would be available. King's Cross was already adjacent to the biggest labour market in Europe, but still had high levels of unemployment. Local residents were competing in a labour catchment area that covered the whole of South East England. What could be done to ensure that a child from Somers Town would have as good a chance of employment in King's Cross, as someone from Cambridge or Tunbridge Wells?

3 Should King's Cross be like Canary Wharf, Singapore or Manhattan, or should it be a piece of London connected seamlessly with its immediate hinterland?

> **For many Camden councillors, King's Cross was also synonymous with drugs, crime and prostitution.**

> **Camden officers were able to demonstrate to their councillors that they had anticipated potential disruptions, understood the political risks, and had managed these.**

4 How would the relationship with (Liberal Democrat) Islington be managed? How could Islington and its politicians be locked into a shared agenda with Camden? Would Islington demand disproportionate benefits from the scheme?

The aim of these four propositions was to generate interest, promote a strategic debate within the council and start to define political objectives for the development. Once the broad objectives were set by the leadership they could be translated into a policy agenda. It would then be possible to work with external organisations such as Islington and the mayor of London, establish their positions and address differences. A firm political agenda would also make it far more difficult for the process to become sidetracked by alternative proposals that might be developed by opposition groups.

The first proposition was addressed by setting up the King's Cross Impact Group (KCIG) to oversee the construction process and minimise disruption not only from the King's Cross development itself, but from the various rail infrastructure projects (see Chapter 3). Work on the underground concourses at King's Cross St Pancras had already started and brought with it substantial deliveries of materials, temporary construction sites and late night working. Euston Road itself was partially closed for several months while underpasses were reconstructed. It was recognised that if these works generated complaints from the public, and if these were not dealt with effectively, they could undermine the standing of the council with local people and raise opposition that might later transfer to the development.

Sir Bob Reid (ex-chairman of British Rail and chair of the King's Cross Partnership) was asked to chair the KCIG. Key stakeholders included Camden and Islington councils, LCR, Argent St George, the Regional Health Authority, the Metropolitan Police and London Underground. The group met fortnightly to review complaints and there was an agreement that those present would personally ensure that any problems arising from within their organisation would be dealt with by the next meeting. Over time the complaints dwindled and KCIG was able to meet less frequently. Camden officers were able to demonstrate to their councillors that they had anticipated potential disruptions, understood the political risks, and had managed these. KCIG also provided an extremely useful mechanism for informal liaison and for building effective working relationships and trust between the key organisations.

The other propositions around the provision of local opportunities in education and employment, the quality and nature of the place, became key policy aims for the council negotiations and are picked up in Chapter 6.

> **The potential scale and content of the development – around 2,000 new homes, a new school and sizeable population increase – would affect every council directorate and the potential gains and risks made it a key concern for the finance directorate.**

One more initiative helped to cement effective officer/councillor working relationships. In the autumn of 2003, a group of planning officers visited Berlin with councillors John Thane and Theo Blackwell (deputy leader and holder of the social inclusion and regeneration portfolios respectively) and Sue Vincent, who was the deputy chair of the development control subcommittee. Over three days the group visited Potsdammer Platz and the newly regenerated areas of East Berlin, met counterparts in the city government and engaged in long debates about architecture, planning and design. As councillor Blackwell said, 'suddenly development and regeneration got sexy'.[23] He had experienced some frustration on the development control subcommittee, seeing good schemes turned down on the opinions of a small group of local activists and conservationists. The visit brought councillor Blackwell into the frame as a key champion of the development, and Berlin provided a useful reference point for the debate about King's Cross.

PREPARING FOR THE NEGOTIATIONS

The potential scale and content of the development – around 2,000 new homes, a new school and sizeable population increase – would affect every council directorate, and the potential gains and risks made it a key concern for the finance directorate. At the start of negotiations, the implications of the project were debated by the council's management team. The potential gains, especially in new affordable housing,[24] were recognised, as was the risk of reputational damage should the council fail to deliver a scheme with real local benefits. Every directorate committed to engage with the development and to allocate staff time to support the negotiating team within planning. This support continued throughout the process.

Camden's chief executive provided an initial fighting fund of £500,000 (to be increased as negotiations proceeded), which was placed entirely at the discretion of the planning team. This helped to address the serious imbalance in resources between Camden and Argent St George. A project as large and complex as King's Cross presented an immense task for Camden's planning department. A policy framework had to be produced and signed off, a masterplan had to be considered, the quantum and distribution of land uses and traffic generation needed to be calculated and agreed, the impact on conservation areas and listed buildings needed to be assessed, as did the type and the design of housing, the quantity and quality of public spaces, the impact on school places and health provision, job creation, building heights, daylight and sunlight, overlooking and environmental impact.

It is usual for a developer to assemble a large team, many of whom are working full time on the project, with the prospect of large performance bonuses. Argent St George would also be able to employ top architectural, planning and legal consultants. Against these forces councils might typically pit a single, middle-ranking planning officer juggling this against 50 other cases and a stream of public correspondence. This is not a fair or winnable contest. The fighting fund enabled Camden to establish an in-house team and to employ top planning and legal consultants. This placed the negotiations on a more equal footing. In subsequent interviews, Argent maintain that far from being concerned by this fighting fund, it welcomed having a well resourced planning team with which to negotiate.

THE NEGOTIATING TEAMS

The negotiating teams are set out in Table 4.2, and these remained in place for the entire period. Both teams were empowered by their respective cabinet/board to negotiate, and either reach agreement or end up at appeal. Both teams had a clear brief and could sign off key agreements as they emerged. In Camden, the leader Jane Roberts and executive member John Thane provided a sounding board and, when difficulties arose, were prepared to back their officers. They also dealt effectively with the internal politics of the council.

The negotiating teams were both led by individuals with a strategic view on the desired outcomes. Roger Madelin's approach was to 'never delegate the critical thinking'.[25] They were supported by colleagues with deep technical knowledge and experience. This balance of strategic and tactical views helped each team to explore and test strategic options, before testing detailed proposals. The operational members of the teams were able to challenge or veto any strategic option that would have been either unworkable or would have significantly

Table 4.2: Executive oversight and negotiating teams		
Camden politicians (provide political overview and policy guidance)	Landowners (set expectations on scheme content and profitability)	
Leader of council – **Jane Roberts** Executive cabinet member for planning and environment – **John Thane**	Managing director of London Continental Railways – **Stephen Jordan**	Director of property at EXEL/Hyperion – **Edwin Davis**
Camden officers	Argent St George	
Director of environment and member of council's corporate management team – **Peter Bishop** Assistant director of environment, and head of planning – **Anne Doherty** Head of King's Cross team – **Bob West** Principal planning case officer – **Richard Kirby**	Chief executive officer of Argent PLC – **Roger Madelin** Representing St George – **Debbie Aplin** Deputy chief executive officer of Argent – **David Partridge** Director of planning – **Robert Evans** Senior project officer – **André Gibbs**	

compromised their respective bottom lines. The negotiations were layered with much of the critical detail resolved between individuals outside formal meetings. As the starting point was so open, the negotiations could focus on objectives rather than haggling over detail. Consequently, when proposals emerged, they were usually well understood and even when contentious, each party could at least understand why the other had put them forward. All specific proposals could then be tested against the previously agreed objectives.

The importance of effective partnership working based on trust comes up frequently in this book. Partnership with the private sector was a relatively new approach for local government that had emerged from the regeneration programmes of the early 1990s. Traditionally, very strict rules of engagement had been enforced and any informal or one-to-one meetings outside a strictly controlled office environment were likely to arouse deep suspicion. Social relationships between the public and private sector remain carefully regulated to safeguard the integrity of the development process, but partnership working is based on joint problem-solving and this requires a different set of relationships from the traditional adversarial culture of mutual mistrust between the planner and developer.

In any negotiation there are moments of deadlock when discussions have to move into exploring alternative possibilities that might be controversial or damaging if taken literally (or made public). There were potential risks in using off-the-record discussions to break the impasse, in particular the perception from outside parties that council officers and Argent St George were getting too close to one another. While the council leadership accepted that less formal working relationships between their planners and Argent St George were necessary (and never expressed any concerns on this), some more conservative councillors viewed it with mounting suspicion (see Chapter 8).

THE NEGOTIATING PROCESS

While Argent St George had no masterplan, it had worked out a process for developing the scheme and was prepared to involve other parties from the beginning. This process worked on the basis of 'convergence'. It started with defining, discussing and agreeing the basic questions around the sort of place that might be created. The aim was to consult widely and move progressively through each element of the development, finishing with the finer details. The rules in the process of building consensus were simple: discuss, propose, consult, evaluate, agree, abide by agreements and move on. The last step was crucial. There was an implicit agreement that once a point was agreed there would be no renegotiation. To have done so might have unravelled the entire process.

For a developer to work in this manner might seem logical, but is far from the norm. The standard approach of most developers is to assemble their professional team and produce an initial design, with plans, models and illustrative drawings, often without any prior discussion. The more cynical developers will add more floor space than they really believe the site will take, to allow horse-trading (or to generate

Figure 4.2: Brindleyplace, Birmingham – Argent's first major development.

excess profits). The scheme is then 'sold' to the planners and marketed to local communities. It is little surprise then, that planning is often seen as an adversarial process of damage limitation.

Although there was initial agreement between Camden council and Argent St George on the process, trust and effective working arrangements had to be established. And of course the negotiations had to be tied into the volatile world of council politics. Fortunately, LCR had already done a lot of the groundwork, and Camden council had already articulated its main objectives for housing, employment and wider area integration.

Establishing a vision

The first stage was to establish an agreed vision for the King's Cross development, describing the kind of place that Argent St George and Camden council wanted to achieve through the development. At their first meeting in May 2001, Roger Madelin invited Camden council's newly appointed director of environment, Peter Bishop, to visit Argent's development at Brindleyplace in Birmingham to gain an insight into its development approach. The invitation was accepted and a day was spent looking around the scheme. On the train back to London, Bishop remarked that he thought that Brindleyplace was, 'good for Birmingham in the 1990s, but would not be good enough for King's Cross in the 2000s'. The lively debate that ensued went on to cover affordable housing, social integration and the importance of streets as public spaces, a point that made an impression on Madelin.[26] There is no doubt that Brindleyplace was impressive (see Figure 4.2). It served as Argent's 'calling card' and confirmed that it cared passionately about what it built. The masterplan was well thought out, Argent had commissioned good architects to design the major buildings, the public realm was of a high, if manicured, standard and the range of independent shops, bars and restaurants was impressive. What was lacking, certainly in 2001, was a sense that Brindleyplace integrated as well with its surroundings, particularly the deprived neighbourhood of Ladywood, as it did with the commercial centre of Birmingham. Brindleyplace felt too corporate. The 'hard edge' to the development and the relatively low level of affordable housing that it provided set clear markers for the forthcoming negotiations.

Camden's politicians feared that King's Cross would be like Canary Wharf (an isolated and elite office precinct cut off from its hinterland), or that it would be a futuristic place resembling Singapore or Hong Kong. The planning officers' response was that King's Cross would be 'another piece of London'. In practice, this meant that the development should be based on public streets, have squares and parks, a mix of uses and a human scale. There were precedents throughout central London. One of the first drawings produced by the masterplanners Allies and Morrison was a projection of King's Cross in a future A–Z map directory of London (Figure 4.3). Using familiar and recognisable graphics, this image aimed to illustrate these basic principles, in particular that the development would link into the surrounding neighbourhoods.

Building on early discussions, Argent St

George produced a set of guiding principles for the development. These were published in its first consultation document, Principles for a Human City, in July 2001:[27]

- a robust urban framework
- a lasting new place
- promote accessibility
- a vibrant mix of uses
- harness the value of heritage
- work for King's Cross, work for London
- commit to long-term success
- engage and inspire
- secure delivery
- communicate clearly and openly.

Jane Roberts wrote a foreword to the document, stressing the importance of the scheme and outlining Camden's own regeneration objectives. Principles for a Human City reflected Argent's particular approach to development. Commercially, it recognised that by creating the conditions to improve and enhance the quality of urban life it would also create long-term

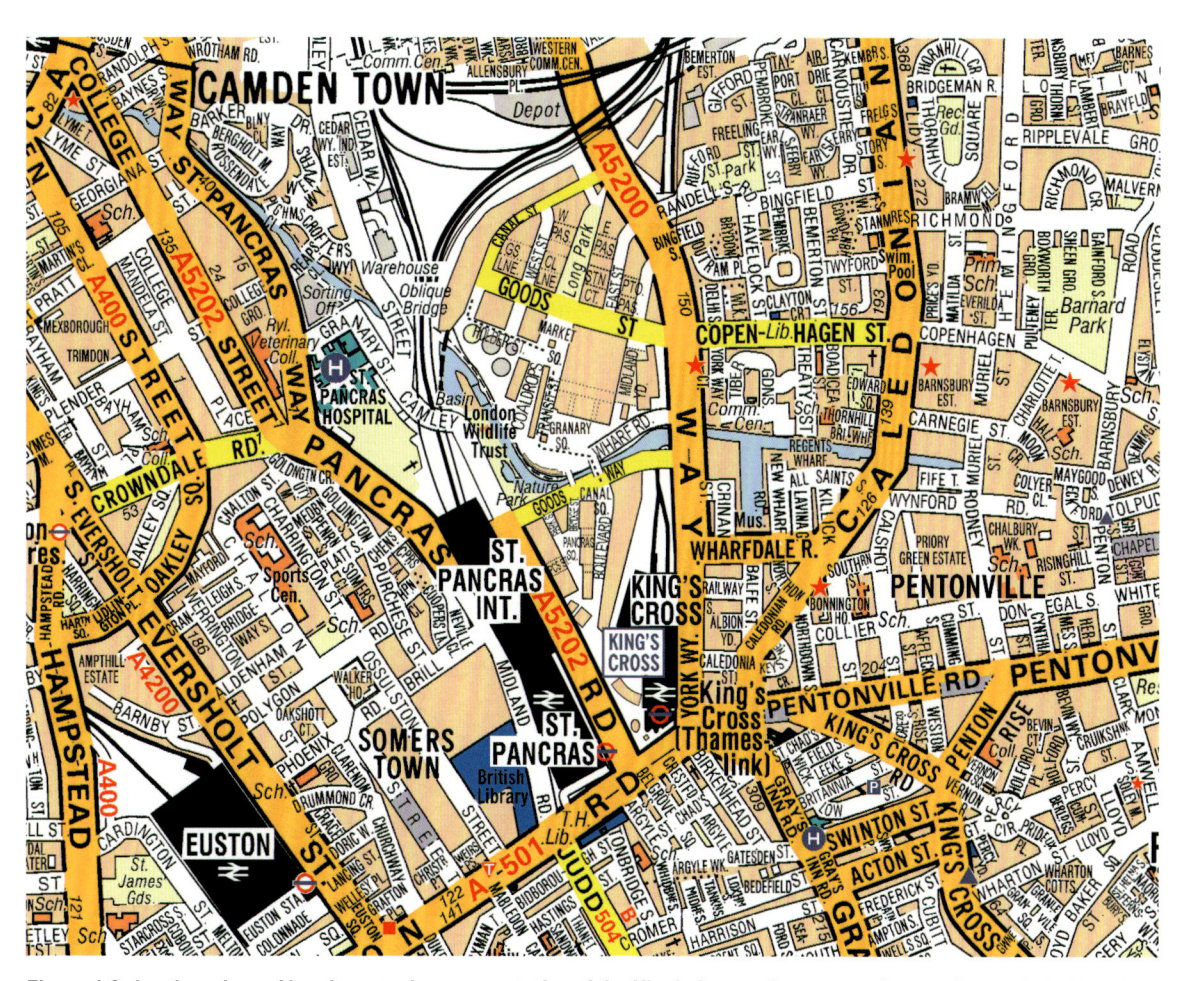

Figure 4.3: Another piece of London – early representation of the King's Cross scheme superimposed on an A–Z of London.

value. It was as simple as that. The document recognised that King's Cross would have an important role to play in the London economy, but it also presented an opportunity to benefit the community. The document's aim was to build a consensus about the fundamentals of the development before embarking on detailed proposals. Argent St George consulted widely on the document (detailed in Chapter 7).

In response to the document, Camden published its own initial objectives for the site – Towards an Integrated City, October 2001.[28] The objective was to create firm physical, economic and social links between the development and the local area so that it would be a well integrated part of London. The document set out the positive qualities that the council wished King's Cross to have. It should:

- contribute to London as a world city, while also relating well to surrounding areas. It should make strong connections with local residential and business communities
- have a mixed character with housing, retail, culture, leisure, offices and open space
- incorporate a rich mix of architectural styles that combine high quality design with lively, safe and attractive streets and public open spaces
- address community safety problems
- respect the Victorian heritage and understand the area's essential character. Distinctive structures to be incorporated into an outstanding contemporary development
- have high environmental and amenity value, especially round the Regent's Canal
- have easy and safe routes, with reduced traffic
- embrace sustainable development principles.

These objectives were summarised in King's Cross – Camden's Vision, 2002, signed by both Jane Roberts and Steve Hitchins, the leader of Islington council.[29] In these two documents, Camden council set out its aims as a basis for consensus-building with Islington and the mayor.

NEGOTIATING TACTICS

Avoiding a public inquiry

Underlying the negotiation strategy was a shared desire by Camden council and Argent to avoid a public inquiry (see textbox on p.57).

Although impartial and rigorous, an enquiry would have taken the final decision away from Camden council and present a risk with an uncertain outcome. Since the negotiations aimed to manage risk, the lottery of an inquiry suited neither party. Both Argent and Camden council also viewed a public inquiry as a sign of failure. Given the complex issues and the number of interest groups involved, an inquiry would inevitably have been long and might have put at least a two-year delay on the project. To compound this, there was at the time a 15-month backlog of appeals awaiting a hearing at the Planning Inspectorate. The costs to both parties would have run to many millions of pounds. Both sides saw this as the nuclear option: it was there if needed, but would benefit neither side (see Chapter 8 for further analysis). At the most difficult and acrimonious stages in negotiations the prospect of a public inquiry acted as a major incentive to problem-solving. That said, Camden council had the resources to fight an appeal and

PUBLIC INQUIRIES

A public inquiry is held by the Planning Inspectorate, an independent agency of the Department for Communities and Local Government (DCLG), to consider planning consent refusal appeals. An inquiry is not a law-court, but proceedings are similar, with representation by advocates, expert evidence and witness cross examination. Lasting days, weeks, or – in the case of major infrastructure schemes – years, they might be triggered if:
- the application was not decided in time (16 weeks) and the developer did not agree an extension
- the neighbouring borough (Islington), the Regional Planning Authority (Greater London Authority), the Environment Agency, or English Heritage objected to the scheme
- Camden itself referred the application to the secretary of state (SoS) for a public inquiry.

Advocacy groups and opposition parties may ask for public inquiries but, unlike statutory authorities, have no power to force one. The SoS also has the power to take over planning applications from local authorities, known as 'call-in'. This is infrequent, usually where development conflicts with national policies, or raises significant architectural issues. A planning inspector is appointed, carries out the inquiry and reports to the SoS who makes a final decision.

CAMDEN'S SUCCESS AT PLANNING APPEALS

Argent knew that Camden council had substantial funds for an appeal, and as negotiations continued, two successful examples influenced how seriously Argent viewed this. Firstly, Camden council turned down an application from London Underground Limited (LUL) for the redevelopment of Camden Town tube station. Camden council supported this long overdue scheme in principle, due to weekend closures and overcrowding. Yet the proposed design was poor, and LUL refused to engage new architects, not believing that Camden council would refuse on design grounds.[30] In December 2003, Camden council did turn it down, fought the appeal, and won.

The second case concerned Union Railways' application[31] for extended working hours for the CTRL into St Pancras construction, due for completion late 2006. Behind schedule, they wanted agreement for 24-7 working hours, for three years.[32] The construction area, however, was within 10 metres of Coopers Close housing terrace in Somers Town.

Camden had been inclined to agree on condition that residents would be compensated with weekend respite in local hotels. When Union Railways rejected this, Camden refused the application and the case went to appeal. Camden funded barristers for the local residents, to mount their own challenge under little used powers of 'general wellbeing'.[33] Camden council also managed to get the hearing held in the community hall – the tenants' home turf. Influenced by the sense of injustice felt by residents, the inspector noted that - since construction had been suspended to allow for disinterment in St Pancras churchyard - 'the living were probably entitled to the same respect as the dead'.[34] The appeal was dismissed, Union Railways was forced to renegotiate, and a suitable compensation package was agreed for locals.

Argent could not be assured of winning. As the textbox on p.57 shows, Camden had proved that it was prepared to refuse applications that it considered unacceptable and had the capability and resources to win appeals.

Some developers, however, see the appeal route as an effective way of threatening planning authorities and short-circuiting the process. Argent was not in this category, but its housing partner St George was and this difference in approach was one of issues that ultimately broke up the partnership. This is covered in more detail in Chapter 6. Paradoxically, some Camden councillors might also have preferred an inquiry. It would have distanced them from the responsibility of decision-making, and would have freed them up to campaign. Should the decision have gone against the council they could blame the inspector, or indeed their own planning staff for failing to put up a sufficiently robust case.

The attraction of raw politics in councils should not be underestimated; councils are at heart political entities. A campaign or public display of resistance can have its advantages and such displays of opposition were familiar territory for some of Camden's long-serving councillors. At times there was even a suspicion among Camden officers that some councillors relished one last great battle. Winning would not have necessarily been the objective; the struggle alone would have been applauded by some members of the local community and the local press. Councillor Woodrow, the chair of the development control subcommittee, expressed the view on a number of occasions that a public inquiry would be the correct forum for determining the King's Cross scheme (see Chapter 8).

Camden and Argent St George constructed parallel negotiating tactics. Stakeholders were divided into those who had the ability to force an inquiry and those who did not. In the first group were Islington council, Transport for London (TfL), the mayor, English Heritage and the two local MPs (Chris Smith and Frank Dobson).[35] The second group comprised all other interest groups, including local community groups, businesses and individuals. While their views were recognised as important, they did not have the automatic right to trigger a public inquiry. This inevitably put them on a different footing. The public consultation processes for King's Cross are covered separately in Chapter 7.

Camden council's tactic was to enter into detailed negotiations with stakeholders who had the ability to force an inquiry, analyse their interests and bottom lines, and provide assurance that Camden would act on their behalf. This effectively denied them a seat at the negotiating table and prevented discussions from becoming unwieldy or over-influenced by a particular party. Negotiations between Camden council and Argent would be difficult enough without other parties being directly involved.

Camden council also wanted to prevent Argent St George from making independent deals with these same stakeholders. As long as they saw Camden representing their interests in the negotiations, they would not be tempted to seek separate agreements with Argent St George. This would have been particularly important in the event of the scheme going to public inquiry. Should this occur, Camden council wanted as many of the key stakeholders on its side as possible in order to present a strong and united case against Argent St George. The upside of this approach was that Camden council took responsibility for building a consensus among public sector stakeholders, thus giving a greater degree of control and certainty to the process. As part of this strategy, Camden council developed specific tactics for Islington, the mayor and English Heritage.

Building a relationship with Islington
As an adjoining borough, Islington council could force a public inquiry if it objected to the development. It was also the planning authority for the 'Triangle' – a small part of the King's Cross site that lay within its borough boundaries (Figure 4.4). Camden officers feared that Islington council could use this position to gain access to the negotiating table and skew benefits (in the form of affordable housing and community facilities) disproportionately away from Camden council. Even if it did not do this, having Islington council as an unknown factor would confuse negotiations and pose significant risks.

Islington council was under a Liberal Democrat administration that was struggling with a severe budgetary crisis and strains on frontline services. There were two possible scenarios: either Islington council would see King's Cross as a source of cash, or it would be too distracted by its internal problems to get involved. Neither scenario was desirable.

Camden council approached Islington council with an offer to conduct all negotiations on its behalf. This was agreed in principle at a meeting between the councils' respective directors. The basis of this agreement was that Camden council would have full control over the negotiations, including areas of the scheme within Islington. Camden council would provide office space for Islington planners within its King's Cross team, and would write Islington council's planning reports. This would relieve Islington's hard pressed planners from a considerable burden of work. Islington council would be kept fully informed of the progress of negotiations and its councillors would make the final decision on that part of the development within its borough boundaries. Camden council would also negotiate a fair distribution of benefits between the boroughs, including access for Islington residents to any facilities on the Camden part of the site. This agreement held throughout the negotiations, and Islington council did not object in 2006 to the final application on the main site. It was also agreed that Argent St George would submit a separate application to Islington council for the 'Triangle' site. The thinking here was that detaching the application for the 'Triangle' from the main site would avoid delays to the main application. Ultimately, Islington council did refuse consent for the 'Triangle' site, and the reasons for this are set out in Chapter 8.

London boroughs are fiercely protective of their respective turfs. Although the two councils were under different political administrations, there were regular meetings between the two leaders, who had previously worked together at the Whittington Hospital. The proposal that Camden council would negotiate on Islington council's behalf was agreed by Steve Hitchins, the leader of Islington council, and he co-signed

PLANNING, POLITICS AND CITY MAKING

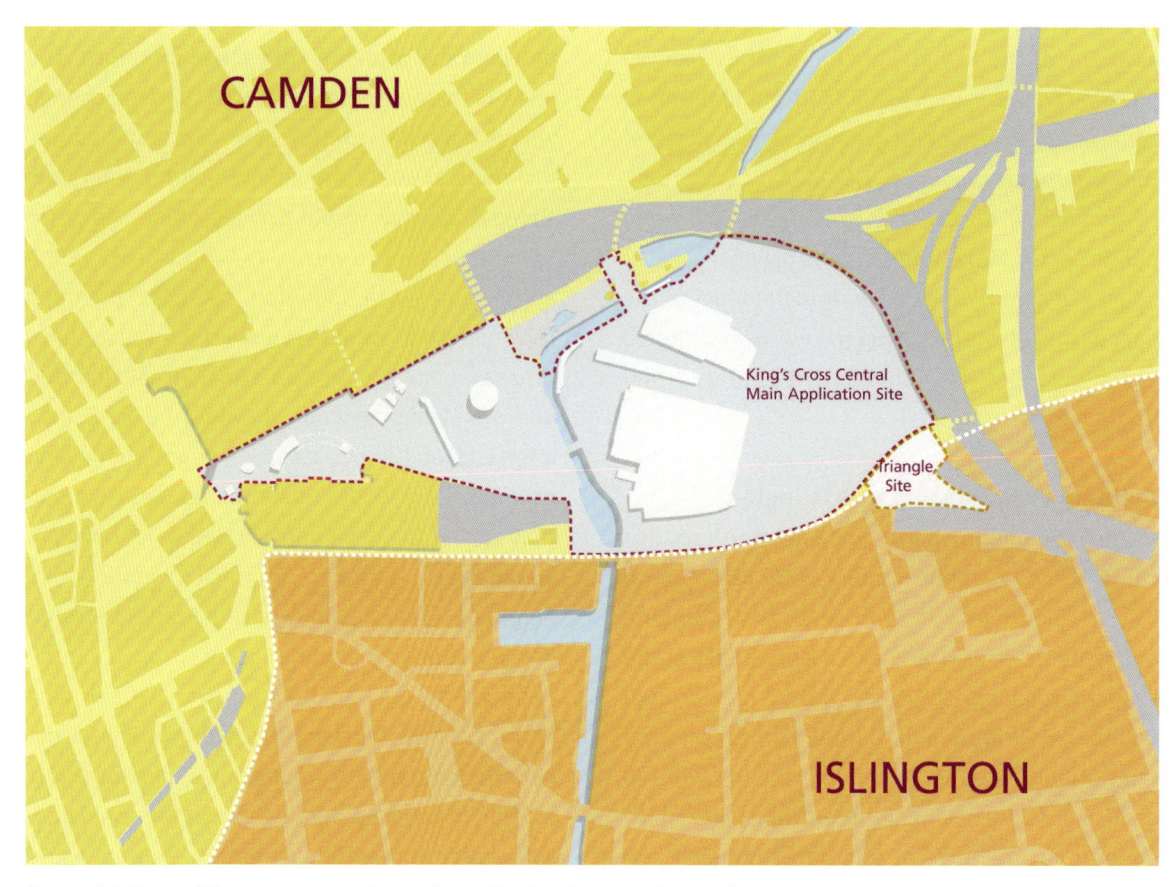

Figure 4.4: Borough boundaries showing main application site and Islington 'Triangle' site.

the foreword to King's Cross – Camden's Vision, referred to earlier. This represented a public commitment by both council leaders to the basic principles of the development.

To cede control over a project of this value and importance is almost without precedent but an element of good fortune came into play. First of all, Steve Hitchins was aware of the appalling underlying social deprivation in the area and of the earlier attempts to regenerate King's Cross. Second, being a newly elected leader with no alliance to the opposition groups who had been active in the area, he was not pulled into opposing the scheme. Third, Islington had the Arsenal football stadium development to deal with and this was occupying a great deal of its energy. In favour of good regeneration schemes, Hitchins trusted Jane Roberts and never considered misusing his position to extract disproportionate benefits from the scheme. Ironically, had Islington remained under Labour control, opposition groups would have wielded greater political influence and it is quite possible that negotiations might have been considerably more difficult.[36]

> **To cede control over a project of this value and importance is almost without precedent but an element of good fortune came into play.**

Working with English Heritage

The King's Cross site was dominated by two Grade I-listed stations and contained a number of important 19th-century buildings, as well as a wealth of industrial archaeology. It was largely covered by the King's Cross conservation area (see Figure 4.5). If English Heritage had opposed the King's Cross proposals, a public inquiry would have been a certainty. Fortunately, LCR had already established trust and credibility with English Heritage through its proposals to move the triplet gasholders and restore St Pancras station, and Argent St George wished to retain nearly all of the historic fabric on site.

The approach to heritage conservation has a wide range of interpretations. The liberal view is that some change can be accommodated while preserving the essential character of historic buildings (see Figure 5.2); the more pedantic standpoint sees little or no possibility of change regardless of the merits of the case. The interpretations of individual English Heritage officers are often crucial in this respect. Fortunately, the two senior officers, Philip Davis and Paddy Pugh, were pragmatic and positive throughout the negotiations, and working relations were therefore open and candid. English Heritage was given access to the negotiations when appropriate, and its technical expertise proved invaluable. It recognised both the importance of creating a new context for the historic buildings, and that the masterplan had to have a clear and robust logic. Where these were in conflict, detailed options studies were commissioned by Argent St George. Issues concerning key buildings are set out in Chapters 5 and 8.

Working with the mayor and the Greater London Authority

The then mayor, Ken Livingstone, represented the biggest unknown. Livingstone was a left wing (previously Labour) politician who had been a Camden councillor in the 1970s. The office of mayor had been newly established in 2000, and had responsibility for strategic planning under the Greater London Authority (GLA), and for transport under TfL. Livingstone wanted to see London established as a leading city on the world stage and was therefore in favour of commercial development. He should have been an ally to Camden council in the negotiations, but there was a suspicion among Camden's officers that he might try to interfere unduly in the scheme. This was confirmed in a meeting between Livingstone, Jane Roberts, Camden officers and Argent St George in September 2001. In their recollections of the meeting, Roger Madelin described him as 'supportive', while Jane Roberts found him 'rude and overbearing'.[37] During the meeting he offered to 'sort out' any problems that Argent might have with Camden

PLANNING, POLITICS AND CITY MAKING

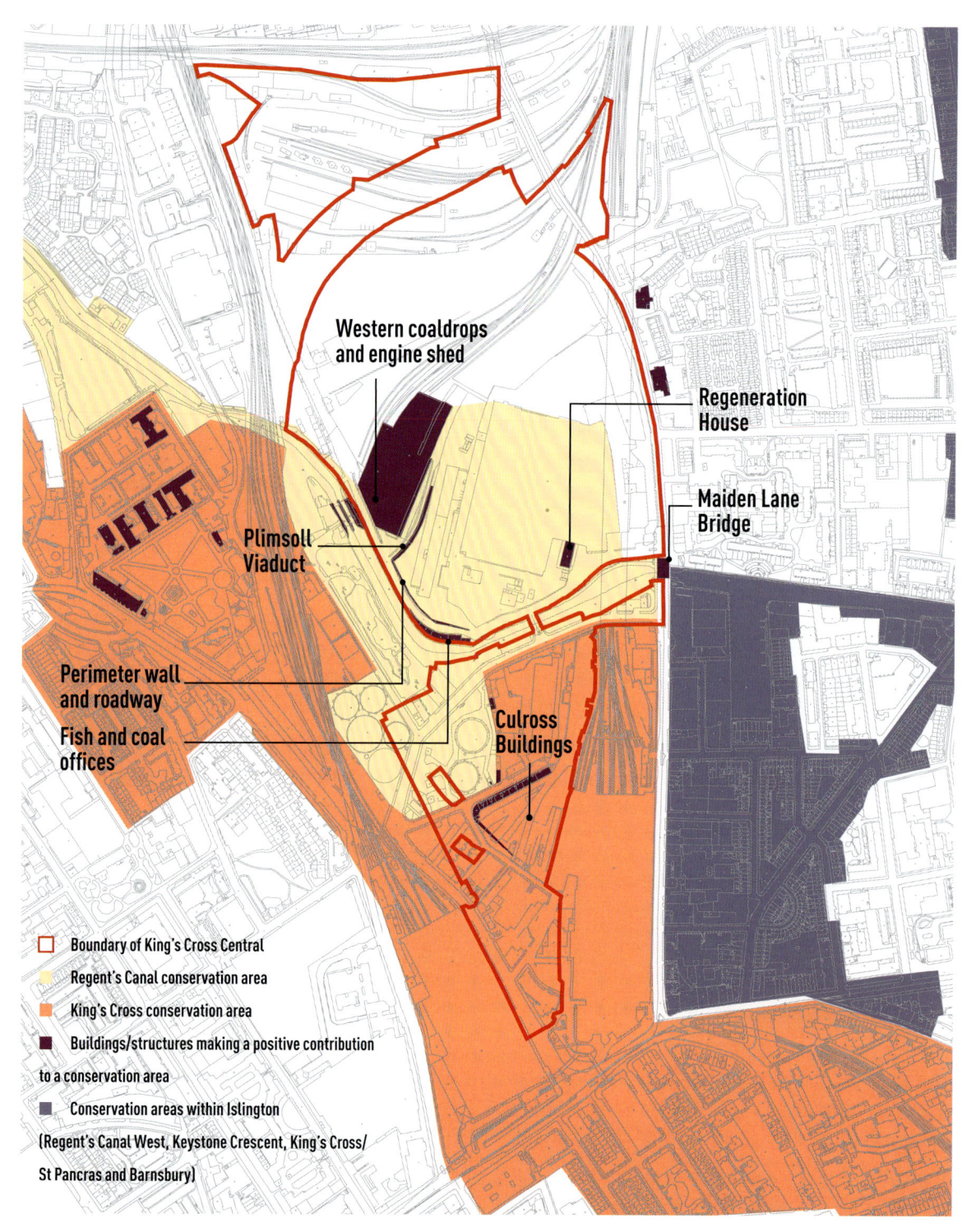

Figure 4.5: King's Cross conservation areas.

Labels on map:
- Western coaldrops and engine shed
- Regeneration House
- Plimsoll Viaduct
- Maiden Lane Bridge
- Perimeter wall and roadway
- Fish and coal offices
- Culross Buildings

Legend:
- Boundary of King's Cross Central
- Regent's Canal conservation area
- King's Cross conservation area
- Buildings/structures making a positive contribution to a conservation area
- Conservation areas within Islington (Regent's Canal West, Keystone Crescent, King's Cross/St Pancras and Barnsbury)

council, and described English Heritage as 'the Taliban'. He also encouraged Argent to build tall buildings, in contravention of his own London Plan policy on viewing corridors.[38]

Camden council had not expected to see the mayor align with Argent, and viewed this as a threat to Camden council's legitimacy in negotiating the scheme.[39] The strategy for working with the mayor and the GLA had to be rethought. Camden council's response was to revise its own planning policy to ensure that it was identical to the emerging new London Plan. It was already revising its policy to increase the requirement for the provision of affordable housing (then at 30 per cent in the existing Unitary Development Plan) to 50 per cent. This would give the GLA no legitimate remit to intervene. It also meant that on issues such as a failure to agree on affordable housing numbers, the GLA would have to support Camden council's position should there be an appeal. The second aspect of Camden council's approach was to set up regular liaison meetings with GLA planners to provide updates on progress, while excluding them from direct negotiations. Notwithstanding Livingstone's support, Argent St George never saw the mayor as a route to gain permission for King's Cross, and recognised that he might promote his own agenda, particularly around transport. As far as transport issues were concerned, Camden council and Argent St George decided to deal with TfL on an issue by issue basis, on the assumption (which proved to be correct) that they did not have the internal processes in place to coordinate discussions.

In practice, though, the GLA took the view that Camden council was capable of getting on with King's Cross, understood that its direct involvement was not welcomed, and was content to focus its energies elsewhere. It was briefed by Camden council, and kept the mayor informed. Later in the process it played a role in the background through representing the planning arguments to the mayor in response to TfL's demands. According to Colin Wilson, now strategic planning manager at the GLA, it is likely that the GLA would have wanted a more central role if the project had taken place at a later date when it was more established.[40]

ESTABLISHING THE POLICY FRAMEWORK

In setting local planning policy, councils have to comply with national and regional frameworks. National guidance had already identified King's Cross as a site where development should support London's position as a global business and commercial centre.[41] When negotiations commenced, Camden council's policy for the site was covered by Supplementary Planning Guidance (SPG) and by Chapter 13 of its Unitary Development Plan (UDP), which had been adopted in March 2000. This had designated the King's Cross railway lands as an opportunity area, with the potential to create a new quarter for London. The policy aimed to protect features of historic and conservation importance, and encourage the development of office, tourism, leisure, housing and community facilities. Local employment was also high on the council's priorities for the area. Outside the site, parts of the King's Cross and Somers Town wards were defined as 'areas of community regeneration', reflecting their status as some of the most disadvantaged areas in the UK. Regeneration of these areas was another clear priority.

The UDP did not, however, have an up-to-date policy concerning the provision of affordable housing. Without policy support, Camden council had no basis to achieve its primary political objective of substantial affordable housing on the site. Camden council therefore decided to fast-track a revision to the chapter of the UDP that specifically covered King's Cross and increase requirements for affordable housing. This process is outlined in Figure 4.6. The reasoning was simple: a new adopted UDP would be subject to extensive formal public consultation, and would carry more statutory weight in negotiations. It would ultimately support Camden council's decision to approve or refuse the development.

The decision to review a policy framework in advance of a major development is good practice. However, negotiating this explicitly with the developer concerned is very unusual. In effect, Camden re-wrote the policy to accommodate the first round of negotiations on the scheme. The rationale was that discussing the policy in advance with the developer would simplify the process of getting the plan formally adopted. The more standard approach would have been to have negotiated with Argent after it had

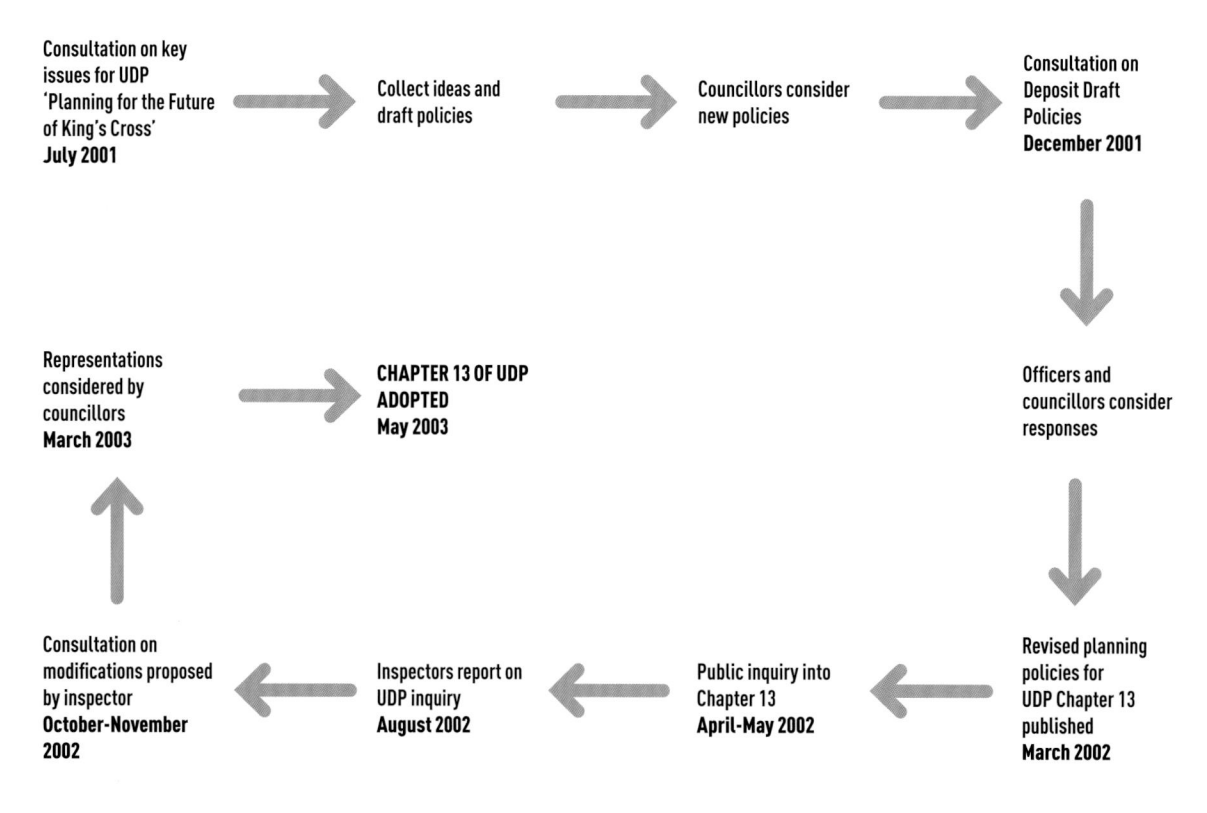

Figure 4.6: The UDP process.

> **The presence of conservation areas and listed buildings meant there was a legal requirement for a detailed application, since the impact on listed buildings had to be assessed with a high degree of certainty.**

objected to policy proposals and then referred any outstanding issues to a public inquiry. The end results were the same. The revised planning framework cleared some of the major issues, in particular setting out a minimum quantum of housing, and the requirement that 50 per cent of this would be affordable. The key designations of the plan as they affect the King's Cross site are shown in Figure 4.7.

Eighteen months later, the UDP was approved by the Planning Inspectorate, following an Examination in Public. Three years later, when the planning application was submitted, the council was able to say that the proposed development was fully in compliance with its UDP. By publishing its revised policy in advance of the London Plan being adopted in February 2004, Camden council effectively ensured that the GLA policy was influenced by it and not vice versa.

DECIDING THE NATURE OF THE PLANNING APPLICATION

An early issue that Camden and Argent St George had to resolve was the nature of the planning application; there were two options – a detailed or an outline application. A detailed application would design every building and public space, while an outline application might be as simple as a statement of the types and quantum of uses, their impact in terms of traffic and job creation, an Environmental Impact Assessment (EIA) and an illustrative masterplan.

This issue was not straightforward. The presence of conservation areas and listed buildings meant there was a legal requirement for a detailed application, since the impact on listed buildings had to be assessed with a high degree of certainty. Argent St George argued that a detailed application would require huge up-front design costs, but the resulting designs would be far too rigid to ever be built over the anticipated long development period. Argent St George would need some flexibility to be able to respond to changes in the market, and it would be costly and cumbersome to have to return to Camden council every time it wanted to change any of the details. Camden council on the other hand could not grant a consent that would be so flexible that it would allow Argent St George (or any subsequently owner) to change the agreement significantly. Both parties agreed that some sort of hybrid application would be required. The problem was that if the scheme departed from the legal requirements this could offer easy grounds for a judicial review (see Chapter 8 pp.165-66). Argent instructed Michael Gallymore of Hogan Lovells and Camden council instructed Stephen Ashworth of Dentons to scrutinise

PLANNING, POLITICS AND CITY MAKING

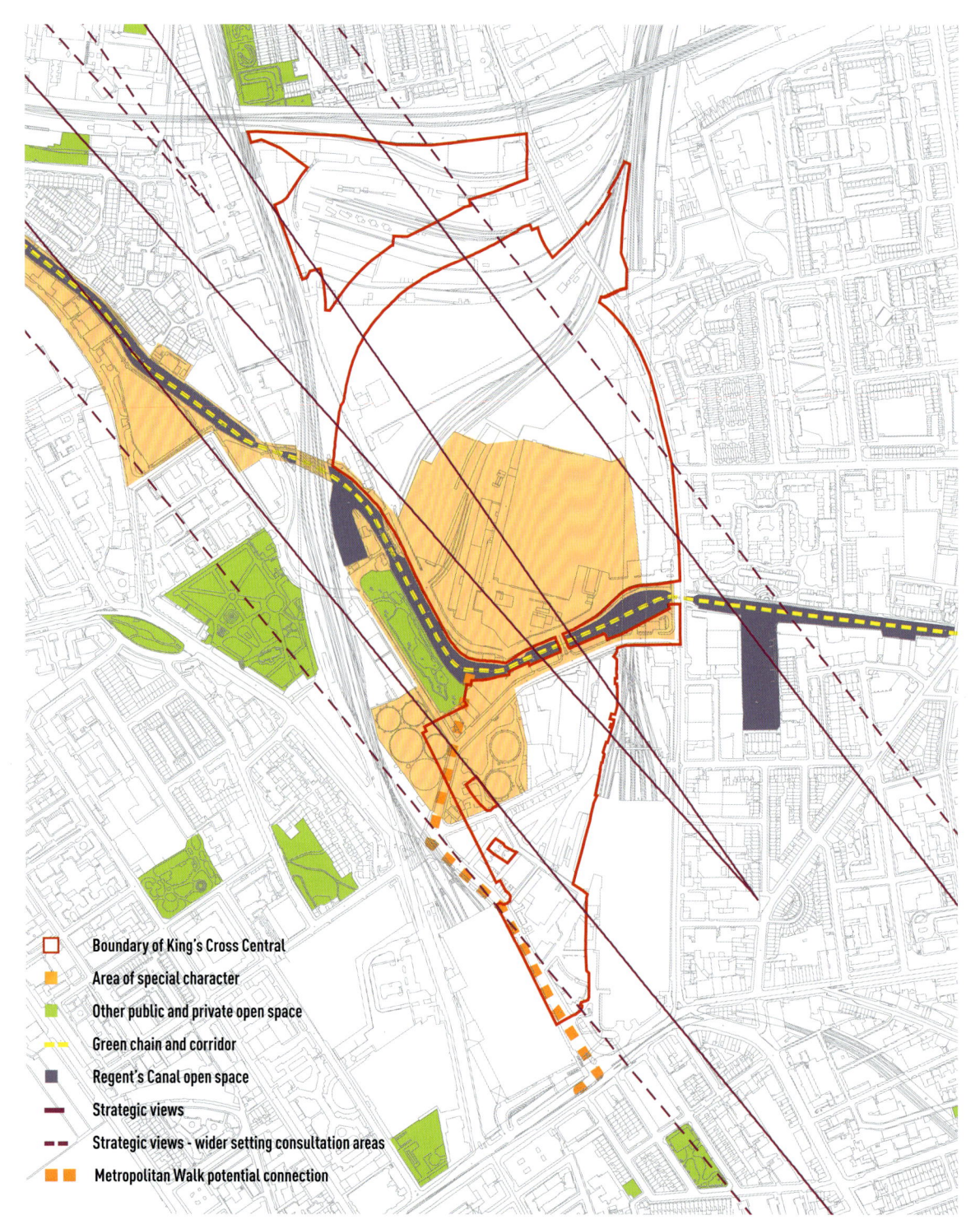

- ☐ Boundary of King's Cross Central
- ■ Area of special character
- ■ Other public and private open space
- ▬ ▬ Green chain and corridor
- ■ Regent's Canal open space
- ▬▬ Strategic views
- ▬ ▬ Strategic views - wider setting consultation areas
- ■ ■ Metropolitan Walk potential connection

Figure 4.7: King's Cross – planning policy designations from Camden UDP.

its work to ensure meticulous procedural compliance. On the critical question of the form of the application, they worked together.

The crux of the problem was that government guidance stated that a planning authority needed to have sufficient information to make a decision. After nine months the legal teams had constructed a new hybrid form of planning application that would comply with planning law. This hybrid application combined the flexibility Argent sought with the level of certainty that Camden council needed. A masterplan would be required to illustrate the form of the development, streets, circulation, specific building plots, building lines and public spaces. A schedule of accommodation was also required, along with the maximum levels for the floor space in each category of use. Argent had the flexibility to draw down the floor space on a series of designated building plots. Each plot had maximum building heights and a minimum environmental specification attached to it. The theory was then tested by the masterplan team. Exhaustive urban design studies considered every combination of height and building use, especially in relation to streets and public spaces.

It was not, however, without its critics. Holgersen and Haarstad[42] suggest that the hybrid planning permission further tipped the agenda in favour of the developers, making it one-way and controlled by Argent. The opposition group King's Cross Railway Lands Group (KXRLG) argued that by allowing a flexible planning permission, Camden council's planners were effectively abrogating their responsibility to consider later development stages in the light of issues such as the developers' performance or later changes in government policy.[43] These arguments ignore the difficulties of developing a site as complex as King's Cross over an extended period. There is evidence set out in Chapter 8 that without this form of application, development would not have taken place at King's Cross. Moreover, the hybrid form of planning application was not challenged, and has since been used in other major developments, most recently at Battersea.

THE BOTTOM LINE

Camden's objectives for King's Cross had been set in the UDP (first drafted in December 2001). To summarise, there were five 'bottom lines'. The first was that a balanced, mixed community should be created at King's Cross. The second was that there should be a significant element of housing, and that 50 per cent of this should be affordable. The minimum quantum of housing, 2,000 units, was specified in the revised UDP, although the maximum was not stated. In the absence of any scientific method of calculation, planning officers thought that 2,000–2,500 units 'felt' right. The third was that the development should successfully address the basic regeneration question, namely how it would make a difference to disadvantaged communities in the immediate neighbourhood. The fourth was a requirement that the public realm should remain public in its nature and open to all to enjoy. In particular, the development should include at least two new parks, should be permeable and connect with the surrounding neighbourhoods. The final requirement was that the development should embody exemplary standards of design

Table 4.3: Argent's initial business plan (June 2000)[44]

Mix of uses	Downside	Target	Upside
Mainstream uses			
Offices	2m sq ft	3.5m sq ft	5m sq ft
Homes	2000	3000	4000
Percentage private	50%	65%	75%
Percentage affordable	50%	35%	25%
Retail/restaurant/leisure	300,000 sq ft	500,000 sq ft	1m sq ft
Other commercial uses			
Hotels	200 rooms	400 rooms	800 rooms
Light industrial/workshops	100,000 sq ft	500,000 sq ft	1m sq ft
Ancillary uses			
Conference/exhibition/performance/sport/people attractor	100–500,000 sq ft	100–500,000 sq ft	100–500,000 sq ft
Education	100-200,000 sq ft	100-200,000 sq ft	100-200,000 sq ft
Other community uses	20,000 sq ft	10,000 sq ft	10,000 sq ft
Common parts			
Circulation (% of total site area)	20%	15%	12.5%
Public open spaces	20%	15%	12.5%

in its architecture, urban design and landscape and, unless completely impractical, retain and refurbish all of the historic buildings on the site.

Despite having to meet the landowners' requirements that the long-term value of the site should be maximised, Argent's bottom lines were more complex. It recognised that an office dominated scheme would be unacceptable to the planners and the community and that a mixed-use development with exceptional public open space would be less risky, more deliverable and in the long term more valuable.

Initial aims were set out in a confidential memorandum from Argent's non-executive director/founder, Peter Freeman in June 2000.[45] The memorandum reflected the need to get St George, LCR and Excel to buy into a planning-led strategy that optimised land values (the principal requirement of the two landowners), while also creating an attractive new quarter of London that would win Camden council approval. In it he stated that:

'The overall financial aim is for the majority of the development to be taken up by Value Creating Uses where the finished value exceeds Total Costs by a significant margin to create both significant land value and substantial development profit after taking account all infrastructure, S.106 obligations and Non Value Creating Uses [...]. However, it is recognised that although a

> **It was agreed that while the development should aim to retain the listed buildings on the site, the Culross Buildings would have to be demolished if a central connecting boulevard was to be built.**

particular point in time on use (e.g. offices) might show the highest margin in terms of pounds per sq. ft., the [...] Planning Interest Parties (i.e. Camden) are likely to favour a mix of homes, employment uses and public uses, rather than a single use development – whether office, residential or retail – which would almost certainly be refused.'

In relation to Argent's initial business plan (Table 4.3) the memorandum states:
'The Parties (Argent, LCR and St George) expect each of the Mainstream Uses to form a significant part of the development. The Parties will seek to minimise the Ancillary Uses unless they can be demonstrated to make a reasonable profit margin on their direct costs and make a contribution of £1m per acre, the Parties will keep the Ancillary Uses to 10% or less of the net developable part of the site, unless those required to build more under Planning Agreements, but will strongly resist those that are excessive.'

The same memorandum set out Argent's aspirations for 20 per cent of the land take to be high quality public realm. Contrary to the mayor's desire for tall buildings, Argent favoured offices of eight to 15 storeys with one or two landmark buildings of 20–40 storeys. The objective for residential buildings was six to 10 storeys with one or two possibly going to 15–25 storeys. The rationale for this approach was summed up by Roger Madelin as 'you build tall buildings – you go bust'.[46] (Comparative quantums for the final scheme, heights, land uses and plot ratios are given in Appendix 2).

Another critical observation on the development was made at an early internal meeting in January 2000. It was agreed that while the development should aim to retain the listed buildings on the site, the Culross Buildings would have to be demolished if a central connecting boulevard was to be built. This observation was later subject to extensive analysis by the masterplanning team and English Heritage, but the loss of the Culross Buildings became a *'cause célèbre'* for objectors (see Chapter 5, pp.89-92).

The objectives of the different parties were not necessarily mutually exclusive. All were in favour of a mixed use development, with a significant quantum of housing, high quality public areas and the retention of the majority of the listed buildings. The fact that the scheme was to be based on public transport was never in contention.

CONCLUSIONS

By the end of the first year of negotiations (2001), firm foundations for the development had been put in place. Camden council had a well resourced team, and the council was engaged both politically and managerially. A negotiating agenda had been translated into political priorities and signed off. Camden council had also updated its policy frameworks and had a firm foundation upon which to negotiate. Islington council and English Heritage were largely on board. The stance of the mayor was still a cause of concern and both parties recognised that the GLA and TfL would require careful management. A dialogue had also started with local communities and was revealing key areas of concern and consensus. The main area for debate was clearly going to be over the amount of affordable housing, the management of the public realm and the levels and costs of community benefits. The battle lines were drawn, there was room for manoeuvre, but the parties were still a fair distance apart. Chapter 6 reviews these negotiating positions further.

5.
THE MASTERPLAN

The King's Cross masterplan sets out the relationship between the buildings and the spaces between them, the through routes and internal circulation, built form and heights and the disposition of land uses. It was the key document that set the spatial context for the negotiations and against which questions such as the quantum of floor space, the quality and accessibility of public space and the scale and location of particular buildings were tested.

Both the Argent and Camden council teams spent a great deal of time working with the architects on the masterplan, and the plan was shaped by that debate. The masterplan evolved over the first two years of the development and it continued to be refined right up to the end of 2005. Two architectural and one landscape practice were involved in the production of the masterplan, as were Argent, Camden council planners and English Heritage. As the masterplan was so entwined with negotiations, it is considered here in a separate chapter. Many of the key objectives, such as wider economic and social regeneration, links to surrounding areas and management of the public realm could only be resolved through the masterplan. As an important element of the plan was the setting and reuse of the historic buildings, heritage issues are also considered in this chapter.

THE ROLE OF THE MASTERPLAN

Masterplanning is a term, often applied too loosely, to describe any large scale development framework, planning strategy or architectural vision. Masterplans are generally prescriptive and illustrate what an area will look like at a particular time in the future. The problem is that the future is seldom easy to predict, let alone prescribe. To have a plan is one thing, to achieve it is another. The process of implementation, often over a protracted period, requires either a high degree of control or a great deal of flexibility. In order to plan and execute a large development, control is needed over land, finances and all the regulatory consents (and variations thereupon) over a prolonged period. To add to the challenge there are external forces over which there is little control, such as business cycles, changing political and planning frameworks, the impact of new technologies and fluctuations in the property market. A good masterplan needs to be robust enough to cope with all of these. As it turned out, the property crash of 2008 provided an extreme test of its strategy, one that the masterplan did indeed pass.

At King's Cross, Argent St George had control over the land and access to finance, two of the basic requirements to undertake development. One of the central roles of the masterplan therefore was to provide a framework for securing the third requirement, planning consents. The masterplan had to:

- show Camden's planners what the project would look like on completion, including its mix of uses, environmental impact and range of local facilities
- show Argent St George the different intermediate states and demonstrate it could be built and let in different phases in response to market conditions
- convince institutional investors by showing a feasible long-term vision for the site with the

flexibility to adapt and renew itself over a long period of time.

An effective masterplan responds to the complexity of the site conditions. It articulates simple and legible hierarchies and relationships between buildings, streets and spaces, and provides a structure and order that allows a wide variety of different architectural styles to be incorporated. This is inevitably a subtle process. The optimisation of the shape and size of individual building plots needs to be balanced against the quality and complexity of the spaces around them. A masterplan needs to understand the conditions on its edges, and wherever possible facilitate rather than inhibit future changes that might occur in the surrounding area. These tensions lie at the heart of good masterplanning. In short, it is part of an open-ended process, a conversation through which the city evolves.

A good masterplan will allow individual buildings a degree of independence from their underpinning infrastructure. This flexibility allows a scheme to be built out in a variety of ways depending on market conditions. In the longer term it will also allow for the eventual renewal and redevelopment of individual parts of the area. The test of a good masterplan is its ability to endure and to remain a relevant element in the continuing evolution of the city. Many of the rules are relatively simple and can be found in historical precedents, such as different geometries, building forms, scales and relationships. Masterplans based on theoretical and abstract geometries that fail to respect the context of the surrounding city tend to be inflexible and potentially sterile.

THE MASTERPLANNING TEAM

Unusually, Argent St George appointed two masterplanning teams, Allies and Morrison and Porphyrios Associates, together with Townshend Landscape Architects. Argent had worked with both teams on the Brindleyplace development, and although they had different approaches to architectural design, their thinking on masterplanning was complementary and mutually challenging. One of the unusual features of the arrangement was that the landscape architects were commissioned at the start of the process, and were able to contribute to the early debates about the arrangement and use of space and circulation in the scheme.

Bob Allies and Graham Morrison shared an interest in the subordinate relationship of buildings to the space that surrounds them; how buildings enclose space, and how this in turn influences the experience of the city. Their practice had developed a refined and understated modernist style and by the 1990s they had completed a series of major commercial buildings and masterplans. The work of Demetri Porphyrios, 'classicism is not a style',[1] reflected his profound understanding of the European architectural and urban planning tradition from the Greco-Roman period to 20th-century modernism.

The critical question was how to masterplan such a large and complex site. All the practices were interested in the constraints imposed by the stations, rail infrastructure and historical fabric, and by the barriers that separated King's Cross from the surrounding area. They recognised that the masterplan had to be subservient and responsive to context.

SITE CONTEXT

Over a kilometre long from north to south, the King's Cross site rises by almost 10 metres to the Regent's Canal – which divides it at its centre – is covered by two conservation areas and contains an important collection of historic buildings and industrial archaeology (Figures 5.1 and 5.2). In the southern part of the site a group of buildings of international, historical and architectural importance reflect the power of the Victorian railway age. King's Cross station (1852) and the Great Northern Hotel (1854), both designed by Thomas Cubitt in a restrained Italianate style, contrast with the Gothic Revival style of St Pancras station (1865–68) designed by William Barlow and St Pancras Chambers (1868) by George Gilbert Scott (see Figures 3.5 and 3.6 on p.21). Between the stations the German Gymnasium (1864–65) is important to the history of the gymnastic movement, and Stanley Buildings North and South (1864–65), are examples of philanthropic housing for workers. Further north stood the unlisted terrace of Culross Buildings and Culross Hall (1891–92) and the Grade II-listed No 8 Gasholder (1883). The unique triplet gasholder had already been dismantled and stored to make way for the extension of St Pancras Station, but with an agreement that it would be reconstructed in a location elsewhere within the site.

The Regent's Canal, completed in 1820, predates the development of the site and provides a focus for a second group of historic buildings – robust warehouses and storage buildings that fan out from the railway sidings that previously serviced them. The centrepieces of this group are the Grade II-listed Granary Building (1851) and Regeneration House, also by Cubitt (see Figure 3.7 on p.22). Originally, a basin existed in the front of the Granary Building, allowing the trans-shipment of goods between the canal and the railway. Two buildings flank the Granary Building with long sheds behind them (the Eastern and Western Transit Sheds). Behind this are other listed railway buildings, dating from 1850–88. The Fish and Coal is a curved range of offices from 1851–60s, overlooking the canal, while completing this group are the

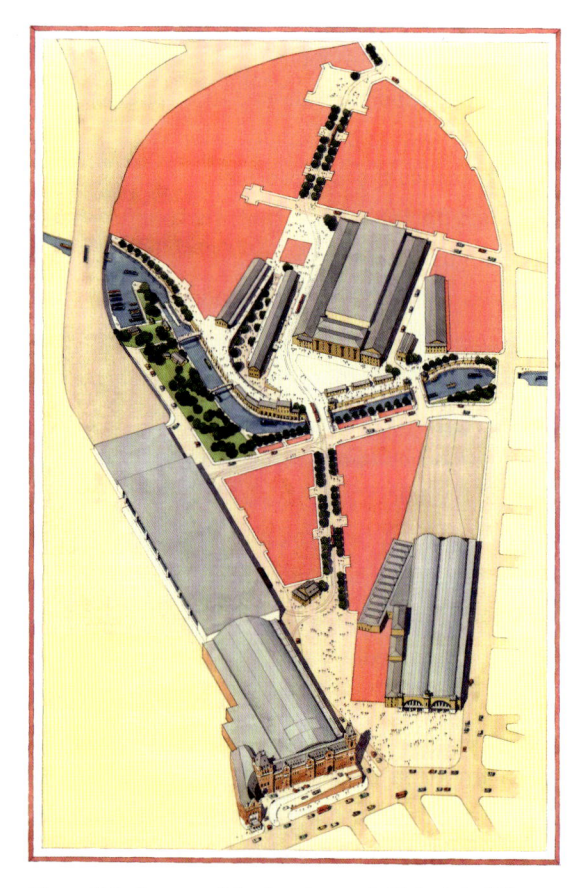

Figure 5.1: Axonometric showing main historic buildings (note: the Great Northern Hotel does not appear on this diagram).

5: THE MASTERPLAN

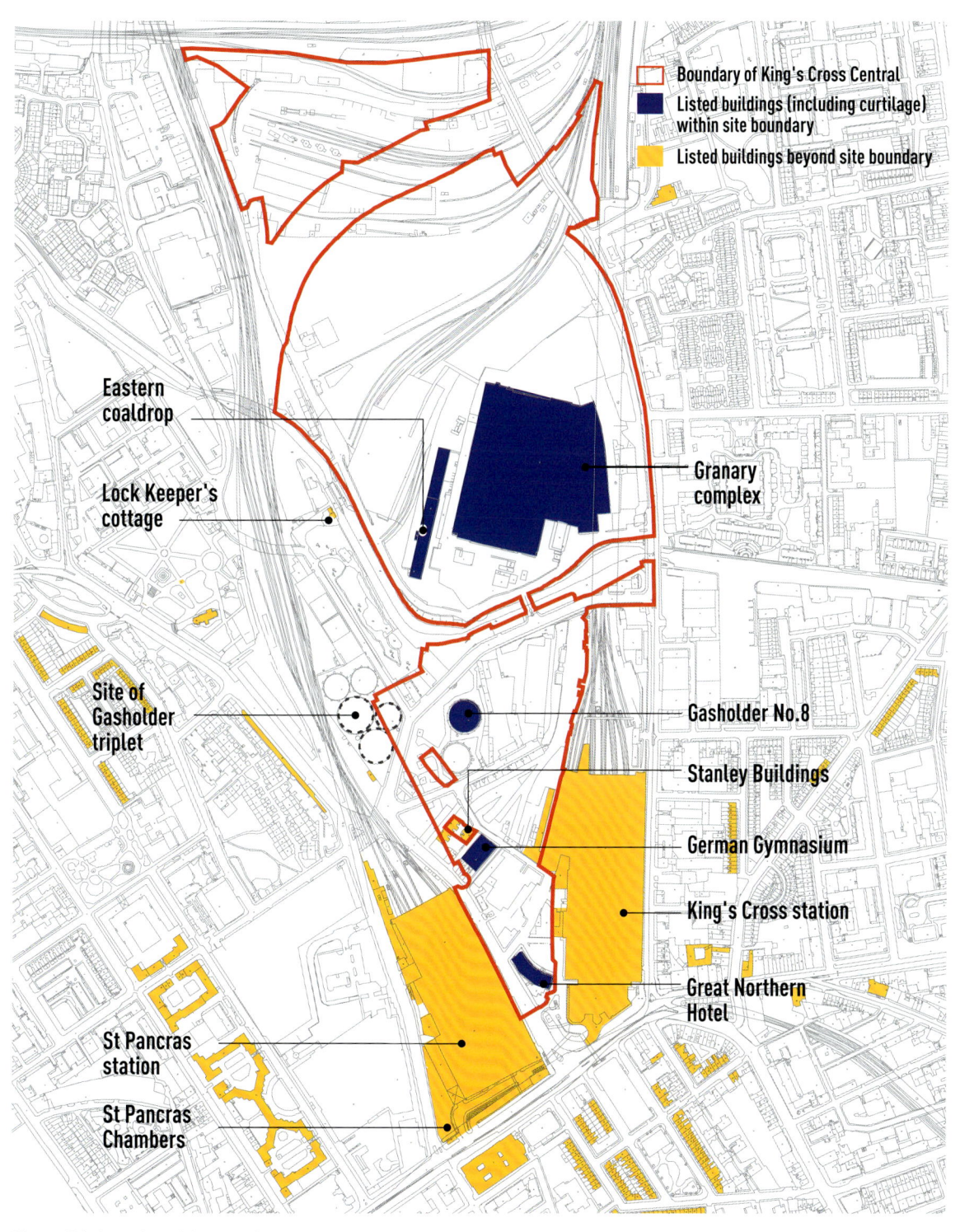

Figure 5.2: Location of listed buildings.

> **The critical question was how to commence a masterplan for a site as large and complex as King's Cross.**

long structures of the Eastern and Western coaldrops. Together they form a historically important group of buildings that enclose a series of spaces containing a rich selection of industrial artefacts such as railway lines, bollards and granite setts. Opposite, on the other side of the canal is the two acre Camley Street Natural Park, owned by Camden council and leased to the London Wildlife Trust.[2] Camden council recognised that any interference with this popular facility would be too contentious to contemplate, given mayor Ken Livingstone's ardent support of the park.

EARLY DISCUSSIONS

The preliminary stage in the preparation of the plan was a two-day design seminar organised by Argent St George, bringing together Allies and Morrison, Townshends and Porphyrios Associates with engineers, environmental consultants and planners. Each party outlined the main influences on their own work and considered exemplars that might inform designs for King's Cross. The objective was to develop 'a visual vocabulary of urban designs and urban schemes'.[3] The presentations provide an insight into the depth of theory underpinning the eventual masterplan.

Demetri Porphyrios started the session with a master class on the history of 19th- and 20th-century urbanism. This ranged from Hippodamus' 5th–4th century BC military base at Miletus (regarded as the first recognisable masterplan), to Priene, Athens and Assos (the visual composition of space) and Pergamon (the use of monumental architecture). He went on to consider the development of the plan for the Roman town, its survival and adaptation in medieval and renaissance Italy, Ledoux's enlightened town of production (Chaux) and Berlin's use of building codes and the reinterpretation of axial routes. He contrasted London to all these examples as 'a collection of major buildings and villages', a city that had 'resisted monumentality'.[4] Porphyrios developed the argument of the differences between London and its European neighbours by looking at Paris under Haussmann, and Barcelona under Cerdà. He also contrasted the almost anti-urban theories of Ebenezer Howard with the work of Le Corbusier, 'the most brilliant architect; the most awful urbanist'.[5] He ended with a critique of post-modernism.

His introduction is outlined here because it set the tone for the debate about the very nature of the place that King's Cross might become. It was not about a sterile argument between modernism and classicism, but a debate about the urban plan (framework) as opposed to the building. Therefore the right plan could accommodate a variety of architectural styles, both now and in the future. Importantly, his illustration of the concept of the public route and its relationship to civic buildings laid down the central spine of the future masterplan (the Boulevard's critical relationship with the Granary). Furthermore, through application of the principles of the Nolli plan,[6] Porphyrios argued that the historic buildings on the site could be embedded into a new urban fabric, as opposed to preservation devoid of context (as in the earlier Foster plan).

The second session, led by Jason Prior of the landscape architects EDAW, focused on the morphology of urban spaces. It looked at the ways in which a hierarchy of routes and spaces could assist orientation and create character. He considered the importance of climate and how spaces work at all times of the day and night. Prior concluded that 'design is not a spray-on, it can not be retrofitted (into a masterplan)'.[7] The group looked at comparable projects elsewhere, including Canary Wharf, 'the office ghetto'; Eurolille 'radical new'; Covent Garden, 'evolution in action'; and Mayfair, 'the highest rents in the country (so obviously doing something right)'.[8] For all these examples, plot ratios, transport, public realm and the mix of uses were analysed and a range of simple design parameters were discussed. These included creating destinations, scale, sequence of spaces, design guidance, active ground floor uses, hours of use, access and choice of access, ability to evolve over time, diversity and flexibility, integrated sustainability and long-term management. These ideas were not radical, but importantly, the whole professional team and Argent St George had derived them collectively, owned them, understood their implications and were willing to apply them throughout the process. Argent's David Partridge said subsequently, that the seminar was about 'manufacturing a consensus' between the design teams and Argent St George.[9]

THE FIRST MASTERPLAN

There were four starting propositions for the masterplan. The first was that the context for the masterplan was already set by the historic buildings, in particular St Pancras and King's Cross stations. Their geometry would determine building relationships in what was essentially a triangular site south of the canal. North of the canal the site tapers, culminating in a second triangle. Here the predominant historic geometry was the railway sidings that splayed out away from the canal. The position of the buildings that they served was directly related to that geometry. The second proposition was a desire to preserve as many of the historic buildings as possible, not as historic artefacts, but embedded within a new urban form. The third proposition concerned the length of the site and the need for devices to draw people northwards from the station interchanges. The space in front of the Granary was viewed as the central public hub of the scheme. The fourth proposition reflected the difficulties of designing a new piece of city that was significantly severed from its surrounding neighbourhoods. In particular, the railway embankments to the west and north meant that although King's Cross was within the political jurisdiction of Camden council, geographically it was part of Islington. The question of how the site could connect the two communities became one of the major considerations in the design.

PLANNING, POLITICS AND CITY MAKING

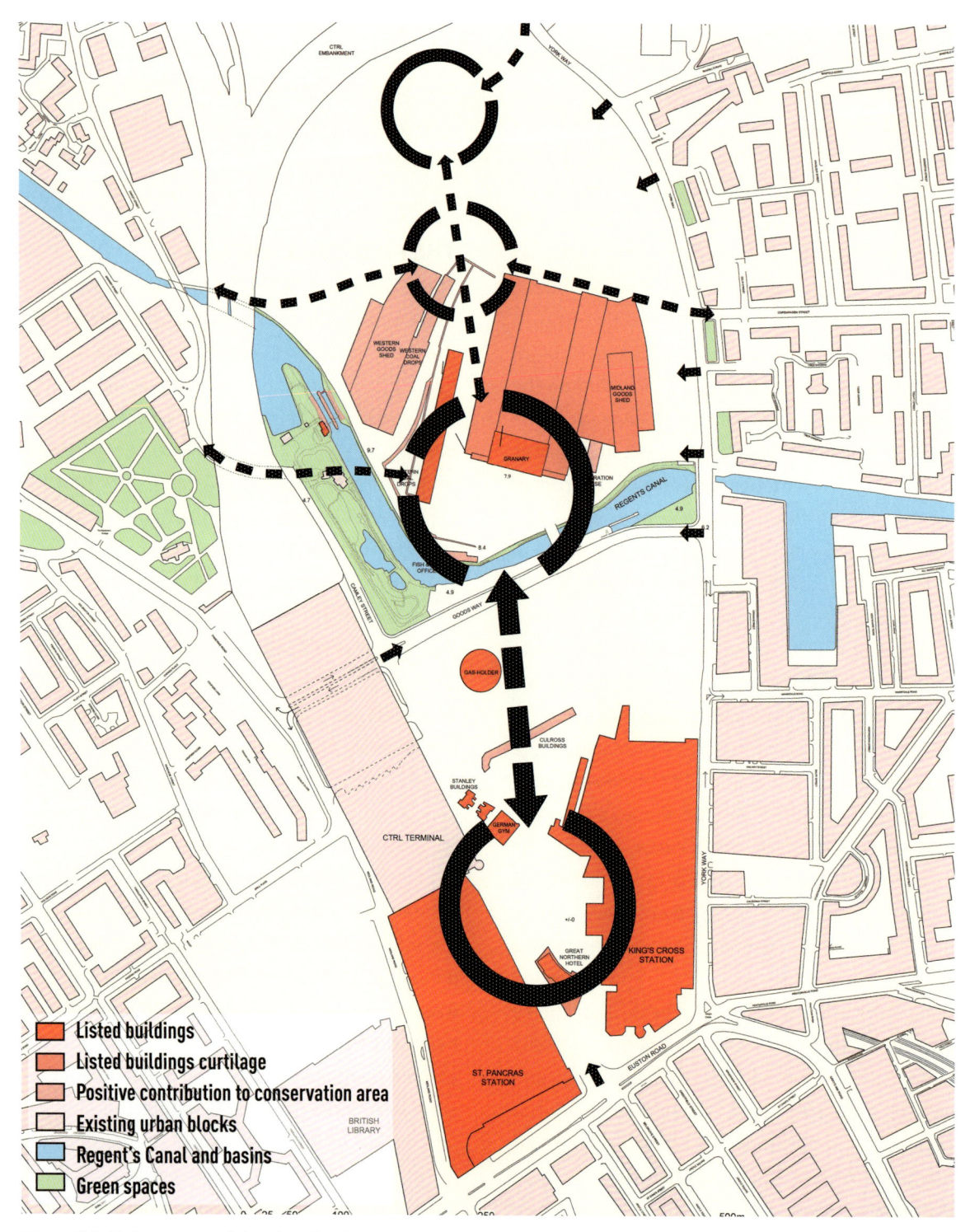

Legend:
- Listed buildings
- Listed buildings curtilage
- Positive contribution to conservation area
- Existing urban blocks
- Regent's Canal and basins
- Green spaces

Figure 5.3: Early conceptual drawing showing central spine route.

5: THE MASTERPLAN

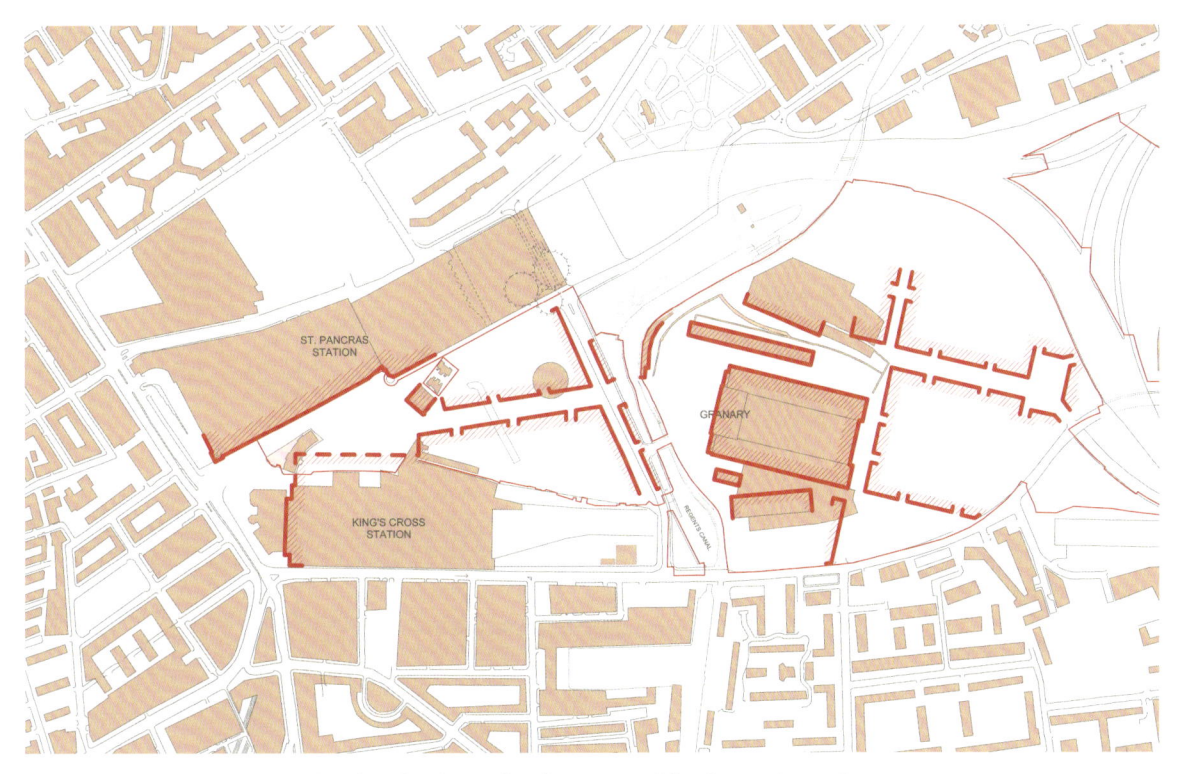

Figure 5.4: Early development drawing showing notional streets and development parcels.

Argent St George, Camden council and the masterplanning team had already agreed that King's Cross should be 'just another piece of London' and reflect the grain, scale and character of the city. The example of Canary Wharf was often cited in early discussions to illustrate a development outcome that would be inappropriate. In particular, it was agreed that the development should connect physically, socially and economically into the surrounding area and should have blurred rather than hard edges.

From these initial stakes, the team agreed the basic structure of the masterplan. The plan for King's Cross was based on the idea of the 'human city', the principles of which are the long-term sustainability of the masterplan's framework; maximum connectivity with the existing city; a physical urban plan with mid-rise high density buildings; and a plan that establishes a dialogue between public and private spaces. The Granary and the space in front of it would become the main focus for the central portion of the site. A simple connecting route or boulevard (civic route) would provide a spine running the length of the site (Figure 5.3). Its position would be determined by the requirement to optimise separate development parcels either side (Figure 5.4). The Granary provided both a destination and a focal point, and its position in the scheme determined the geometry of the north of the site, in particular by deflecting the central spine route westward

PLANNING, POLITICS AND CITY MAKING

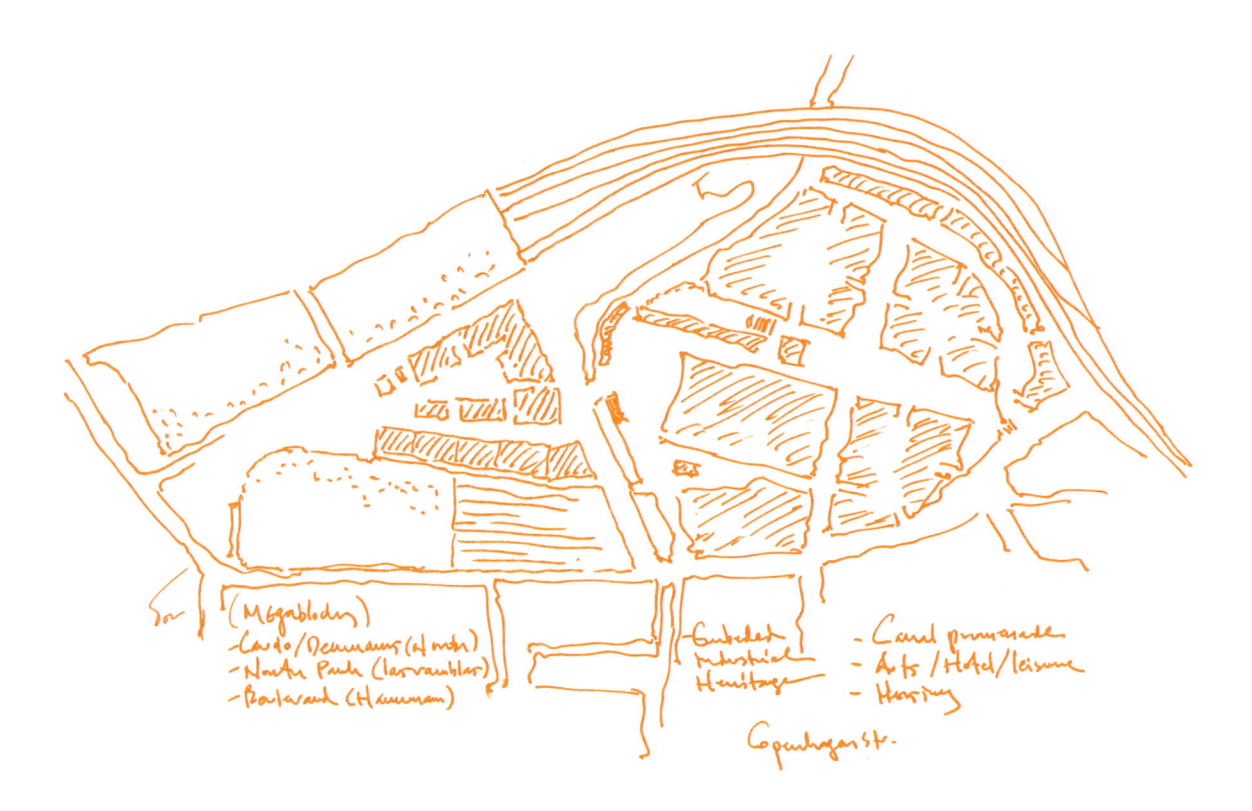

Figure 5.5: Early masterplan sketch showing links to Copenhagen Street and the Boulevard.

before it eventually rejoined York Way at the top of the site. By extending the alignment of Copenhagen Street into the site, a simple division of the northern portion of the site was achieved with four development parcels (Figure 5.5). The precedent cited for the north-south route was Las Ramblas in Barcelona.

This simple plan gave a point of connection to the Islington street grid with crossroads at Copenhagen Street (Figure 5.6). It also set up the conditions for a variety of different development phases. But it was more subtly referenced than that. As seen in Figure 5.3, the spine route connected three new spaces, in the south between the two stations, in the centre in front of the Granary, and at the north on York Way. In the centre, the Granary acted as a 'basilica' or 'cathedral' with a piazza, and Porphyrios cited Blondel's 1765 plan for Strasbourg as a precedent. The division of the northern part of the site into four quadrants roughly on a north-south, east-west axis resembled the Cardo Decumanus of the Roman city. The central hinge of the intersection north of the Granary would be marked by the park. At this stage in the design process it was assumed that the Great Northern Hotel would be demolished and a major new public space between the two stations would be created. The initial proposition was for this space to be framed by simple colonnaded buildings.

5: THE MASTERPLAN

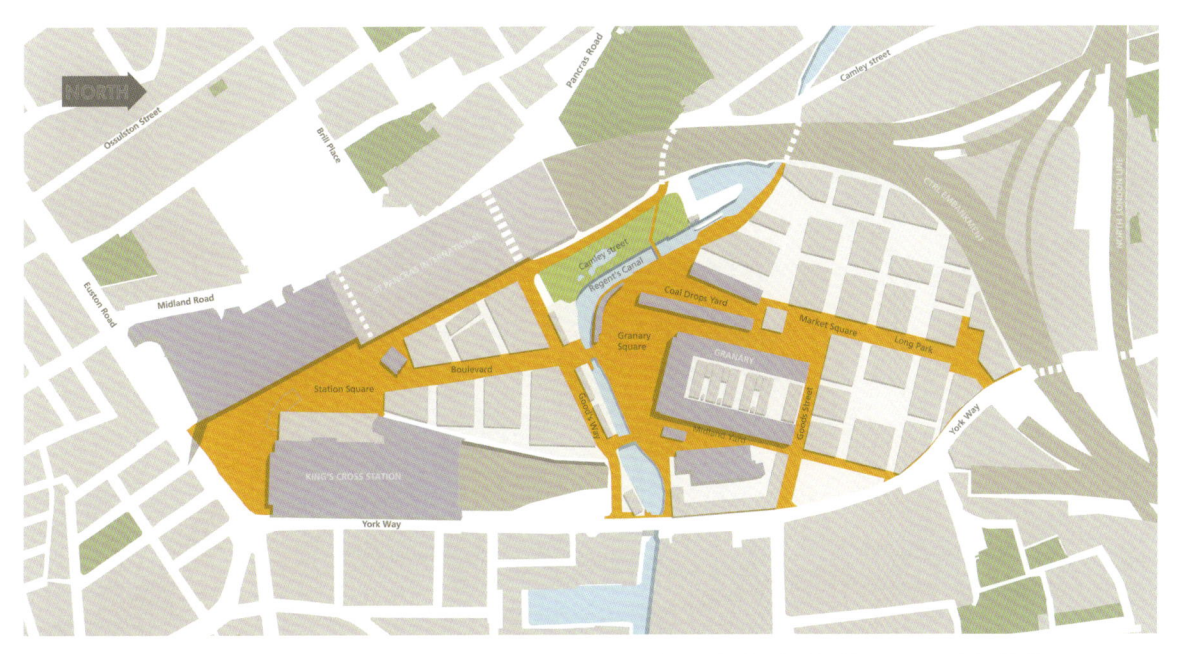

Figure 5.6: Masterplan in February 2002 prior to presentation to the Commission for Architecture and the Built Environment (CABE).

The use of historical precedents was never meant to be literal or nostalgic; instead it allows a set of propositions to be tested, referenced and communicated. It is the interpretation and application of lessons that make them powerful tools. Straightforward replication can produce a theme park. The precedents, of which there were many in the King's Cross masterplan, were used to begin, rather than end, the design process. From these initial concepts the masterplan went through many adjustments and refinements.

DEVELOPING THE MASTERPLAN

The first refinement was to interrogate the orthogonal geometry set up by the principle routes. Regular grids have many advantages; they are legible and create standard sized building plots, optimal in terms of development economics. Much of central London is in fact grid based, but these grids are not uniform. The piecemeal development of the city in the 18th and 19th centuries meant that grids are usually offset, are of different proportions and do not align. In the areas adjoining King's Cross there were three such grids aligned on different geometries.

The team concluded that a simple geometric grid referenced to the central space would be inappropriate. There were two principle reasons for this. The first was the difficulty posed by the retained listed buildings. These sat in relation to the geometry of the former railway sidings that had fanned out as they entered the site from the north (Figure 5.7). Forcing them into an orthogonal grid would, at best, create an uneasy relationship between them and new buildings,

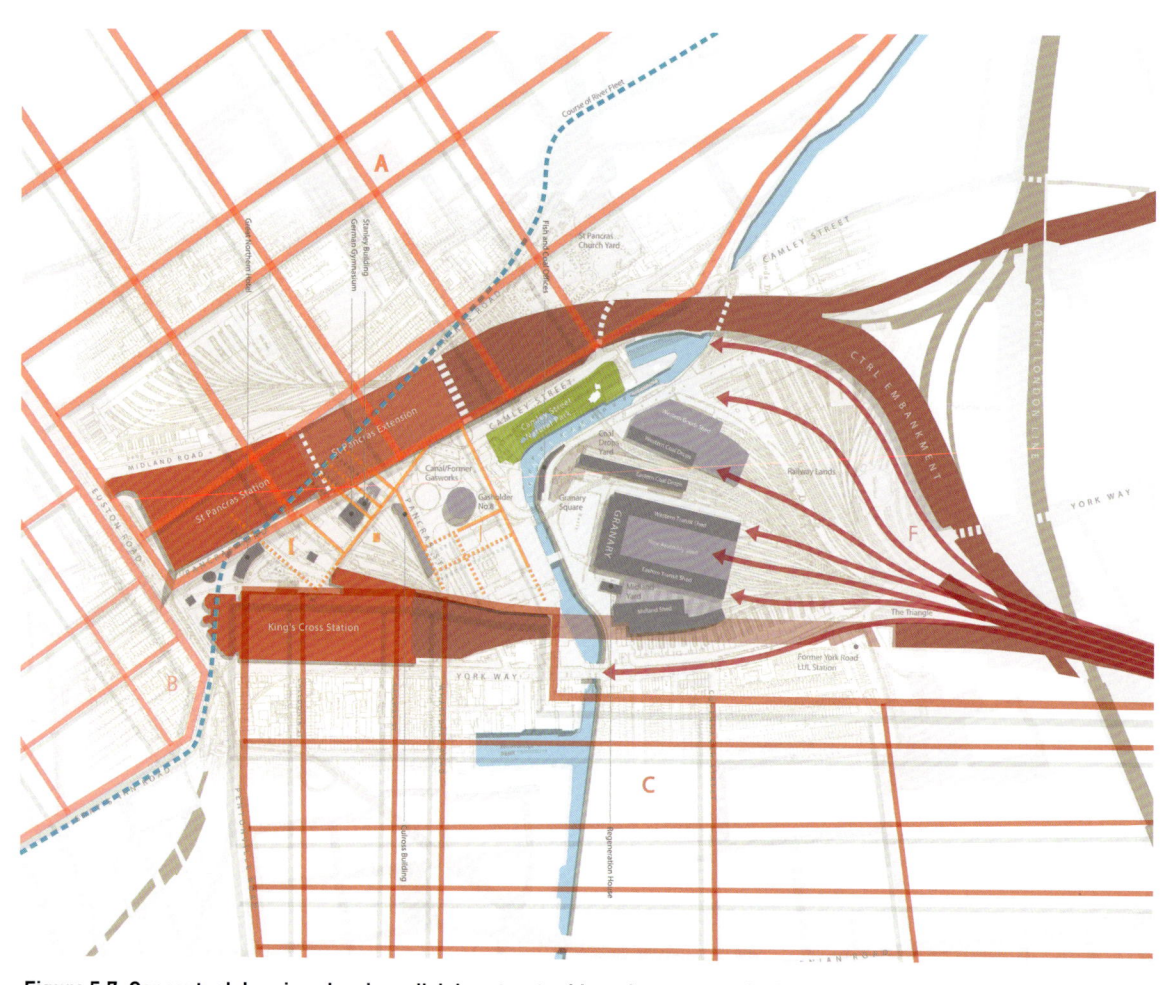

Figure 5.7: Conceptual drawing showing adjoining street grids and geometry of railway sidings.

and at worse, leave them as objects removed from any urban context. Incorporating the geometry of the railway tracks into the masterplan resolved this problem, and introduced a degree of informality that allowed intervening spaces to be adapted in a more sophisticated manner (Figure 5.8). In particular, the widening of the spaces on the spine to the north of the Granary allowed a new public park (Long Park) to be created.

The second reason came from a deliberate decision to explore the use of perspective to inform the pedestrian experience of the site. By widening the Boulevard as it approached the Granary, perspective could be manipulated and the distance appear foreshortened. It also created a more efficient geometry for the adjacent development parcels. To the north of the Granary the reverse takes place; the buildings converge, effectively lengthening the perspective and emphasising the size and proportions of the public spaces (Figure 5.9).

5: THE MASTERPLAN

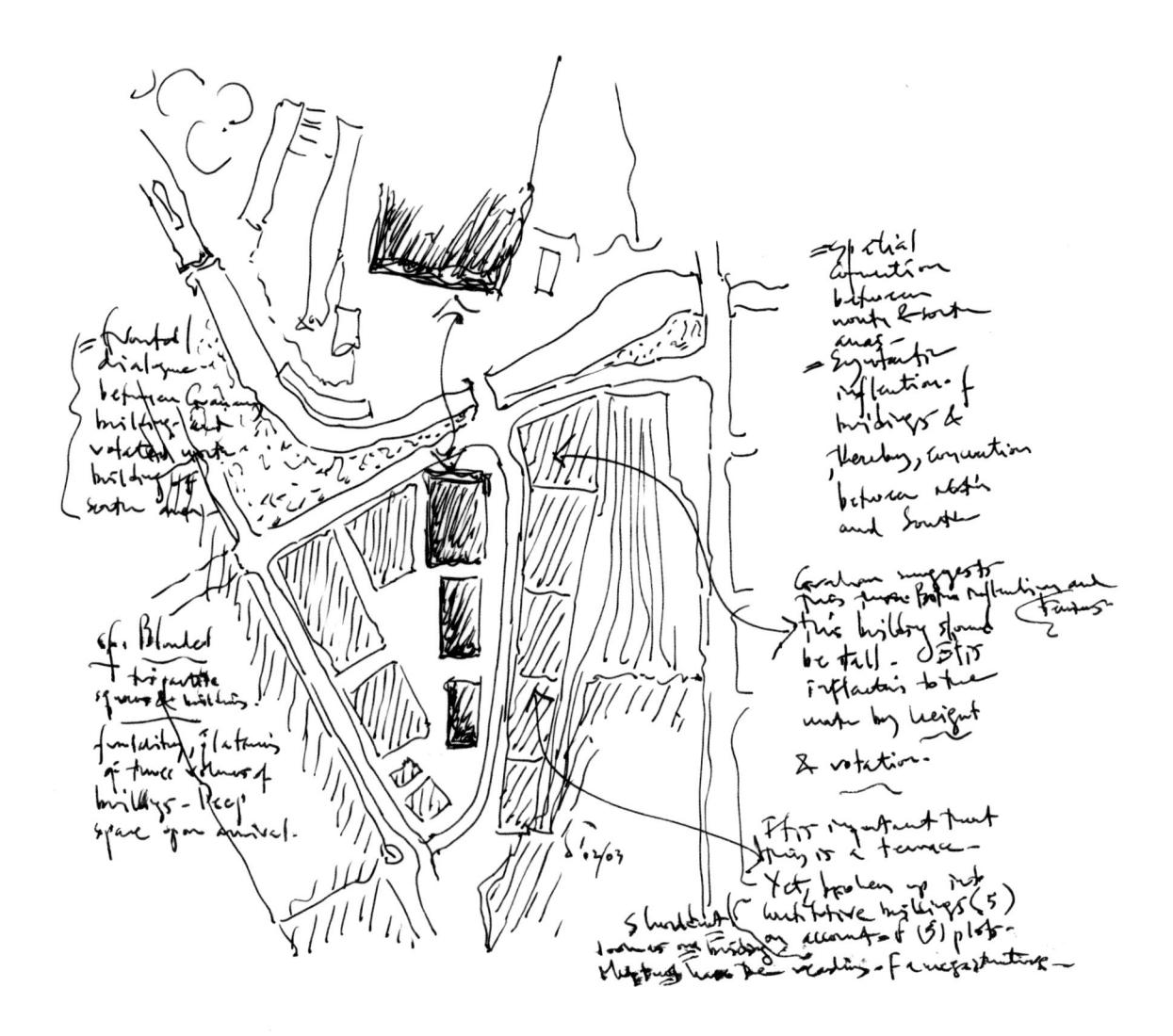

Figure 5.8: Working development sketch.

Notes from top left:

1) Frontal dialogue between Granary Building and rotated north of building of south area;

2) CF Blondel – tripartite squares and buildings, functionality of three volumes of buildings. Deep square upon arrival;

3) It is important that this is a broken terrace. Yet, broken up into buildings (5) on account of (5) plots. Should not look as one building. Must not have the reading of a megastructure;

4) Graham (Morrison) suggests this building should be tall. Inflection to the north by height & rotation;

5) Spatial connection between north and south areas. =Syntactic inflection of buildings & thereby connection between north and south. (Taken directly from Demetri's notes on the drawings.)

Scale and building heights

With the basic framework in place, the masterplanning team could start to consider scale.[10] The question of what constitutes a human scale is vexed. The centre of most European cities, including London, was developed with traditional load-bearing structures, and the resulting scale tends to be four to six stories. Within and between buildings, land uses are mixed (as opposed to being rigidly zoned) and the urban form is both complex and comfortable in its familiarity. The building technologies of the 20th century have challenged these premises, along with the automobile and increasingly specialist requirements of present day commercial buildings. New urban forms have emerged that pose challenges to today's designers.

The two-day design seminars had already agreed that the mayor's advocacy of tall buildings (see p.63 in Chapter 4) might be in conflict with the scale of the emerging masterplan. Argent did not support tall buildings, believing them to be a risky commercial proposition. It considered 10–12 storeys to be the optimum, as it could be let to a single office tenant and optimised building costs. Above a certain height, structural costs increase and floor plates diminish. Ten to 12-storey buildings were also easier to fit into a conventional street-based masterplan. The King's Cross site sat within viewing corridors from Parliament Hill and Hampstead Heath to St Paul's Cathedral and long-established planning policies restricted the height of buildings within these corridors. These were firmly embedded in the mayor's own London Plan. Although the mayor had offered to ignore these policies,[11] Argent St George was content to comply with them, and a prevailing 10–12-storey height was incorporated over most of the site.

Design review

The first masterplan was largely in its final form by the beginning of 2002 and Camden council was mostly satisfied with progress. The decision was made to take it for design review by the Commission for Architecture and the Built Environment (CABE). CABE had been set up by the government as an independent organisation to promote good design in the built environment and was well-regarded and powerful. Its views were non-statutory but carried considerable weight. The first design review took place in February 2002. While CABE acknowledged the thoroughness of the approach, it was critical of the emerging masterplan:

'We found the plan disappointing. There was no sense of the excitement of this enormous development opportunity [...] we saw little in the ideas presented which appeared new or challenging, or attempting to push the boundaries. The modest nature of the vision of the streets and squares seems to us to be at odds with the character of the site.'[12]

The letter went on to say that while the routes through the site were anchored well enough in the south they were not adequately resolved to the north and east, particularly around York Way: '[...] the proposed grids do not seem to derive from anything in particular'. Regarding the open spaces, CABE suggested that greater consideration was needed concerning 'what each is for, and what is the appropriate size for it. In some cases, the spaces proposed seem too large, so that it may not be possible to achieve

5: THE MASTERPLAN

Figure 5.9: Masterplan development sketch showing exaggerated perspectives.

PLANNING, POLITICS AND CITY MAKING

> **It was not that the masterplan was poor, it was more a case that it could have been better.**

the life and activity hoped for.' CABE's summary was damning:

'development on this site could develop a strong character and identity of its own, based on the distinctive nature and history of the site, while at the same time making strong connections with its surroundings. These two things need not be in conflict. The present scheme, however, does not go very far towards achieving either of them.'

In March 2002 the plan was also taken to English Heritage's London advisory committee. The committee was a key statutory consultee in the planning process, and its support was essential. Its response was to: '[…] applaud your approach […] the analysis of the area's history, architecture, urban characteristics and heritage significance has been exemplary'.[13] However, English Heritage had concerns over the loss of a number of listed buildings and the incorporation and setting of others within the masterplan. It expressed particular concern on the unresolved nature of the southern part of the site and its failure to 'consolidate the frayed urban fabric in this area'. It delivered a clear note of opposition regarding the proposed demolition of listed buildings in this area, in particular the Great Northern Hotel.[14]

REFINEMENT OF THE MASTERPLAN

CABE's comments were met with a degree of shock by Camden council and the project team. There was some suspicion that CABE had an innate bias in favour of a modernist rather than traditional approach to masterplanning and that it had failed to understand the scheme. There were however, clear and important messages from both CABE's and English Heritage's responses. A project of this complexity needs to go through a number of iterations. The scheme presented, although fundamentally sound in its research and intentions, was still only partly formed. In Graham Morrison's words, 'it was the last 10 per cent of the design development, to make the plan work, that occupied most of the remaining time'.[15] It was not that the masterplan was poor, it was more a case that it could have been better. Design review plays an important role in the evolution of schemes. It is an external challenge, and when the parties believe they have done enough, it forces a critical rethink.

The design team reconsidered the plan, particularly the concern that the initial plan was too rigid. First, the scale, grain and size of individual development parcels were reviewed. Initially Porphyrios suggested that the grain should be broken down into a series of far smaller buildings within larger street blocks (Figure 5.10). He argued that the very objective that King's Cross should be 'just another piece of London' supported a very fine grain with significant variations in heights from one building to another. Allies and Morrison advocated a different approach based on the requirement

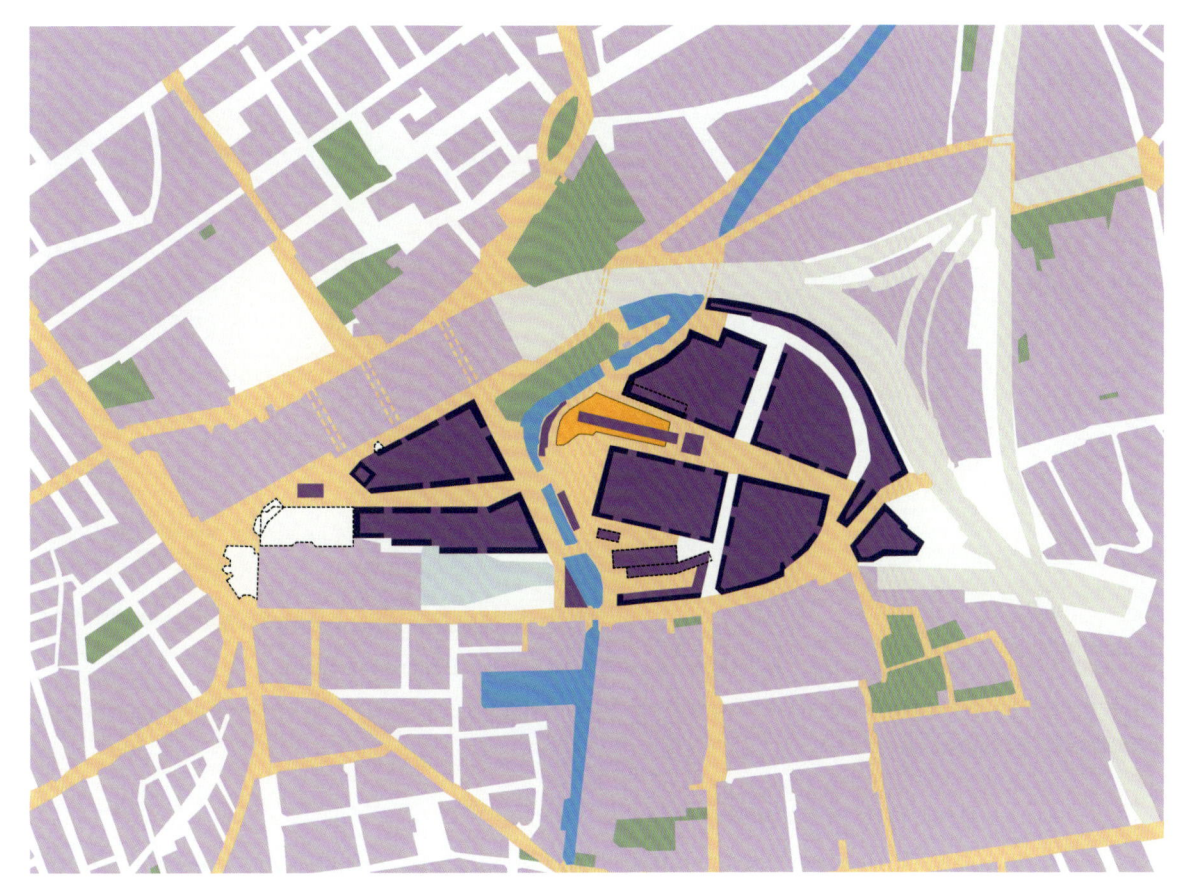

Figure 5.10: Refinement of masterplan into network of street blocks.

to achieve street blocks better tailored to commercial needs. Further development between the teams arrived at a compromise where the mega blocks were retained but were divided by streets that allowed smaller buildings to be accommodated (Figure 5.11).

The Great Northern Hotel

The future of the Great Northern Hotel still had to be resolved. Although Argent St George and Camden council recognised its importance, the Grade II-listed structure was in poor condition and formed a serious bottleneck between the stations at exactly the point that the taxi and bus stops should be. Moreover, TfL's aspirations for segregated bus and cycle lanes would occupy the entire space, and pedestrian movement along Pancras Way would be impossible. Although it was clear that English Heritage would oppose the loss of the Great Northern Hotel, both Camden council and Argent St George were convinced that its demolition would open up opportunities for a far better resolution of the southern part of the scheme and a new concourse for King's Cross station. It was, they surmised, what the Victorians would have done.

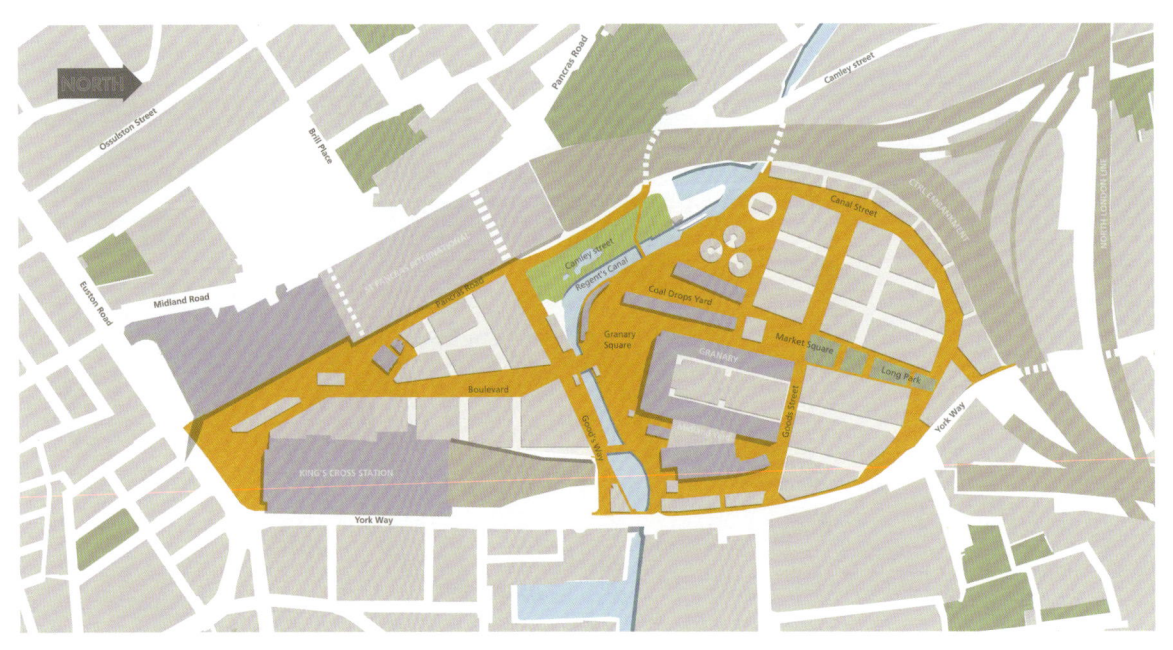

Figure 5.11: Revised masterplan (August 2002) following CABE and English Heritage comments. (Major changes include repositioning of the Boulevard, reinstatement of the gasholders in new position next to canal and inclusion of larger public spaces.)

Various studies were carried out, including the construction of a glass station box alongside King's Cross and even the positioning of a tall building between the stations (Figure 5.12). The removal of the hotel would, however, have left a poorly defined space around the front and side of King's Cross station, which would have been filled with taxis, bus canopies and all the paraphernalia associated with transport operators. Although the responsibility for a new concourse for King's Cross rested with Network Rail, and their architect John McAslan, the land upon which it was to sit had been transferred to London and Continental Railways as part of the development agreement. Camden council brought together the teams to ensure an integrated solution was found.

Although the constraints posed by the underground concourses were significant, McAslan proposed using the curved façade of the Great Northern Hotel to determine the geometry of a new curved concourse roof that rested above the colonnaded ground floor of the hotel (see Chapter 9). The decision to retain the Great Northern Hotel satisfactorily resolved the southern part of the scheme, accommodated TfL's transport requirements and removed the significant threat of opposition from English Heritage (Figure 5.13). The southern space would be divided into two, each with clear and distinct functions. The southern space on Euston Road (later designed by Stanton Williams) is a city square providing a formal setting for the newly revealed frontage of King's Cross station.

5: THE MASTERPLAN

It unites a group of outstanding, if stylistically different, grand Victorian buildings. The space to the north, in contrast, is a functional interchange framed by the two new station concourse buildings (see Chapter 9). This forms a natural and legible entrance to the Boulevard. Once the issue of the Great Northern Hotel had been resolved, the southern part of the masterplan could be finalised.

The Culross and Stanley Buildings

The Culross Buildings were built in the 1890s as workers' housing by the Great Northern Railway. This simple four-storey terrace crossed the route of the Boulevard in the centre of the site. Although not listed, they were considered of local importance, despite the group of which they had once been a part having largely disappeared. To the south were the two Stanley Buildings, again workers' tenements, but slightly earlier and more ornate, meriting a Grade-II listing.

Peter Freeman had already recognised that the Culross Buildings would pose significant design problems if they were to be retained, as they blocked the important visual link that the Boulevard would make between the stations and the Granary. They would also be extremely difficult to embed in the masterplan without significantly reducing the scale of the commercial development. Argent St George argued strongly that the Culross Buildings would jeopardise the development of the central part of the site and as they were not listed, advocated their demolition.

The fate of the Culross Buildings (see Figure 5.14) became a *cause célèbre* for the scheme's opponents. There was a strongly held view

Figure 5.12: Feasibility drawing for a tall building to replace the Great Northern Hotel.

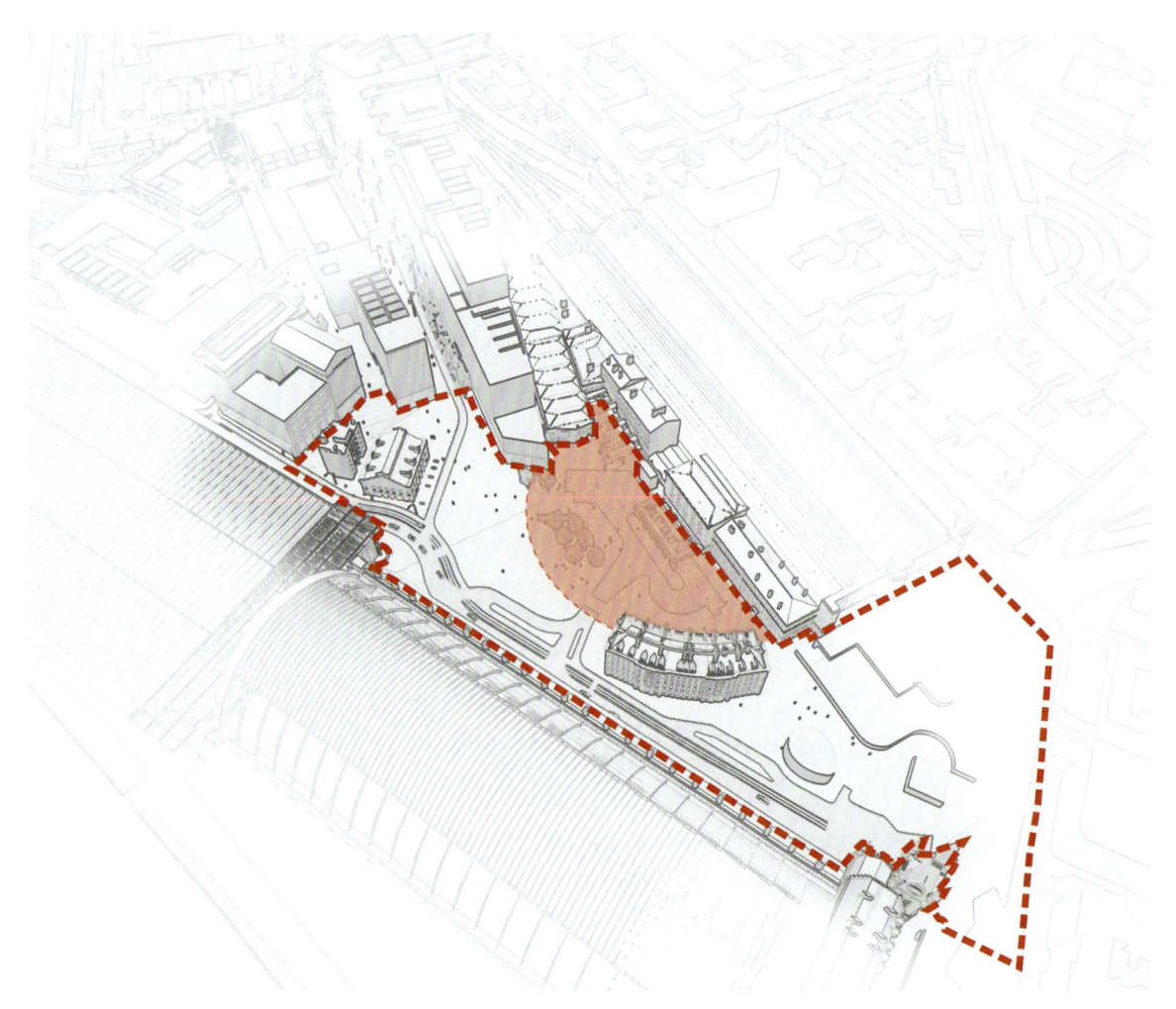

Figure 5.13: Station concourse area, public realm and location of new concourse.

among conservation groups that the buildings were a key part of the overall assemblage of heritage structures and should be retained. Several local and national groups supported an alternative scheme for the Culross Buildings proposed by the King's Cross Conservation Area Advisory Committee (KXCAAC). The committee argued strongly that the building should be preserved as residential accommodation and proposed cutting an arch through the structure so that, walking along the Boulevard through the Culross Buildings would be like entering a walled city.[16] A small extension to the Culross Buildings was proposed to double the amount of residential accommodation, making it more viable and allowing the creation of a semi-public residential square.

The fate of the Culross Buildings was seen by Camden council as having considerable potential to derail the entire scheme, as should

5: THE MASTERPLAN

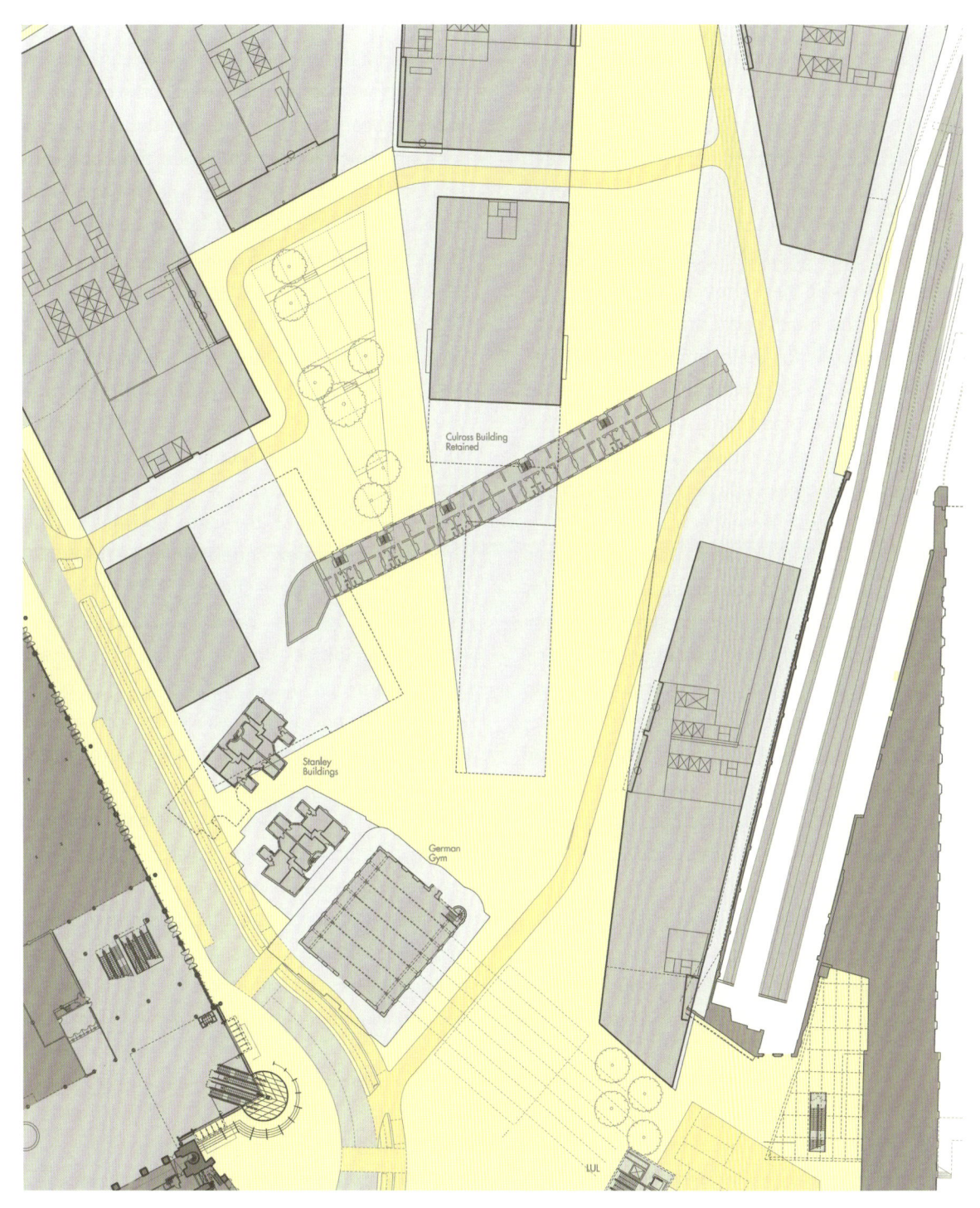

Figure 5.14: Design study showing the implications of retaining the Culross Buildings in relation to the Boulevard and proposed development blocks. Source: report by ARUP, April 2004.

English Heritage not be convinced that its demolition was unavoidable, it had the power to object to the development and therefore trigger a public inquiry. On the other hand, if Camden council had insisted on retaining the Culross Buildings, then Argent St George would probably also have gone to appeal. Camden council and Argent St George therefore went to considerable lengths in the masterplan process to examine different options for their retention. ARUP was commissioned to carry out a study, and its report in April 2004 examined options for retention but concluded that they should be demolished.[17] This recommendation was accepted by Camden council and English Heritage.

Argent St George and Camden council favoured the retention of the southern Stanley Buildings but accepted that the straightening of Pancras Road, after the completion of Foster's extension to St Pancras, was logical, but would necessitate demolition of the northern Stanley Buildings. The alternative of looping the road around them (and there was a temporary construction road in this position), would have left them as an isolated group, devoid of their original historical context.

The Boulevard

The blocks on either side of the Boulevard were designed around shared service basements and parking. On the western block seven commercial buildings were placed around a new triangular public space, St Pancras Square, thus effectively resolving the geometry between the Boulevard and St Pancras Way. The Boulevard was also moved eastwards to allow larger development footprints around St Pancras Square. On the eastern block four separate buildings were proposed.[18] Beneath these would be a service yard, shared with Network Rail and accessed via a ramp from Goodsway. The final change was to realign the northern end of the Boulevard, turning the northern section to align with the front of the Granary.

In the centre of the site, in front of the Granary, a major new square would be the public centrepiece of the scheme, its proportions determined by the canal and surrounding historic buildings (Figure 5.15). The scale and dimensions of the square were carefully examined, and design exercises considered whether new structures might be incorporated, including a series of pavilions along the canal (Figure 5.16). In another design variation, Porphyrios proposed an elevated podium and promenade along Goodsway to resolve the topography of the site as it falls away to the west and reduce the apparent scale of the commercial buildings. His proposition was that the archways beneath would open up the basements for small

❝ The scale and dimensions of the square were carefully examined and design exercises considered whether new structures might be incorporated, including a series of pavilions along the canal. ❞

businesses, as in 19th-century railway viaducts, an idea that was not ultimately pursued.

The new square was always seen as the centrepiece for the scheme. Early ideas to restore the canal basin in front of the Granary were rejected in favour of a more traditional and lively public space. The key move by Townshends was to open the canal onto the square through the construction of a series of south-facing steps, a proposal originally criticised but now one of the most popular features of the scheme. The landscape strategy for the square had to strike a balance between the reuse of historic fabric and the creation of a new, useable public space, (Victorian granite steps might look good, but are an unsuitable surface for cyclists or people with disabilities). Townshend's approach was to retain the historic fabric that had been part of the site, for example the railway lines, turntables and bollards, but to resist filling the spaces with historic bric-a-brac.

Back to design review
The revised scheme was taken back to CABE in July 2002. Although it was essentially the same masterplan, the design had matured and had acquired greater sensitivity both to its surroundings and to the historic buildings on the site. In particular, relatively subtle changes had been made in the geometry, not just in the realignment of the central boulevard but also in the relationship between the street grid and the buildings and spaces that it framed. This time CABE was more positive. Its letter states: 'the committee offer warm support for the new direction in masterplanning', while ironically referring to the 'strength of the earlier framework'. In particular, CABE welcomed the further development work that had taken place around the canal and York Way. It put down a significant marker regarding the nature of the public realm:[19] 'it will be important to identify which of the roads are to be adopted by the local authority. The streets should foster a sense of citizenship and be accessible 24 hours a day [...]. In our opinion, the Canary Wharf model, where the streets appear to be public but a private company controls access and monitors behaviour, is to be strongly resisted.'[20] This point formed a significant part of negotiations with Camden council, as discussed in the next chapter.

Testing the masterplan
The next stage was to interrogate the masterplan in order to be certain that it could work in different permutations. Design exercises tested the relationships between each of the buildings and intervening spaces (Figure 5.17). Extensive design studies were carried using models, axonometrics, line drawings and watercolour renditions (Figures 5.18, 5.19 and 5.20). The proportions of streets and the dimensions of public spaces were also tested and referenced against comparable examples.

The final test of the masterplan concerned the notional positioning of appropriate land uses and activities on the ground floor frontages (Figure 5.21). There was always an intention that the whole site should be active, and if not the 24-hour city, it should at least be enjoyable, accessible, safe and stimulating through both day and night in all of its zones (Figure 5.22).

LINKING THE PLAN TO THE WIDER AREA

Physical connections

If King's Cross was to be a seamless part of London, the masterplan had to connect to the wider area. Connecting the site to Islington in the east was difficult, as much of the historic urban structure had been destroyed by the 1960s housing renewal programmes. To the west, Goodsway was the only road connecting to Somers Town and physical integration was virtually impossible due to the railway embankments. The early stages of the

Figure 5.15 (above): CGI showing Granary Square.
Figure 5.16 (right): Same view of Granary Square – watercolour showing canal-side pavilions.

5: THE MASTERPLAN

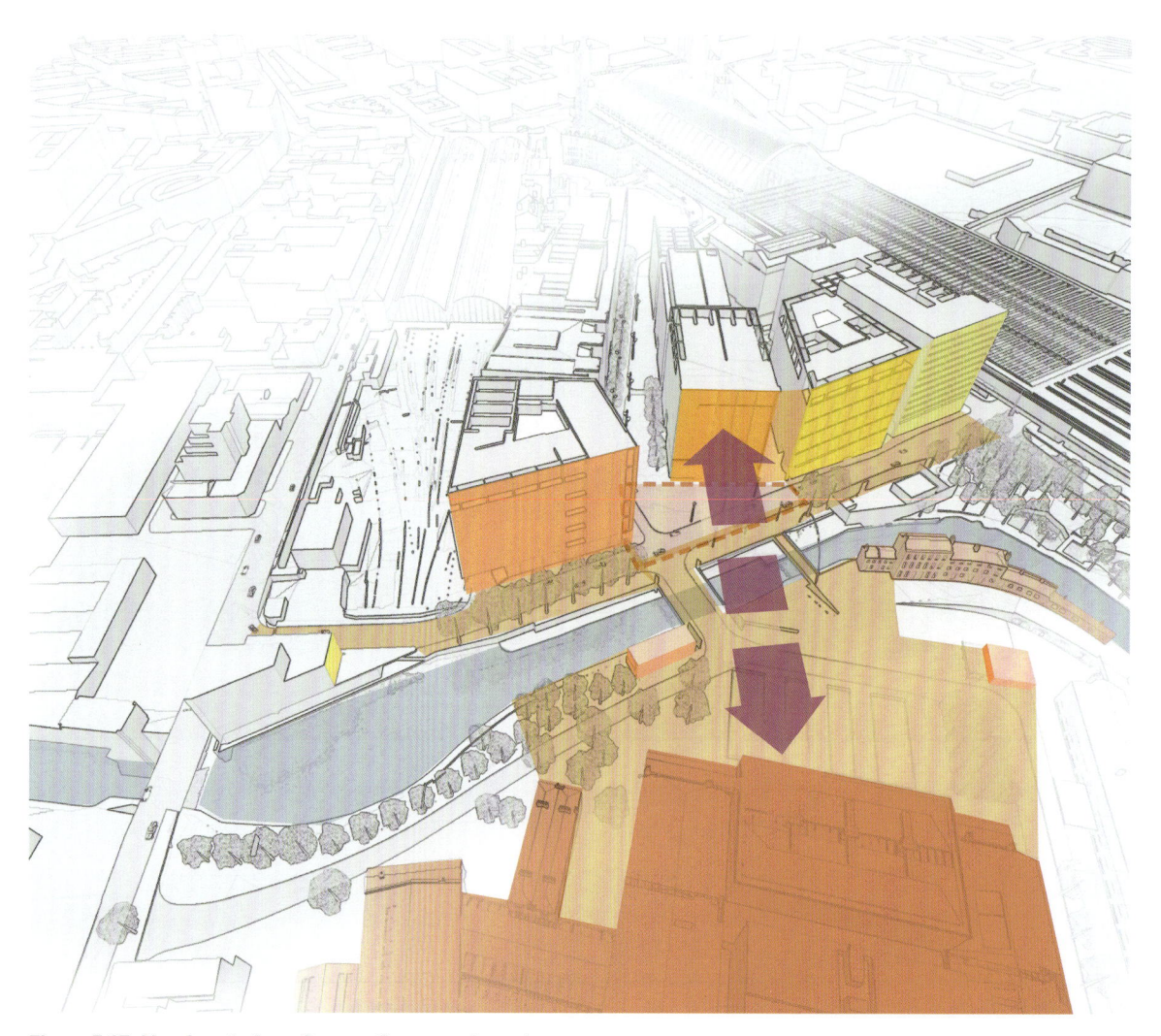

Figure 5.17: Massing study on Granary Square and canal.

masterplan had evaluated all the options to overcome the barrier of the tracks and Arup had been commissioned to look at options for bridges and tunnels. Bridging over the embankments was not feasible due to the sheer height problems. Tunnelling did not work either, as the canal passed under the railway and under that were the Thameslink rail tunnels. Any tunnelling option would have had to start and finish way beyond the site boundaries, effectively defeating its purpose.

The final masterplan is shown in Figure 5.23. To the east, the masterplan proposed linking the King's Cross road network directly into Copenhagen Street. To the south of this, the railway lines into King's Cross station made further road connections unfeasible due to level differences. North of Copenhagen Street,

5: THE MASTERPLAN

though, there were opportunities as Islington council was in the process of restructuring the Bemerton estate. It would have been possible to connect streets from the northern part of King's Cross through to Caledonian Road, in effect restoring the street grid that had been obliterated in the 1960s. Argent funded landscape architects EDAW[21] to carry out a feasibility study, but the idea was never entertained by Islington council and a major opportunity was lost.

Psychological connections

Attention moved away from physical connections to consider devices to overcome the psychological barriers that might dissuade local people from entering the site. The idea was to make King's Cross such an attractive destination that local people would see it as part of their own neighbourhood. Camden council and Argent St George analysed a range of factors that would impact on the experience of visiting King's Cross, particularly how it could be made to look and feel familiar. Again, the example of Canary Wharf, with its hard impermeable edges, corporate urban realm and estate security was something all parties wanted to avoid. The critical issue of Camden council's adoption and management of the urban realm is covered in Chapter 6, but these discussions laid down the basic condition that King's Cross should be open and inclusive and should feel familiar to those living in surrounding areas.

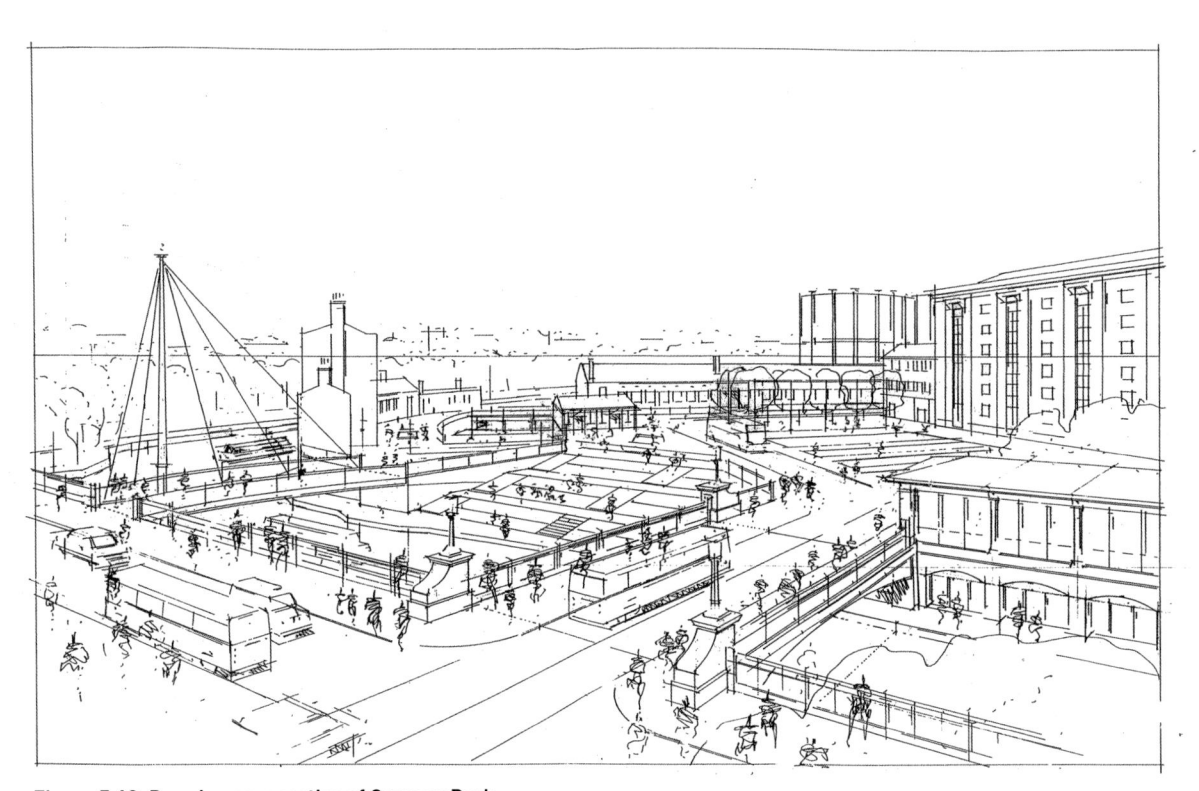

Figure 5.18: Drawing perspective of Granary Park.

PLANNING, POLITICS AND CITY MAKING

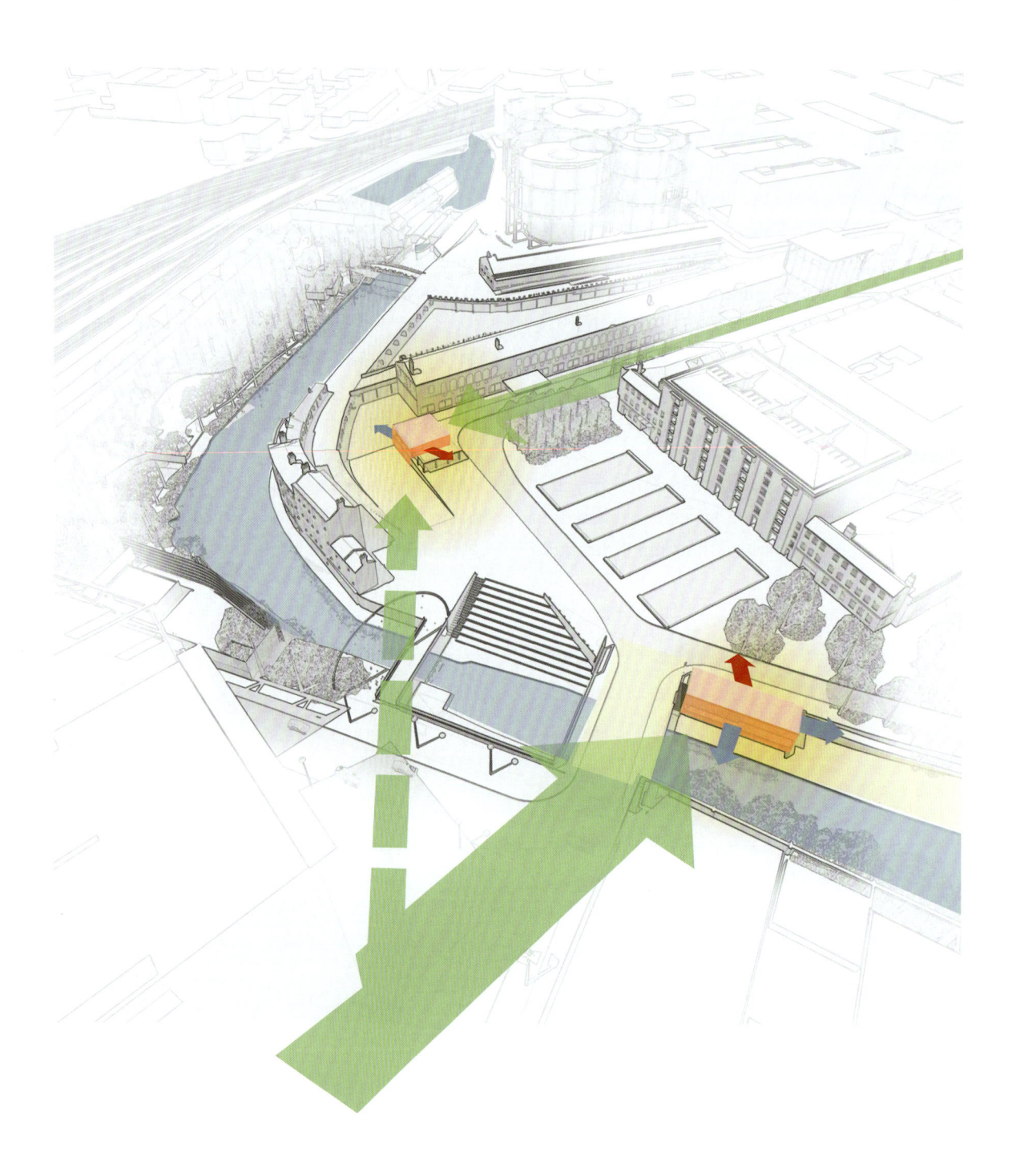

Figure 5.19: Design study of Granary Square.

5: THE MASTERPLAN

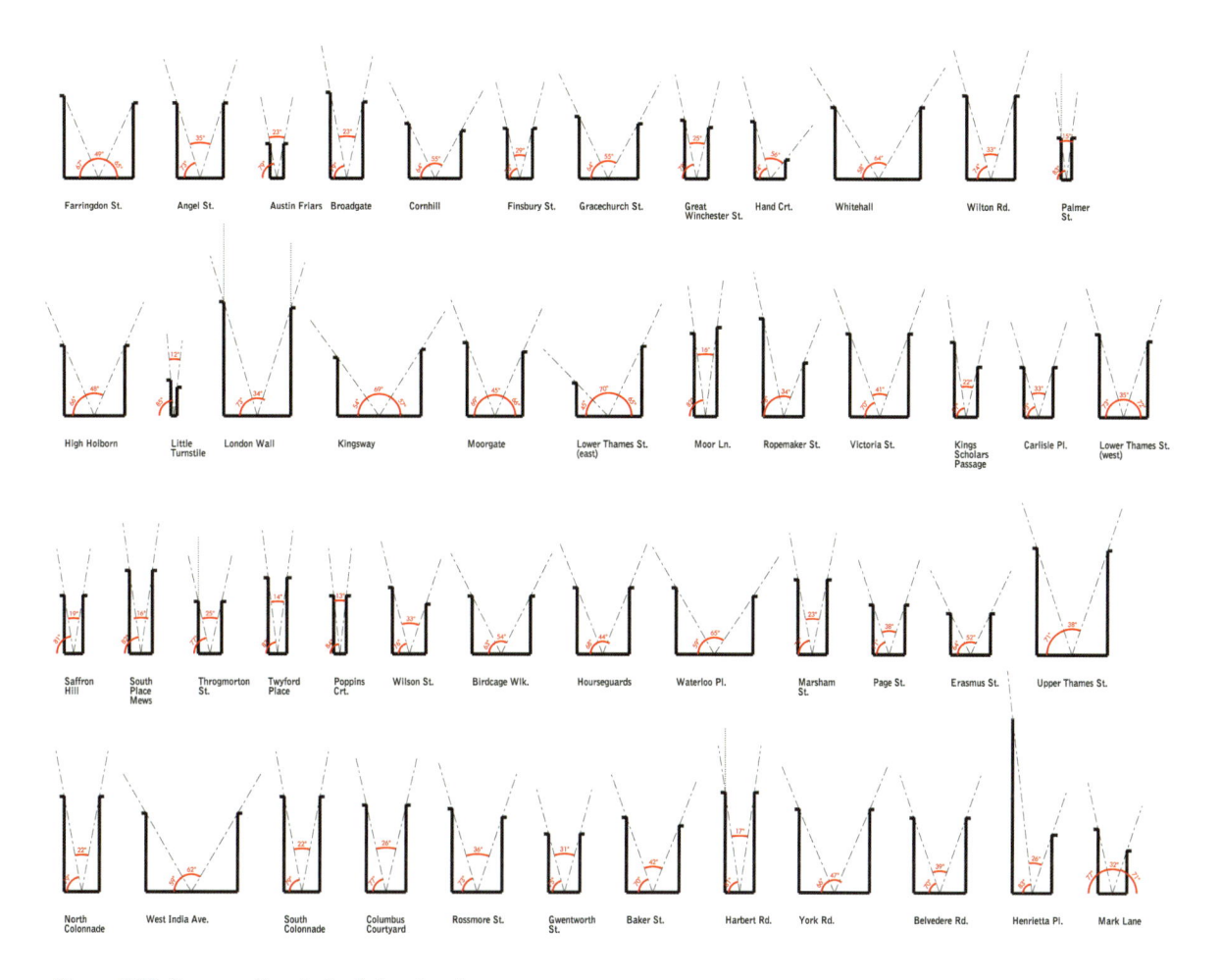

Figure 5.20: Comparative study of street scales.

To reinforce this concept, Camden council and Argent St George agreed that key buildings would be placed in specific locations within the masterplan. The public swimming pool and gym were sited at the end of Goodsway, as near to the western edge of the site as possible and at a prominent entry point. This location was further reinforced by Camden council's subsequent decision to take a long lease on the entire corner building for their town hall offices. The primary school, nursery and health centre, however, were placed in the heart of the site, presupposing that unlike visits to sports facilities, which are voluntary journeys, walking children to school and visiting a GP are not. By placing these facilities deep in the heart of the scheme the idea was that these would become journeys of exploration and familiarisation. Granary Square and its fountains have subsequently become a popular destination for the wider community.

PLANNING, POLITICS AND CITY MAKING

Figure 5.21: Final masterplan – rich mix of ground floor land uses.

Figure 5.22: Night time economy.

5: THE MASTERPLAN

Figure 5.23: Final masterplan.

Parks and open spaces

Despite some calls for a full sized football pitch, it was accepted that the site was just too small to accommodate leisure facilities on this scale. The concept of the London square was used as a familiar model to incorporate open space into the city. London's Bryanston Square provided the model against which the size of spaces was tested, and Argyll Square provided a model for the blend of active, passive and children's play that could be accommodated. It was agreed that formal spaces such as Granary and Pancras Squares would be important new civic spaces. Although these were to be managed by Argent St George, 24-hour public access was guaranteed, together with a commitment to manage as if they were publicly adopted.

CONCLUSIONS

A masterplan is not an abstract exercise; numerous commercial imperatives need to be embedded, building heights and plot sizes have to be optimised, and circulation and servicing

> **" A good masterplan arises from a dialogue between an informed client, other professionals within the team and the public at large. This takes time to develop. It also helps if this dialogue is based on a deep and scholarly understanding of design precedents and, importantly, how to apply them. "**

routes must work. David Partridge, managing partner of Argent St George, summed up a good masterplan as one that is legible: 'it needs to have simplicity of navigation; it needs to have front doors. Without this legibility it will be extremely hard to sell properties to potential investors'.[22] It is surprising how many masterplans fall at this first hurdle.

Without the ability to control land and finance, masterplanning can be a whimsical exercise. The masterplan must be able to guide development through implementation, and respond to changes in external conditions. It must be able to accommodate changes in phasing and be flexible enough to adapt to changes in the market. It needs to open up rather than close down future possibilities.

A good masterplan arises from a dialogue between an informed client, professionals within the team and the public at large. This takes time to develop. It also helps if this dialogue is based on a deep and scholarly understanding of design precedents and how to apply them. Research into the history of the area gives important clues to the potential urban form. Working with historic fabric and embedding this into new relationships is not easy, but it can produce distinctive places. Generally, the best masterplans are those that rise to the challenge of complexity.

Commissioning three practices to produce the masterplan avoided stylistic bias, and allowed time for a debate to take place and for the plan to mature. The three teams provided a creative tension, and ideas emerged from this dialogue that made the masterplan more subtle. The practices had a deep knowledge of the history and theory of architecture, landscape and city planning, and applied this to the challenges of the site. Inevitably, some architects have criticised the scheme. Zaha Hadid described it as dull and a missed opportunity.[23] Others, such as architectural critic and journalist Rowan Moore, have been more complimentary.[24] At the heart of this debate are the fundamentals regarding the nature of urban form. The masterplanning team opted for a particular form based on a legible street pattern. This does not necessarily make the scheme less radical.

The final masterplan developed over a period of more than four years. In reviewing its evolution, it is noteworthy that although aspects of its final form were clearly recognisable in its early stages, later changes, subtle as they were, resulted in significant improvements. Good masterplans are complex and display a deep understanding of their contexts. In contrast, masterplans based on abstract geometrics and parametrics struggle to produce good places.

The relationship between the masterplan and the historic buildings was central to the scheme. The historic fabric provided a constant challenge to the emerging design, but the strategy of embedding it into a new urban form, has resulted in buildings like the Granary sitting very naturally in relation to the new buildings and spaces that surround it. Paradoxically, it was the inability of the masterplan to embed the Culross and northern Stanley Buildings that led to the justification for their demolition. The tests of logic were exactly the same.

At the end of the day, one of the key tests of any masterplan is whether it gets built. King's Cross is under construction and the plan has proved robust enough to adapt to extreme economic circumstances. It is too early to judge its success in creating a new piece of city; that will be up to future generations of Londoners.

6. THE MIDDLE GAME

By the beginning of 2003, a policy framework – the basic principles of the scheme and the main elements of the masterplan – were in place, key stakeholders were on board and a firm foundation had been established for the negotiations. However, key details remained to be thrashed out. Getting this detail right occupied the next three years of negotiations.

Due to the complex nature of the discussions, this chapter is structured thematically, rather than chronologically, around these major areas of contention. It examines the differences between the parties and how agreement was brokered. A planning consent is usually granted with conditions. The quantum and type of housing and adoption of public realm would normally be contained within the permission itself or covered by conditions. The detailed arrangements, for example the allocation of the housing, or management arrangements for street and parks' maintenance, would be included in section 106. In this chapter we have dealt with housing and public space separately as they were substantive items, even though they occupied a significant part of section 106. (For more explanation on this see pp.107-17.)

It was also becoming clear, however, that there were significant differences in the aims and approach of Argent and its housing partner St George, and this was creating tension.

THE BREAK-UP OF ARGENT'S PARTNERSHIP WITH ST GEORGE

St George had brought specialist housing expertise to the partnership, but there were significant differences in the operational culture of the two firms and these were apparent from the start. At an early meeting during a visit to a St George scheme at Vauxhall Cross, a senior member of the St George team took Bob West of Camden council aside and said, '[...] if you think you are going to get any planning gain out of King's Cross, you've got to be joking'.[1] In St George's view, planning was adversarial and a lottery. It was more inclined to go to appeal believing that even if a scheme was refused, it would at least know where the battle lines had been drawn.

This difference in approach reflected the parties' different development models. Argent intended to retain as much of the commercial property as possible and collect an increasing rent over time. The St George model was to develop and move on, meaning that it focused on short-term value at the point of sale. Although both commercial and residential developments are subject to market fluctuations, housing will usually sell at a price. Offices, however, need occupants; discounting rents alone will not result in lettings, especially in an economic downturn. The two partners therefore also had different risk profiles. At the time of Argent's bid, Berkeley Homes, St George's parent company, was considering becoming a broad based property company that would have aligned their approach more closely with Argent's. When Berkeley decided to remain as a volume house builder, the consequences for the partnership were significant.[2]

St George was pushing to bring negotiations to an early conclusion and to submit a planning application. When it was clear that Argent would

> **For Argent, the critical question was the amount by which Camden council was likely to try and reduce overall quantum of floor space in the scheme.**

not do this, St George suggested dividing the site and developing housing in the north. Argent resisted, as this would certainly have impacted on the long-term value of the whole estate. Increasingly, St George became less involved in meetings, eventually taking what Roger Madelin describes as a 'monitoring role', reporting back progress (or its perceived lack of it) to its board.[3] London and Continental Railways and Exel shared Argent's misgivings about the partnership and in October 2004 a decision was made to end the partnership and for Argent to buy out St George's interests.

Argent was concerned at the cost of a buy-out, and reconsidered its business plan before making an offer to St George. For Argent, the critical question was the amount by which Camden council was likely to try and reduce overall quantum of floor space in the scheme. Madelin sought assurance on this point in a phone call to Peter Bishop. He stated candidly that the maximum floor space that Argent could lose would be 10 per cent; any more and the scheme would be unviable. Bishop's response was that Camden council did not have a target, and that it was essentially agnostic about the quantum of floor space as long as the affordable housing was delivered and the Environmental Impact Assessment (EIA), retail and transport assessments all worked. Some members of the Camden council team believed that this response was a tactical mistake and that if a 10 per cent reduction in floor space had been accepted it could then have been 'traded' back in negotiations, in return for other benefits.[4] This would have been a standard approach under conventional negotiation practice. However, the whole focus of the negotiations was about achieving a good scheme, not about quantum. In Bishop's view, a blanket 10 per cent reduction in the quantum of floor space would have been meaningless at such an early stage in the scheme's development. He was also concerned that a reduction in overall floor space would make the negotiations on housing numbers and the percentage of affordable housing more difficult to resolve in Camden's favour.

In November 2004 Argent bought out St George's interest and severed the partnership, albeit at a high cost. Argent then restructured and took on expertise in residential development. As the sole developer, Argent could pursue the negotiations more constructively, and with the long-term aim of consensus building.

HOUSING

The most significant area of contention in the negotiations over the section 106 agreement was in relation to housing – particularly the amount of affordable housing that the scheme would accommodate.

The quantum of housing

Expectations on the amount of housing to be accommodated on the site ranged from a minimum of 1,074 units (in Camden council's Unitary Development Plan (UDP)), to a minimum of 1,250 units (in the London Plan), and a target of 2,000 units (in Camden's Housing Strategy). Community consultations indicated a desired target range of 2,000–3,000. Frank Dobson, the local MP, wanted at least 3,000 and some community groups were pressing for 4,000. The question of quantum was not abstract. Bob West had outlined the constraints in a briefing to the leader.[5] The government's Regional Policy Guidance (RPG3) had effectively concluded that 3,000 houses could not be accommodated at King's Cross without prejudicing commercial floor space around the transport interchange.[6] The historic buildings further constrained development on over eight hectares of the site. Camden council would also require community facilities and a school, and accommodating these with family housing would not be easy in a very high density development. The briefing concluded that 1,800 units might be the upper limit.

Argent needed a minimum amount of commercial floor space to make the scheme financially viable, but knew that cramming too much onto the site would ultimately depress values. The quantum of development flowed from the masterplan, and was always secondary to the objective of creating a successful place.[7] Both parties were prepared to consider 2,000 as a target, but minor shifts from housing to offices or vice versa would have significant impacts on the overall value of the scheme. The appropriate quantum of housing could not be calculated until a detailed masterplan had been signed off, but as the negotiations progressed and the masterplan was refined, the quantum of housing gradually increased.

Affordable housing

The percentage and type of affordable housing was to prove the most difficult area for agreement. For Argent it represented the greatest drain on the value of the scheme.

A BRIEF HISTORY OF AFFORDABLE HOUSING PROVISION IN THE UK

The principle of state intervention in the UK to provide decent housing for less wealthy sectors of society was established in the 19th century, and notions of social and moral reform were embedded in the early town planning movement. The establishment of the planning system in the post-war period coincided with the need for reconstruction and slum clearance. The metropolitan councils established large and powerful architecture and housing departments and planning delivered the land and the utopian ideals. Government intervention occurred on a massive scale.

The restructuring of the state under the Conservative government of the 1980s saw council housing programmes curtailed and provision moved to independent housing associations – Registered Social Landlords (RSLs). Initially RSLs were supported through public subsidies, but these were progressively reduced in the 1990s. Instead, the government began to rely increasingly on the planning system to require developers to provide 'affordable' housing within new developments through the section 106 agreement (for more on the section 106 agreement see Figure 6.8 on p.126).

> **The principle of state intervention in the UK to provide decent housing for less wealthy sectors of society was established in the 19th century, and notions of social and moral reform were embedded in the early town planning movement.**

For Camden council it was the absolute key to political agreement. Without a level of affordable housing approaching 50 per cent, as sought in Camden council's policy, the scheme would undoubtedly have been refused.

For councils facing a major housing shortage and with long waiting lists, the provision of any additional accommodation is important. In practice, when viewed against need, the amount provided through the section 106 agreement is relatively small. But this is not the point. Achieving affordable housing is symbolic; it demonstrates a commitment to deal with the problem and tenants' groups often hold councils to account on this. For planners, a specific affordable housing target also provides a tangible and demonstrable measure of success.

Despite the long association between planning and housing policy, the provision of affordable housing through planning is still contentious. While it is a role of the planning system to identify sufficient land for housing needs, it is questionable whether it is the role of developers to provide social housing in return for planning consents. Arguably, the private sector has no more responsibility to provide social housing than other services such as schooling or healthcare. In effect, this policy is replacing a government programme delivered through direct taxation to one delivered locally through indirect taxation. Although in theory this should be reflected in land values, in practice the provision of affordable housing represents an opportunity cost, and other benefits including design quality are often compromised.

Whatever the arguments concerning affordable housing, planning should have a responsibility to achieve social mix. A mix of house types, values, sizes and tenures is a strong characteristic of London and creates balanced neighbourhoods.[8] In many neighbourhoods the wealthy and poor live alongside each other, rather than being segregated into ghettos or gated communities (an unacceptable feature of many new developments). Social mix was viewed as one of the keys to achieving the objective that King's Cross should be just another piece of London, and it drove Camden council's negotiating position at least as powerfully as the housing need argument. Camden planners suggested that for a neighbourhood to be socially sustainable, with functional schools, a good range of local shops and community facilities, wealthier or poorer households should not constitute more than 70 per cent of the population. Clearly this was rule of thumb, but the argument was accepted by Argent.

Definitions of affordable housing

There are strict definitions of what constitutes affordable housing under planning policy.[9]

These rest on a calculation of the percentage of housing costs in relation to household income. This sets affordability thresholds. At the time of the King's Cross negotiations, the upper limit of affordability was based on an income of just over £50,000 for a couple in a two-bed unit. Within this definition there are different affordable housing options targeted at different income levels. These range from fixed cost rent to forms of shared ownership.[10] All affordable housing is usually delivered under an agreement between a developer and an RSL, and the council has the first option to nominate potential tenants from its waiting lists.

Types of affordable housing

There are various types of affordable housing (Table 6.1). In simple terms, social rented housing is aimed at individuals on lower incomes than forms of mid-tenure housing. At the time of the negotiations, grants were available to support affordable housing and Argent was able to sell land to RSLs, albeit below market value. The opportunity cost of each house negotiated from market to affordable amounted to £250,000 off the total value of the scheme.[11]

Negotiations over affordable housing

The percentage of affordable housing

The Three Dragons Report,[12] commissioned by the Greater London Authority (GLA) in 2001, suggested that all housing developments of more than 15 units could provide 50 per cent affordable housing on site. A target that developments should achieve up to 50 per cent affordable housing was then incorporated in the 2004 London Plan.[13] Camden council's revised UDP had already included this target.

Argent had always recognised that it would have to provide some affordable housing but had set 25 per cent as its preferred level. Camden council started negotiations with an expectation of 50 per cent. These positions were aired early in negotiations, during work on the revised Camden UDP (see Chapter 4).[14] As the quantum of housing could not be calculated until a detailed masterplan had been signed off, a working compromise was agreed. Of the first 1,000 additional units (over and above the replacement of the 74 units that had existed on the site in Culross Buildings), 50 per cent would be affordable (35 per cent social rent and 15 per cent intermediate), but above this the council would seek 50 per cent with the same social rent/intermediate mix. Argent also guaranteed that affordable housing would be built in each

Table 6.1: Definitions of affordable housing

Housing type	Definition
Social rented	100% rent paid to an RSL
Specialist social rented	100% rent to an RSL but for groups requiring extra care
Key worker housing	Discounted market rent through an RSL
Shared ownership	50% purchased on a mortgage, 50% rented from an RSL. Occupier can 'staircase out', i.e. progressively buy equity
Shared equity	50% purchased, but no rent. Occupier can 'staircase out' but the RSL retains any uplift in the value of the remaining equity

Source: interview with Robert Evans, 6 November 2015

phase of development and that the social and market housing would be integrated, rather than segregated, within the site. The policy was supported by Camden council's housing needs strategy and by policy in the GLA's emerging London Plan. The policy was designed to be flexible enough to allow negotiations to continue and to incentivise Argent to increase both the quantum of housing overall and the percentage of affordable housing.

From the outset, both sides agreed that a polarised scheme comprising the very rich and the very poor would not be a satisfactory outcome. It was a private conversation between Madelin and Bishop that opened up the next round of talks. In October 2002 they met by chance at a conference in Birmingham and agreed to review progress on King's Cross. The issue of affordable housing had to be resolved urgently and Bishop set out an offer. Camden council's position of at least 2,000 units of housing with 50 per cent affordable was non-negotiable. If Argent could agree this, Camden council could be flexible and would be willing to look at new models of mixed tenure, as long as they fell within the broad planning definitions of affordable housing. If this was agreed, Camden council would use all reasonable efforts to make a scheme work. The offer was accepted.

Although Camden's policy was to seek 50 per cent affordable above the first 1,000 units, Islington's policy on the 'Triangle' site was 35 per cent. An overall target of 50 per cent affordable housing across the whole site was not therefore supported by policy. To resolve this problem, Camden council indicated a willingness to reduce the social rented housing below 35 per cent and have a higher percentage of mid-tenure housing. Argent in return suggested developing new mid-tenure products. The first was 'Homebuy', whereby Argent would subsidise Camden council's nominees with a 25 per cent interest free loan. The second, 'Right to Buy – Homebuy' made the same product available to council tenants who wanted to transfer their right to buy discount (which Argent would cover) to a property in King's Cross. This had the advantage of freeing up council housing for re-let. These products were within the council and the GLA's strict definitions of affordable housing.

An inherent problem in negotiations on levels of affordable housing is that the amount of government grants or subsidies fluctuates. It was implicit that the Shared Equity, Homebuy and Right to Buy – Homebuy products would be delivered without grant funding. The remaining tenures were, however, expected to require an element of grant funding. Argent argued that in order to be able to agree the baseline affordable housing offer, safeguards would be required should the government significantly reduce the grants. Camden council responded by proposing a cascade mechanism. Under this, Argent would receive a minimum index-linked price for completed units. The price would be based on the cost of delivering these units, excluding land and infrastructure costs. The level of grant needed to achieve this price was benchmarked against levels secured in 2004–06 within the borough. Should the RSLs be unable to pay the agreed price for the unit, the cascade mechanism allowed for adjustments to the affordable housing and eventually for the mix to change.

Notwithstanding this, the gap between Argent's offer and Camden council's policy still looked intractable. The negotiations were again taken offline and new solutions sought over cups of coffee. Three further areas were explored to provide Argent the reassurance it needed to increase the level of affordable housing: child density, the location of the affordable housing, and Camden council's nomination policy.

Family units and child density

Camden council wanted to see as high a percentage of larger family units as possible, in order to address the problems of overcrowding in its own stock.[15] However, family units were more expensive for Argent to provide and more difficult to fit into a high density mixed-use development. Argent was also concerned that too many large family units would create a disproportionate number of young children on the estate. This would cause management problems. There was little research available to back this view, although Camden's housing department had experienced problems on new developments in Camden Town. Argent commissioned the Rowntree Foundation to produce an independent research report.[16] The report concluded that the maximum child density (the percentage of children aged 5–18) should not exceed 18 per cent.[17]

This placed Camden planners in a difficult position as they were under pressure to negotiate as much family housing as possible. However, they accepted that a clause in the planning agreement might allow negotiations to be concluded. In return for additional very large family units Camden council agreed to adjust the housing mix and abide by an allocations agreement that limited child density to 23 per cent. In retrospect, it is difficult to assess how serious a point Argent was making here. The issue of child density was a novel concept that Camden had not seen in previous development negotiations. Argent maintains that its primary concern was the welfare and impact of high numbers of children on the management of a large mixed-use estate in Central London.[18]

Camden council had set out its view early in negotiations that the social and market housing should not be segregated into separate enclaves, but mixed ('pepper potted'). After several meetings it was agreed that affordable housing should be distributed throughout the scheme and that the buildings should be tenure neutral, that is, indistinguishable from one another (Figure 6.1). In return, Camden council conceded that mixing tenures within blocks would be difficult due to the impact service charges would have on overall affordability. The implication would have been that only tenants on the lowest incomes and receiving housing benefit (which covered service charges), would be able to live in the social housing. This would have polarised the social mix in the scheme and squeezed out key worker housing.

Council nomination rights

The final part of the affordable housing deal concerned council nomination rights of prospective tenants. Allocation is usually on a points system based on individual need. It is a fair system, but it does mean that a developer has no say on the occupants of the social housing in their scheme. Argent wanted a guarantee that

6: THE MIDDLE GAME

Figure 6.1: Intermediate, affordable and student housing from the park.

Camden council would not 'dump' its problem tenants into King's Cross. This appeared to be a fundamental disagreement and negotiations were again suspended. Camden council considered refusing the scheme and going to appeal. After a period of two weeks in which there had been no contact, an informal meeting took place to explore ways out of the impasse. Argent proposed that it would increase the percentage of affordable housing in return for guarantees by Camden council that it would not use King's Cross as a 'sink estate'.

A solution was found by adapting an existing policy. Due to the strong association in the King's Cross area with crime and drug use, Camden had a policy to not allocate housing to vulnerable tenants or those with a record of anti-social behaviour.[19] This was adapted for the King's Cross development as a 'sustainable lettings policy'. Under this, prospective tenants had to meet the basic requirements, including no recent record of anti-social behaviour. With this agreement in place, the way was clear for the housing details to be finalised.

Student housing

The final element of the housing negotiations concerned student accommodation. Although not within the planning definitions of affordable housing, it did introduce another diverse element into the community and an increase in the size of the resident population. For Argent this was a good commercial proposition; for Camden council it took pressure off housing stock elsewhere in the borough. Both agreed that student housing would contribute to the creation of a mixed community.

How good was the deal on affordable housing?

In the end, a total of 2,013 houses was agreed, plus 650 units of student housing. Calculating the final quantum was not straightforward due to the many variables. The figures presented to the development control subcommittee for approval were:

Main site	1,700 units
'Triangle' site	246 units
St Pancras Chambers	67 units
Student housing	650 units
Total	2,663 units

How good was the deal on affordable housing, and did the parties achieve their negotiating objectives? Camden council achieved its initial target of 2,000 units of housing and Argent had a balanced mixed-use scheme with enough office floor space to make it profitable. There is a question as to how much affordable housing was actually achieved. Under strict planning definitions and using the information presented to councillors in the March 2006 committee report, the figure was 43 per cent on the main site, or 47 per cent when the portion of the site within Islington was included. This excludes the 650 units of student housing. Although there was a need for student housing, it does not come under the definition of affordable housing. If these are added in, however, the percentage of market housing becomes less than 40 per cent of the total.

While negotiations at King's Cross were proceeding, London and Continental Railways

6: THE MIDDLE GAME

(LCR) was also negotiating planning consents for its site at Stratford, where the percentage of affordable housing was agreed at 35 per cent. In subsequent interviews, Roger Madelin believed that Argent might have conceded a further 3 to 4 per cent in affordable housing, while Robert Evans believed that the deal was right at the limit of what Argent and the land owners could accept.[20] King's Cross is comfortably within Camden's 70:30 definition of a mixed community (i.e. that no more than 30 per cent of residents should be poor or rich). The opportunity cost of affordable, as opposed to market, housing was approximately £250,000 per unit, or about £210 million. The difference between achieving 47 per cent affordable housing and 35 per cent (the London norm), was around £50 million.

Percentages are open to interpretation. What really mattered for politicians on King's Cross was the political deal. No other major scheme in London was achieving over 40 per cent affordable housing at the time, and the mayor accepted that King's Cross was in compliance with the London Plan. The total offer constituted a mixed community.

MANAGEMENT OF THE PUBLIC REALM

Chapter 5 described the physical difficulties of linking the site to its immediate hinterland, and the options for overcoming the psychological barriers that might deter local people from entering and using the site. Central to this was the design and management of the public realm.

Figure 6.2: Study boards on public realm.

Since its first document, Principles for a Human City, Argent was committed to high quality, well designed public space (Figure 6.2), and Camden council had similar aspirations. The main area of disagreement was over who should manage the public space. Argent wanted the public realm to be maintained through an effective management regime under its control. Failure to do so, it argued, would impact on rents and land values. Its concern was that in the recent past, Camden council's maintenance services had been near to collapse and Camden's ability to maintain the estate to the standards demanded by commercial tenants was questionable. Camden argued that the council was now one of the best in the country, with high standards of cleaning and maintenance. Moreover, if King's Cross was going to be 'just another part of London', its streets must look like London streets, rather than have the sanitised character of a commercial estate.

The issue of public realm management is important. Adopted streets and open spaces are fully accessible to the general public for use within the bounds of the law, and are maintained and cleaned at the public expense. In recent times many developers have sought to retain the control of public areas, and some cash-strapped local councils see the privatisation of such space positively. But public access to privately managed space can be restricted through a plethora of rules and enforced by private security. Under a heavy-handed regime the young and the poor might be made to feel unwelcome, and effectively excluded.

Two widely publicised incidents helped Camden council's case. In the first, cleaners who had been laid off by a firm in Canary Wharf had tried to demonstrate against their treatment. Since the streets were not publicly adopted they had been removed by private security guards. Mayor Ken Livingstone had been particularly angered by this case. The right to demonstrate became a test of whether public realm was really public. The second incident concerned two young men who had been removed from the Bluewater shopping complex in Kent purely because they wore the hoods of their jackets over their heads. This led to the 'hoodie' test – a breakthrough in resolving the impasse.[21]

Argent accepted that individuals should have the right to use public space lawfully, regardless of their dress or appearance, but this could not be put into any meaningful planning condition. Should it dispose of the estate in the future, or take another management approach, then the entire character and feel of public spaces could change. It would only take one incident of a parent being told that its children were not allowed to play in the park, for word to spread locally that 'King's Cross is not for us'. Although the subtleties of day-to-day estate management

> **Argent accepted that individuals should have the right to use public space lawfully, regardless of their dress or appearance, but this could not be put into any meaningful planning condition.**

practice could not be enshrined in a legal agreement, the adoption of streets could.

The agreement that was reached is still unique to the development. Camden council has the option to adopt the main streets and open spaces, and Argent retains control over the larger formal squares.[22] This allows higher quality maintenance and event management in the formal spaces, but Camden council still retains public control over the rest of the site. The feel of the place would clearly be public. Under the agreement, Camden council maintains and cleans to its usual standards, but if Argent requires higher standards, the maintenance specification and budget can be topped up from the service charge.

ENVIRONMENTAL PERFORMANCE

By 2004, environmental performance was featuring on political agendas and it was clear that it would become an increasing concern for future tenants. Addressing it now was good business strategy for Argent. Successive rounds of public consultation had already demonstrated local support for strong environmental performance in new developments. On the political front, the Green Party was challenging John Thane's seat in Highgate.[23] Environmental performance was important, but came below affordable housing and local employment on the council's priorities. The overriding political concern was not to leave this flank open for attack by the opposition, the mayor or community activists.

Although Argent was committed to providing environmental performance at or above Camden council and the GLA's policies, the main area of difficulty was in translating such aspirations into practical measures. There was a gap between planning policies and the cost-effectiveness of the environmental technologies available. Emerging technologies were largely untested, policy prescriptions had rarely been thought through and the GLA target of 10 per cent for on-site renewable energy was impracticable. Early calculations[24] demonstrated that the developable part of the 27-hectare site could not physically accommodate these requirements and that the costs would have been prohibitive:

- Photovoltaics: 12 hectares of roof space would contribute 1.58 per cent of energy needs at a cost of £78 million.
- Solar water heating: 3.9 hectares would contribute 4.87 per cent of energy needs at a cost of £27.3 million.
- Wind: 525 x 9m diameter or 5 x 70m diameter turbines (as in off shore wind farms) would contribute 4.87 per cent of energy needs at a cost of £27 million and £8 million respectively.
- Ground source heat pumps: a 27.5-hectare footprint would contribute 7.42 per cent of energy needs at a cost of £27 million.

The planning report 'accepted that full use of these technologies is not compatible with size, townscape and other technical constraints within the site. For example, there is no place on either the main or "Triangle" site that would accommodate or provide sufficient wind speed for even a single 70 metres diameter wind turbine.'[25]

Argent's Andre Gibbs was tasked with resolving the problem.[26] Camden council was content that most of the negotiations on energy

Figure 6.3: Energy centre.

were conducted between Argent and the GLA in order to comply with London Plan requirements. The London Plan had policies requiring developments to produce energy assessments, but no one was sure what these policies meant in practice. Each policy was tested against practical technologies under the principle of 'great idea, but what problem are you trying to solve?'. Ultimately the agreed approach was to invest primarily in energy efficient buildings and district heating (Figure 6.3).[27] It was reasoned that a district heating plant would pay in the long term and that the necessary pipework could be laid alongside the development's other infrastructure. The problem was that a district heating system would be required before the first development was completed and therefore required significant upfront investment. Argent solved this by building a temporary boiler (that has now been replaced by the energy centre).

TRANSPORT

Transport for London

London's medieval street patterns and offset grid systems are not able to cope with unrestricted car usage. For many years, therefore, policies have directed commercial development to major transport interchanges and have restricted on- and off-street parking. With the re-establishment of London government and the election of its first mayor in 2000, an integrated strategic transport authority, Transport for London (TfL), had been created. Mayor Livingstone was himself a daily user of the tube and bus systems and a strong advocate of public transport. TfL introduced a congestion charge over central London, and invested in new infrastructure for the underground, buses, walking and cycling.

At the time of the negotiations, TfL was still a young organisation and the task of welding a disparate collection of powerful departments into a coordinated organisation had hardly begun. Each department was focused on maximising its own operational efficiency and there was little internal coordination. A standing joke between Camden council and Argent was that at the beginning of any meeting they had to introduce TfL staff to each other.[28]

The mayor was clear that if there was substantial opposition to the King's Cross proposals from TfL, he would oppose the scheme and direct refusal. Had this occurred, it is likely that Camden council and Argent would have joined forces at a public inquiry. It is difficult, even in retrospect, to see what grounds he would have had as Camden council's transport policies were aligned with the mayor's. Nevertheless, the threat had to be addressed. TfL was inexperienced, and somewhat naively saw the mayor's powers as an opportunity to extract significant money from the King's Cross development.

Transport interchange

The space between King's Cross and St Pancras stations had to accommodate a new concourse, buses, cars, taxis, cyclists and pedestrians, but the details of this transport interchange still had to be resolved. The Great Northern Hotel formed a pinch point (see Chapter 5) that left only 2 metres of the space to accommodate these requirements beyond the existing carriageway. All the TfL divisions submitted their own plans for separate bus, cycle lanes, taxi ranks and pavements. At the time, TfL had little interest in the public realm and the result was as complex as a motorway junction. It took over a year of negotiation before matters were formally resolved towards the end of 2005. The solution, which involved collonading the Great Northern Hotel (see Chapter 9 for details), did not work when set against the transport models (which predicted gridlock). It was the experience and perseverance of LCR that finally persuaded TfL to accept what it considered to be a less than optimal solution. It now works perfectly well, and justifies the scepticism at the time about the accuracy of transport models.

The Cross River Tram

King's Cross St Pancras was already the best connected interchange in the UK, handling over 100 million passengers a year (Figure 6.4). There was adequate transport capacity for a major commercial development; it just required minor interchange improvements, sensible traffic restraints, and improvements to local public transport in the form of taxi drop-off points and local bus services.

TfL thought differently. During the late 1990s feasibility work had examined the options for new tram lines in London and one, the Cross River Tram, was planned to be built from Peckham in south-east London to King's Cross (Figure 6.5). Although Camden council and Argent welcomed this in theory, the problem was its engineering specification. 'Tram system'

is something of a misnomer. In reality it was a light rail system requiring the extensive re-routing of underground services, wide turning circles and lane priority throughout. A route along Euston Road terminating in front of King's Cross station seemed the most logical and least disruptive, but was ruled out by TfL on engineering grounds. Instead, it proposed taking the tram through Somers Town and into the site along Goodsway, terminating at the southern end of the Boulevard. This posed two problems. The first was that the stations (with raised platforms, sidings and cross-over lanes) would all but destroy any possibility of the Boulevard

Figure 6.4: Walking times from King's Cross St Pancras.

6: THE MIDDLE GAME

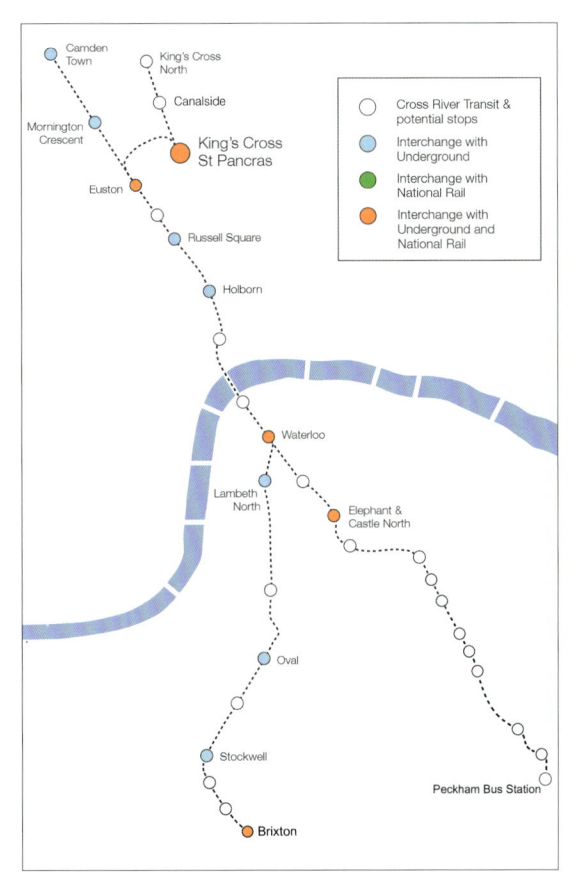

Figure 6.5: Route of proposed Cross River Tram.

becoming a high street and a public space. The second was that the proposed route through Somers Town raised opposition from the local councillor (Labour), Roger Robinson.

It might appear that a new tram through Somers Town would bring significant benefits to local people, but Robinson saw the tram as a noisy and intrusive safety hazard and mobilised local opposition against it. The tram threatened to alienate local opinion and there was a danger that this could, by association, feed back as opposition to the King's Cross scheme. To make things worse, TfL engineers saw a large amount of conveniently empty land at King's Cross, which could house a tram depot, and believed that Argent, with the mayor's insistence, would gift them the land. They proposed an open depot of approximately 7.5 hectares or 15 per cent of the land area.

The tram posed a significant threat to King's Cross. The £300 million project was not funded, the land was not owned by TfL and a depot, sited along York Way, would have completely severed the development from Islington. Nevertheless, TfL saw no need to negotiate or compromise. The mayor saw the tram as critical to improve access to jobs in central London for residents in the deprived areas of south-east London. Camden council and Argent feared that any accommodation for the tram would lead to further demands from TfL for the development to fund the scheme. Camden council's first response was to suggest alternatives. The first, with Islington council's agreement, was to extend the tram northwards to Holloway and look for a depot in south-east London. The tram would then only pass through King's Cross with a simple set of stops rather than a terminus. The second was to suggest a depot on a Camden-owned industrial estate to the north of King's Cross. In return for the land, Camden council would retain the development rights over the depot. Both options were rejected out of hand. Finally, in exasperation Argent approached the mayor directly. He agreed that the depot would be unworkable and asked TfL to turn its attention to Peckham, where a site was eventually found. This resolved the problem of the depot but not the terminus. Camden council suggested moving the terminus 100 metres into Midland

Way between St Pancras Station and the British Library. This was rejected by TFL as it was 'not at King's Cross'.

The problem of the tram was really one of politics. The mayor had given a direction that he would not sabotage King's Cross, but neither would he see his proposals for the tram shelved. He asked David Lunts, the executive director for planning at the GLA to intervene and sort out the problem. Lunts played the critical role of public sector 'fixer'. In the autumn of 2005, with negotiations completed between Argent and Camden council, he stepped in and brokered a deal between TfL and Argent. Argent agreed to accommodate the tram in King's Cross as long as TfL reduced the specification of the project. The masterplan was amended and building lines moved back to allow the tram to turn into the Boulevard from Goodsway. Lunts went back to the mayor and described the deal as, 'as good as you can get'.[29] Ironically, the project was never implemented. Boris Johnson, the next mayor, finally scrapped it in 2008, but it had run out of steam long before that. By the time it was abandoned, the Argent scheme had been approved and Argent did not want to re-open negotiations in order to remove the safeguarding lines.

Buses

The *quid pro quo* of the mayor's intervention to remove the threat of the tram depot was a request for some help with buses. He accepted Argent's offer of a temporary bus depot on the site while construction was taking place. This was accepted by TfL and two acres in the centre of the site were leased to them on a temporary basis by the landowners (Exel). Due to poor wording in the agreement, however, TfL returned with a demand that this land should be gifted to it in perpetuity. Once again it claimed the mayor's support and waved the threat of a 'call-in' if its demand was not supported. LCR eventually agreed to relocate the depot to land at the north (and outside the site), in the so-called 'linear lands' that were under its control.

Cycling

Both Argent and Camden council were keen to make provision for cycling in the scheme. It came as a shock, however, when in 2004 TfL proposed that Argent should provide the cycle parking required for the two stations. After lengthy negotiations, the scaled-down option of a cycle hub was included in the section 106 agreement (despite the fact that TFL could not come up with an operational model).[30] In the end, accommodation was reached with TfL on all these issues, but it took almost 18 months of protracted negotiations. Most of TfL's demands, well intentioned though they were, fell well outside the demands that a planning authority could legitimately make on a developer. Ultimately, there is only so much public benefit that a development can fund and still remain viable, and Camden council's priorities were affordable housing, employment and local facilities. While the lack of proper coordination within TfL was a major problem to all parties, it did bring Argent and Camden council together in common cause.

Car parking

In line with policy in the London Plan, the commercial floor space needed very little parking due to the proximity of the transport interchange. Camden council also sought to restrict residential parking and insisted that a proportion of housing should have no parking provision at all. Argent argued that the requirement for 50 per cent affordable housing had already put a severe strain on the scheme, and car-free housing on top of this might depress market values to the point of making the scheme unviable. To resolve the impasse, Argent suggested siting all parking in a multi-decked building on the edge of the site. It argued that the role of the planning system was to regulate the use of private cars rather than ownership. The 10-minute walk to the car park from people's homes would dissuade the use of cars for short journeys. Camden council accepted the argument.[31]

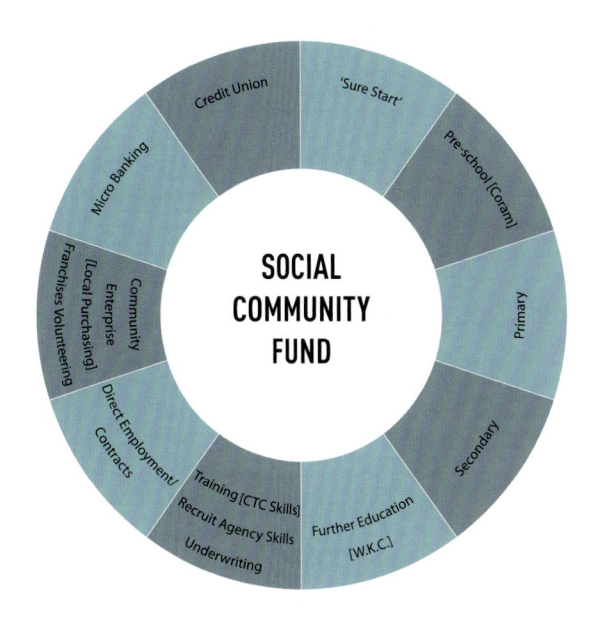

Figure 6.6: 'The Wheel'.

OTHER PLANNING BENEFITS

In early 2004, with the main areas of contention – affordable housing and adoption of the public realm – nearing resolution, the negotiations turned to the other planning benefits that would be included in the section 106 agreement. Argent proposed taking the negotiations 'off site' to a neutral venue to thrash out the principles. Aware of the sensitivities of using expensive venues, Argent hired a children's play hut in nearby Coram Fields. The main aspects of the deal were agreed here over two days in March 2004, with minimal heating, sitting on child-size plastic chairs.

Camden council and Argent started discussions by focusing on the problem of why local people were not finding work in the vicinity, and Camden council returned to its early proposition: 'how could King's Cross make a difference to the lives of local people?' (see Chapter 4). To answer this 'The Wheel' (Figure 6.6) was constructed. The Wheel allowed Camden council and Argent to frame

> ❝ **It argued that the role of the planning system was to regulate the use of private cars rather than ownership. The 10-minute walk to the car park from people's homes would dissuade the use of cars for short journeys.** ❞

a benefits package around the life cycle of a local child. Starting with the council's existing 'Sure Start'[32] programme, it looked at what was missing in terms of local provision throughout the educational life cycle, asked what specific interventions might improve life opportunities, and considered how contributions from Argent might fill the gaps.[33] By mapping the first 16 years of a local child's life, it was possible to assess how Argent's investment could best be targeted to complement existing programmes.

Primary school and health centre

The initial proposal for a new primary school on the site came from Argent. Camden council checked the demographic projections and for a scheme of 2,000 new homes, somewhere between a one-form and a two-form entry primary school and pre-school facility would be necessary. Both parties accepted that a larger school serving a wider area would help community integration. The same went for the health centre. Since the provision of educational or medical facilities to serve areas outside the development could not be justified under section 106, it was agreed that Argent would provide the shell for both buildings, Camden council would fit-out the school, and the medical practice would fit-out the health centre.

Secondary schools

Negotiations over contributions to secondary education were less conclusive. There was no demographic case for a secondary school on site; indeed, the nearby South Camden Community School had spare capacity. Argent resisted a request for £3 million to improve facilities at the school on the grounds that there was no planning case, which was for the most part true. Underlying this was a concern shared by many developers that monetary payments for facilities outside the site constitute a loss of control, the money simply disappearing into council coffers.[34] This was one area of the section 106 agreement that went down to haggling; eventually Argent agreed what was essentially a 'goodwill' contribution of £1.5 million towards secondary education in the immediate area.

Leisure centre and library

Public consultation had established an overwhelming demand for a swimming pool and leisure centre. Although under no strict obligation, Argent recognised the importance of responding positively to community demands and was sympathetic to the request. A swimming pool could also be put into a basement and act as a heat sink in the district energy scheme. Initially, Argent opposed Camden council's desire to run the pool and leisure centre, but after meeting Camden's leisure managers, conceded that Camden could be trusted to manage the facilities. As Camden would be earning a revenue stream from the new centre, it was agreed that it would make a contribution towards its fit-out.

Local employment opportunities

The provision of tangible local employment opportunities is generally one of the easier issues for a council and developer to agree. It does, after all, resonate with private sector thinking around personal improvement and wealth creation. For Camden council, it was

Figure 6.7: King's Cross construction training centre.

second only to affordable housing on the political agenda. Despite being only a short walk from central London, the most vibrant employment area in Europe, unemployment in the locality remained high. There was no reason to suppose that new jobs at King's Cross would go to local people unless something positive was done to improve their chances.

Early discussions centred on the provision of low cost (i.e. subsidised) workspace. Argent opposed this on the basis that subsidised rents would just lead to inefficient businesses. Public sector management of business and community space has had a tortured history in London, and the council accepted Argent's argument. In return, Argent agreed to provide a range of smaller commercial units that might be more suitable for startups. Discussion then switched to the best means to help local people gain employment and entrepreneurial skills.

The 20-year construction programme represented a substantial and sustainable source of new local employment. A standard approach to the provision of local employment is for major schemes to incorporate an element of local training for construction jobs. Most developers are willing to agree to this, but pass the obligation on to their contractors who agree to comply as long as they can choose who they take on as trainees. At best, they reject many local people as unsuitable, at worse they are actively prejudiced against them. However, a package of construction training is a useful entry point to well-paid local jobs if the right vehicle can be found.

Although the Single Regeneration Budget (SRB), LCR and the King's Cross Partnership (KCP) had already established a training

PLANNING, POLITICS AND CITY MAKING

Creating shared value

Secondary school age
- MUGA [J]
- Gas holder 8 [J]
- Floating classroom [K]
- Bus service improvements [HH]
- New indoor leisure facilities [L]
- New health facilities [M]
- Local streetscape/open space improvements [O/P]
- New affordable homes [NN]
- Business volunteering programme [F]
- Social and community fund [H]
- Community schools improvements [I]
- Secondary school contribution [J]

Young adults
- Construction training/apprenticeship [A]
- Social commitments fund [G]
- New community facilities [H]
- Community safety improvements [I]
- MUGA [J]
- New indoor leisure facilities [L]
- New affordable homes [NN]
- New health facilities [M]
- Local streetscape/open space improvements [O/P]
- Canal and waterscape enhamcements [T]
- Bus service improvements [NN]

Primary school age
- Business volunteering programme [F]
- Social and community fund [G]
- New community facility [H]
- Community safety improvements [I]
- New primary school academy [J]
- MUGA [J]
- Gas holder 8 [J]
- Exploratory centre [K]
- Floating classroom [K]
- Handyside Park new indoor leisure facilities [L]
- LEAP/LAP [L]
- New health facilities [M]
- Local streetscape/open space improvements [O/P]
- Public art as play [Q]
- Canal and waterscape enhancements [T]
- New affordable homes [NN]

Adults (working age)
- Construction training/employment [A]
- Skills and recruitment programme [B]
- Support for community enterprise initiative [C]
- Small business space provision [D]
- Voluntary sector space provision [D]
- Local business support and legal purchasing [E]
- Business volunteering programme [F]
- Social and community fund [G]
- New community facility [H]
- Community safety improvements [I]
- Gas holder 8 [J]
- New indoor leisure facilities [L]
- New health facilities [M]
- Local streetscape/open space improvements [O/P]
- Canal and waterscape enhancements [T]

Pre school
- Social and community fund [G]
- New community facility [H]
- Sure start/children's centre [J]
- LEAP/LAP [L]
- New health facilities [M]
- Local streetscape/open space improvements [O/P]
- New affordable homes [NN]
- Public art as play [Q]

Elderly
- Extra care affordable homes [NN]
- Social and community fund [G]
- New community facility [H]
- Community safety improvements [I]
- New indoor leisure facilities [L]
- Local streetscape/open space improvements [O/P]
- Canal and waterscape enhancements [T]
- Shopmobility [FF]
- Bus service improvements [HH]
- Nursing home [MM]

Figure 6.8: Development of 'The Wheel' as presented in the section 106 agreement (letters refer to sections in the section 106 agreement).

programme, Argent agreed to provide funding to ensure that it continued and a centre was established on land belonging to Argent on York Way (Figure 6.7). To overcome contractors' reluctance to employ local people, a model was adopted based on the success of the West Paddington Partnership. Here the partnership acted as an intermediary between business and the community, and was trusted because it did not put anyone forward for a job unless it was convinced that they had the skills and the aptitude to do it. Such has been the success of the King's Cross centre that after the section 106 agreement had been signed, Argent and Camden council agreed to increase its size, sharing the extra costs between them.

Argent's direct funding of the training centre was complemented by initiatives to link the local further education college to new jobs at King's Cross,[35] and to encourage future occupants to recruit locally. The result was King's Cross Recruit; its impact is considered further in Chapter 9. Another part of the package considered how members of the local community might benefit through setting up their own enterprises to exploit new business opportunities in the scheme. Provision was made in the section 106 agreement for training packages, small amounts of venture capital and access to cheap credit for business start ups. This was important since many local residents did not have access to bank accounts and were vulnerable to the usurious levels of interest charged by the unsecured credit sector. The final element was a 'community chest' of £1 million for local investment to support a range of different access to employment initiatives.

Development of the Wheel
The first development of the Wheel focused simply on the life cycle from an education and employment perspective, as discussed above. However, it was later developed by Argent into a working programme that covered all aspects of the section 106 agreement (Figure 6.8).

'The Wheel' represented a comprehensive and credible package that might begin to break the cycle of deprivation in the surrounding communities. Argent's board was persuaded that its contributions would complement existing programmes and potentially achieve large benefits.[36] It also addressed Camden council's starting propositions and represented a powerful and persuasive political package that Camden councillors were able to approve.

In summing up the negotiations on the section 106 agreement, Robert Evans of Argent commented, 'it is what planning is supposed to be about – mitigation and enhancement of impact. The Wheel focused on services rather than contributions. It allowed us to describe what we as a company wanted to achieve. Regeneration is not the same as development; it has a social dimension. In marketing Argent as a company we are proud of this. This for us is our point of difference.'[37]

CALCULATING THE VALUE OF THE SECTION 106 AGREEMENT

Government guidance on the negotiation of planning benefits is clear; a planning authority can only negotiate benefits that are required to offset the impacts of a development in accordance with its adopted policy. So, the provision of affordable housing and public space are legitimate, as is investment in transport, schools and leisure facilities that cope with increases in demand arising from the development. Provision of benefits also needs to be phased as the scheme is built. Developers will invariably resist up-front payments as, in Roger Madelin's words, 'it's a bit like paying your income tax before you have earned anything'.[38] There is a very fine line between legitimate planning benefits and extortion; at best, many developers see planning benefits as a form of tax on their development profits. There may be arguments for tax on developers' profits, but this is for national, not local government. Successive administrations have been trying to work out an appropriate formula for such a tax for decades,

> **The real question is whether the development is, on the whole, a good one and whether it improves the site and wider area. In this respect, planning benefits should rightly be restricted to those needed to make a scheme work and to offset any adverse effects.**

but so far none has been forthcoming.

Notwithstanding these arguments, a cash-starved public sector will inevitably see section 106 benefits as an opportunity to extract as much money as possible. Inevitably the question will arise at some time in the decision-making process as to whether the council has got enough, or more crudely, have they been taken for a ride by a tougher and more professional developer? To counter this, a planning authority will usually ask for a financial appraisal and Camden commissioned property consultancy DTZ, to do this.[39]

With so many complex variables in the King's Cross scheme, this was a difficult and expensive task. Argent was approached to provide financial data, a request that it refused on the grounds that it was not required to provide such commercially sensitive information. After a heated exchange, Roger Madelin elegantly summed up development finance: 'there are only three scenarios. Number one you lose your shirt, number two you break even and number three you make shed loads of money.' He hesitated before adding, 'fortunately I've always come somewhere between breaking even and making shed loads of money, which is why I still have a job'.

In the end, DTZ had to use comparative data from other schemes and fill in the detail with educated estimates. The modelling exercise confirmed Madelin's views. It tested a range of scenarios using different assumptions about content and external market conditions. One result in particular stood out. DTZ had allowed a period of 36 months from the first pile going into the ground to Argent receiving the full rent on an office building (allowing for any discounts and rent free periods). At the height of the commercial office boom in 2004 this was realistic. Extending the construction period to 48 months would effectively wipe £120 million off the value of the scheme.

It is now possible to speculate whether Camden council did get a good deal on the development. Our interviews with Argent confirm that the affordable housing provision at 44–47 per cent was probably as close as the landowners would have accepted, although throughout the negotiations Camden council was at a considerable disadvantage. Despite being well resourced, development finance, price indexing and construction costs were not fields in which Camden council had any significant expertise. Moreover, many of the sums in the section 106 agreement were inevitably based on Argent's figures. In Robert Evans's words, 'planners are not trained to be tax collectors or financial analysts'.[40] Camden council also lacked specialist support on housing finance, which Argent admits put it at a significant advantage (although it maintains that it did not exploit this).[41]

Ultimately, the scale of the possible market fluctuations makes the question of whether Camden got enough, rather pointless.[42] The real question is whether the development is, on the whole, a good one and whether it improves the site and wider area. In this respect, planning benefits should rightly be restricted to those needed to make a scheme work and to offset any adverse effects. If at the end of the day a developer makes a high level of profit, this is irrelevant to the planning process. The major items of the section 106 agreement are set out in Appendix 1.

REFLECTIONS ON THE NEGOTIATION PROCESS

While neither the Camden council nor Argent teams had been schooled in negotiation theory, both did contain experienced negotiators. Therefore, it is worth reflecting briefly on the negotiating process and relating this to current theory. This does not seek to be a comprehensive analysis of the theory, but is a simple attempt to compare practice to theory. Negotiation theory is well established, particularly in business deals, wars and labour disputes, although there are fewer references to its use in the public sector, or planning in particular. There are four basic elements of good practice in principled negotiation:[43]

1 Separate the people from the problem

It is important to maintain credibility and create positive personal relationships through honesty, trust, respect and diplomacy, and to ensure that neither party is forced to lose face. The ability to understand the situation as the other side sees it, is a key skill. The better the relationship, the more cooperation and information sharing there will be. This can involve informal discussions that can help negotiators get to know one another.

Good working relationships had already been established between the council and LCR through the King's Cross Partnership. This legacy carried through into the development discussions. On King's Cross, the negotiators established a good working relationship based on trust and honesty. They also recognised that the negotiation process would be lengthy and that positive working relationships had to be maintained. As Argent planned to retain ownership of the estate, it was particularly important for it to maintain a long-term relationship with Camden council.

Both sides also understood and respected the constraints under which the other side was operating. Argent understood the difficult internal politics in Camden council, and Camden recognised Argent's commercial requirements. Both teams avoided pushing the other into corners by seeking to extract the last drop of blood from the negotiations. There was also an agreement concerning fair conduct and reasonableness; once an element of the negotiation had been agreed it was never revisited.

This principle implies a very different relationship to that commonly observed in planning negotiations where an atmosphere of mutual suspicion and aggressive bargaining often predominates. Both parties did have to tread a delicate line between having an effective working relationship and not compromising (or being seen to compromise) their integrity. It is certainly true that some Camden councillors and some in the opposition groups believed that Camden council's planning officers had overstepped this line. Informal and off-the-record discussions did take place, but these were instrumental in breaking the deadlock at critical stages.

2 Do not bargain over positions or stated stances

Instead, identify the interests underlying an issue. This allows negotiators to focus on issues of mutual concern with greater creativity, understanding and flexibility.[44] Behind apparently opposing positions there may be shared and compatible interests.

Camden council and Argent specifically spelled out their own bottom lines (or positions) on many occasions and there was sufficient trust between the parties for these to be believed. Having done so, the negotiations always looked at the deeper agenda, constantly asking 'what are we really trying to achieve here?' (in relation, for example, to the affordable housing targets), or 'what does this really mean?' (in relation to public management of public space). As a result, both sides were able to generate creative options to solve problems, rather than operating from entrenched positions. There is no evidence to suggest that either party tried to bluff or horse-trade during the negotiations. If there had been a difference in this respect, it is unlikely that agreement would have been reached.

3 Invent multiple possible solutions to problems and look for mutual gains

Identifying options promotes creative thinking, expands problem-solving capabilities and provides a clearer understanding of the interests at stake. There were times when the King's Cross negotiations were suspended over disagreements, but each side was able to regroup and think creatively about how to break the deadlock, for example by developing new affordable housing models.

4 Insist that the results should be based on some objective criteria

Such criteria might include precedent, scientific judgment, professional standards, efficiency, costs, moral standards, equal treatment, tradition or reciprocity. These provide a basis for logical decision-making, and ensure that parties can look back on the negotiated solution as legitimate. The basic principles for the King's Cross development were derived from objective research (such as that on child density commissioned from the Joseph Rowntree Foundation) and this common ground formed a firm foundation for negotiations to proceed.

The theory also emphasises the importance of preparation in understanding the strengths and weaknesses of the opponents' position. In the King's Cross negotiations each side spent time analysing each other's bottom lines and strengths and weaknesses (and those of other interest groups). This assessment allowed them to calculate where trade-offs might occur. It also

> **The approach to stakeholder management paid dividends at this stage, and Camden council and Argent were largely able to resolve the key issues between them.**

revealed the relative strengths that each party would have in the event of an appeal and inquiry. Clearly, a negotiated settlement will only endure if all parties are fully empowered to make and honour binding commitments.[45] Camden council's officers spent a great deal of time in preparing the ground internally for negotiations. Some of the most important aspects of this were structural – setting up internal liaison and consultation arrangements; others were conceptual – translating the issues into political statements of priority. Camden council then aligned its own planning policy documents to its negotiating position. Perhaps unusually, Camden's officers were given a high degree of autonomy by their senior politicians within the parameters set by council policy.

Another principle of negotiation is that all stakeholders should have a place at the table. This is certainly where opposition groups such as the King's Cross Railway Lands Group (KXRLG) wished to be. Here, practice certainly diverged from the theory, and some of the reasons for this are explored in Chapter 7. Argent and Camden council exercised a high level of control to limit the direct participation of external parties. They adopted a strict definition of stakeholders as those with statutory powers, but agreed to keep them out of direct negotiations. As discussed in Chapter 4, those who could force an inquiry – Islington, GLA, TfL and English Heritage – were consulted, but their place at the negotiating table was restricted. Those writing on the pitfalls of multiparty negotiation do point out that involvement of more than two parties can lead to the formation of coalitions, holdouts, vetoes and betrayals that may reduce the scope for mutual gains.[46]

CONCLUSIONS

This chapter has looked at how a series of technical issues were resolved. Setting the policy frameworks had been relatively easy. Translating them into practice was at times fraught, and on a number of occasions nearly led to a breakdown in negotiations. These issues were resolved largely because the early negotiations had established good working relationships based on objective research, mutual trust and respect. The approach to stakeholder management paid dividends at this stage, and Camden council and Argent were largely able to resolve the key issues between them. It is also important to note that both parties resisted the temptation to haggle, or simply to split the difference where there were disagreements. Instead, arguments were based on well-researched positions and the study of precedents. Where there were genuine sticking points, the parties resorted to informal meetings to look at different ways to break the deadlock.

In formulating agreements, the importance of the masterplan cannot be underestimated. It provided a framework for testing both the quantum of development and the distribution of land uses across the site. It is unlikely that key issues such as the public realm and the integration of the site with its hinterland could have been resolved in abstract without reference to the plan. There were aspects of the scheme that were truly innovative, such as The Wheel, the public realm management agreement, and some of the intermediate housing options.

Unexpected issues will always emerge during negotiations and the tram was one of them. For a period of time it posed a significant threat, creating uncertainty and potentially pitting the mayor against the scheme. Perhaps more dangerously, it also threatened to turn the local community against the scheme. While the relationship with TfL was the most difficult to control, it did bring together Argent and Camden council.

On the content of the final section 106 agreement it is apparent from interviews that Camden council might have achieved a little more at the margins. Had it adopted a more adversarial approach and employed a degree of brinksmanship, it might have avoided paying the fit-out costs on the school and swimming pool, even though there was no planning basis for this. Eventually, a deal was done, the planners felt they had achieved a good scheme, and the scheme is being built. Whatever financial contributions are agreed, they are relatively small compared to the risks of building in difficult market conditions, as we shall see in Chapter 9.

7. COMMUNITY CONSULTATION

Both Camden council and Argent put considerable resources into consulting very widely with local communities, both at the pre-application stage and on the planning application itself. Community consultations started in July 2001 with the publication of Camden's Key Issues for UDP: Planning for the Future of King's Cross and Argent's Principles for a Human City, and continued throughout the negotiation process (see Figures 7.1 and 7.2). The parties estimate that over 30,000 people were contacted over the course of this work and the processes have won awards for their innovation and thoroughness. Despite this, there remains cynicism among some activists that the development was a foregone conclusion and that the parties were merely paying lip service to any meaningful process of stakeholder engagement.

This chapter presents an account of the consultations that took place, and explores the extent to which these influenced the emerging scheme. It also explores objections to the scheme and to the consultation and decision-making processes, and examines whether a process of 'consensus-building' was ever capable of accommodating significantly different views.

PRE-APPLICATION CONSULTATIONS

Local authorities are required under planning law to consult widely with stakeholders and local communities on all planning policy documents. National planning guidance also emphasises the need to 'front load' consultations, in advance of the submission of planning applications. In order to create binding commitments on consultation, local authorities are required to

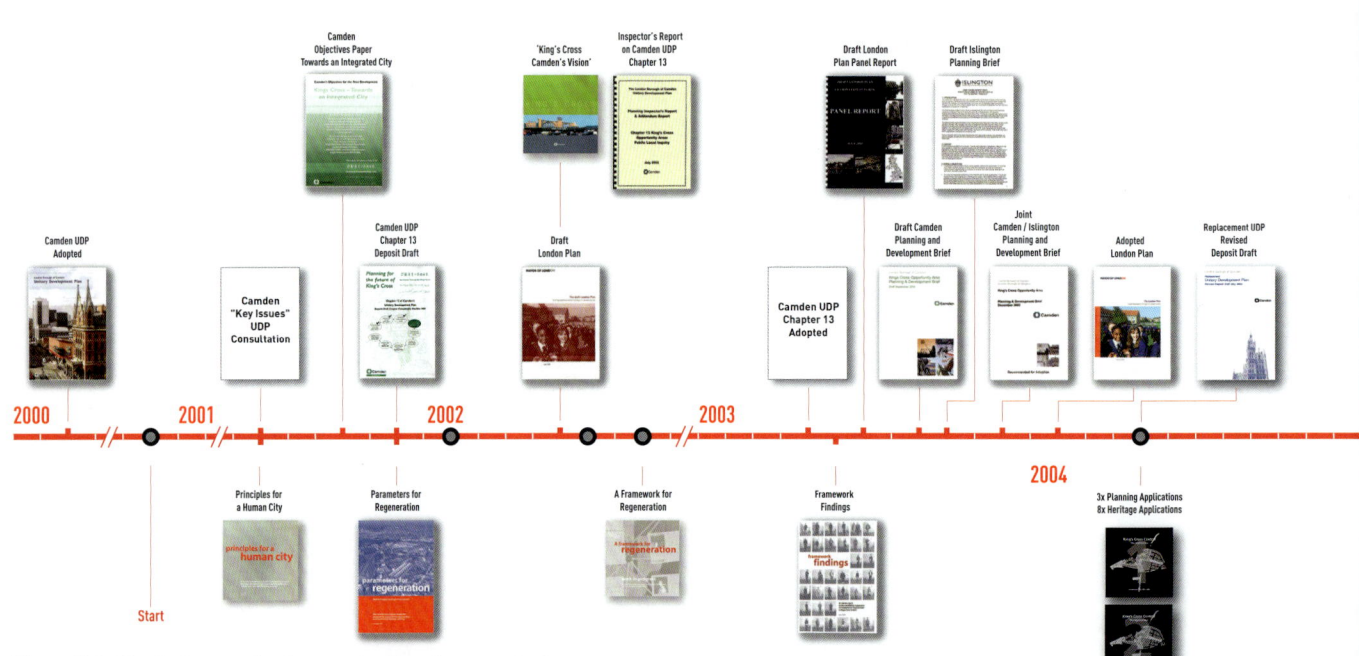

Figure 7.1: King's Cross – the journey to planning permission.

produce, consult on and publish a Statement of Community Involvement (SCI).[1] This is a statutory document that accompanies their local plan (the Local Development Framework). There is no such requirement on developers to consult at the pre-application stage, although government guidance to local planning authorities suggests that their SCI should encourage developers to engage in early consultation on significant applications. The rationale underpinning this guidance is that pre-application discussions could 'avoid unnecessary objections being made at a later stage',[2] and save time.

At the start of the negotiations, Roger Madelin stated that as chief executive of Argent he 'would go anywhere, anytime, and speak to anyone about the King's Cross development'. According to Argent, Madelin alone met with nearly 4,000 people in over 200 meetings in the four years from March 2000.[3] Argent's offer put a human face on the development. Unlike many corporate bodies, here was a person (who often turned up on a bicycle and wearing cycling gear), that one could talk to directly and argue with. If Madelin gave his word, he was personally accountable. This contrasts starkly with the approach of many developers who use PR companies to front up and sell their proposals to a sceptical public.

This offer also meant that Camden council could not possibly be outdone on consultations by the developer. This was not just a matter of local politics and public relations; the council wanted to avoid any possibility that Argent could build alliances with local consultees and capture hearts and minds. Bearing in mind that a working relationship with Argent had not been established at this stage of negotiations, officers feared that a marketing operation from the

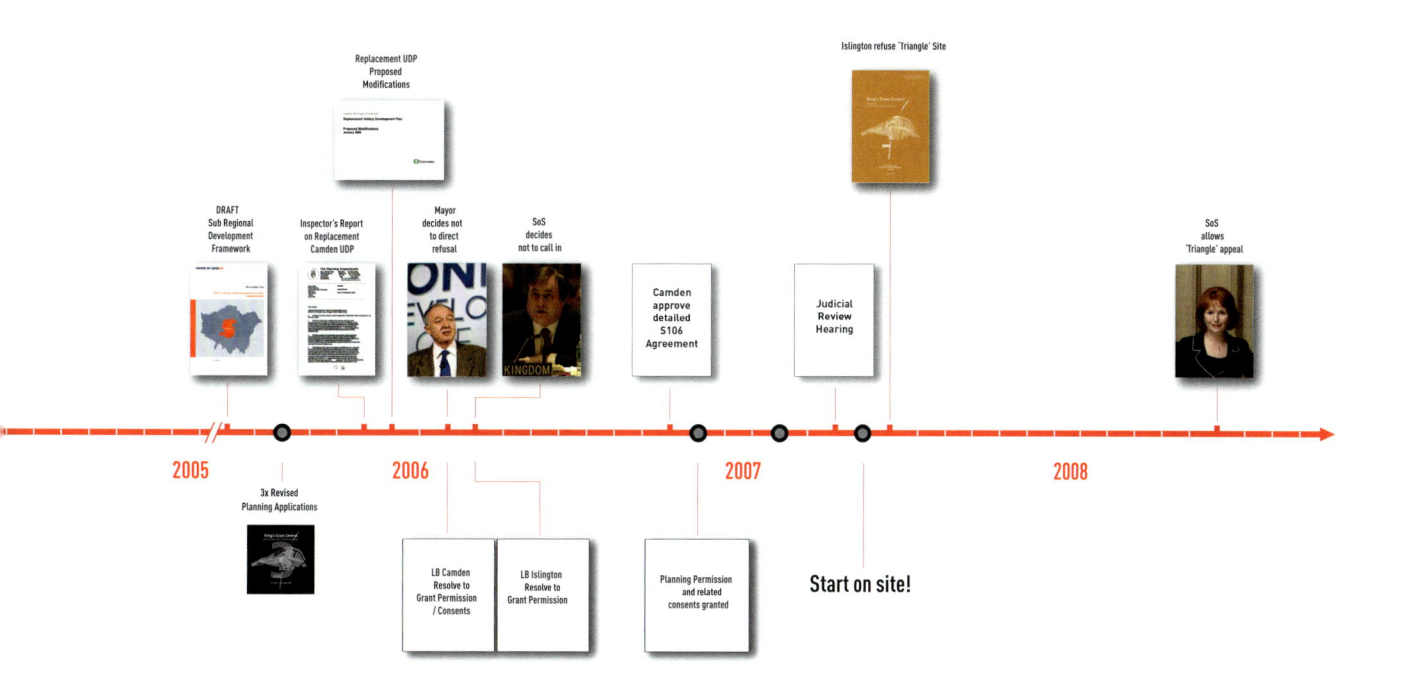

Consultation timeline

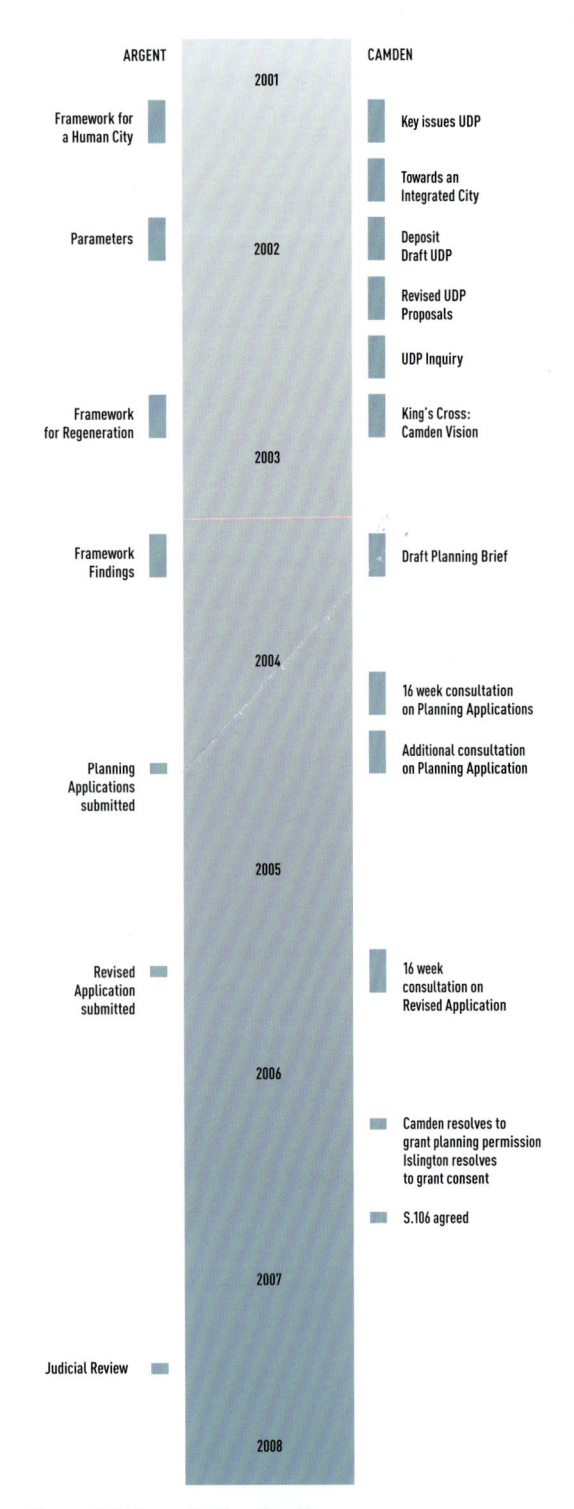

Figure 7.2: Consultation timeline.

ARGENT / CAMDEN

- 2001
  - Framework for a Human City
  - Key issues UDP
  - Towards an Integrated City
- 2002
  - Parameters
  - Deposit Draft UDP
  - Revised UDP Proposals
  - UDP Inquiry
- 2003
  - Framework for Regeneration
  - King's Cross: Camden Vision
  - Framework Findings
  - Draft Planning Brief
- 2004
  - 16 week consultation on Planning Applications
  - Additional consultation on Planning Application
  - Planning Applications submitted
- 2005
- 2006
  - Revised Application submitted
  - 16 week consultation on Revised Application
- 2007
  - Camden resolves to grant planning permission Islington resolves to grant consent
  - S.106 agreed
- 2008
  - Judicial Review

---

developer might in effect buy local support and undermine local councillors. In the event of an appeal, Camden council needed the community on its side. Madelin's statement therefore triggered a dual (and slightly competitive) process of extensive consultation.

Camden council's consultation strategy

The initial consultation strategy for King's Cross was based on the following commitments:[4]

- maintain high quality publicly accessible information
- maintain the King's Cross development forum in representing local opinions as inclusively as possible over the whole King's Cross area
- continue consultation with hard to reach groups not wishing to attend the forum, including minority groups
- continue the planning advice and support programme for black and ethnic minorities, and for any others that request it
- continue working in schools, with young people and youth clubs
- continue working with the principal community groups at conventions, events, etc
- set up focus panels or workshops on particular topics, such as accessibility (including disabled people, the elderly and those with young children), safer and better streets, local priorities, etc
- develop ways of bringing local people into design development, such as designs for streets, shopping/leisure/health uses, etc
- develop ways of easier access to decision-making processes
- encourage and support community groups working together on wider regeneration initiatives

- create innovative ways of sustaining long-term and widely representative community involvement.

The consultation processes

As noted in Chapter 4, the negotiation process between Camden and Argent was based on 'convergence'. This implied working together and moving from the first principles to more detailed proposals. The consultation processes reflected this. Both sides consulted separately on each of the documents that they produced as they jointly refined the scheme from principles to proposals (Figure 7.2). The consultation results were then fed back into the negotiations and were used to challenge or validate proposals as they developed.

Camden's formal consultations started with the revised chapter on King's Cross in the Unitary Development Plan (as discussed in Chapter 4). Proposed changes were summarised in a consultation document on Key Issues in July 2001.[5] This was published at the same time as Argent's Principles for a Human City.[6] In response to the Principles document, Camden published its own initial objectives for the site in King's Cross – Towards an Integrated City in October 2001. Argent St George's next consultation document in December 2001 was Parameters for Regeneration.[7] This put all the factual information that Argent had amassed on the site and the surrounding neighbourhoods into the public domain. The thinking here was that if consultation was to have any value then the public had to have access to information on constraints and opportunities. To do otherwise would have resulted in too many ideas and suggestions being dismissed as unfeasible. In June 2002 Camden council then summarised the emerging policies for its draft of the new UDP chapter on King's Cross in King's Cross Camden's Vision.[8] All of these documents went out to public consultation. Figure 4.6 summarises all the stages in Camden's consultation on its new UDP chapter for King's Cross.

Argent developed its ideas in A Framework for Regeneration,[9] which contained tear-out pages for responses and was accompanied by a consultation roadshow in Camden and Islington. It also appointed a specialist consultancy, Fluid, to run consultation events for harder to reach groups, such as youth and women's groups. The responses were compiled into nine short films on the Argent website. Nearly 200 people attended workshops in December 2002. By mid-March, Argent had received 133 written responses to the framework document, which were summarised in Framework Findings in June 2003.[10]

Camden council went on to produce and consult on a Draft Planning and Development Brief for the King's Cross Opportunity Area in September 2003,[11] which was itself informed by several workshops with the King's Cross development forum and other groups.[12] In this process the King's Cross Team contacted over 100 individual community groups to reach as wide an audience as possible, with a specific focus on hard to reach and non-English speaking groups. More widely, officers contacted over 700 groups offering to attend one of their meetings and over 40 sessions were held with local community groups. Over 4,000 people took part in discussions. In addition, there were flyer

> **To support the consultation processes, the council undertook a mapping exercise to identify all local business, amenity and residents' groups.**

drops, workshops and stalls at local festivals. The council supported these meetings with interpreters, translation services and crèche facilities. Findings from consultations were reported back to the leader, senior politicians and to groups themselves, and fed back into the development of the planning brief.[13]

To support the consultation processes, the council undertook a mapping exercise to identify all local business, amenity and residents' groups. Argent commissioned a database of all employers within a mile of the King's Cross site, as a basis for outreach and dialogue. The developer, Camden council and the King's Cross Partnership also jointly commissioned a study and consultation process with creative industries to identify the scope to develop the sector.[14] A growing understanding of the diverse communities in and around King's Cross, as well as lessons learned from the consultation phases were constantly fed into the negotiations.

The influence of the pre-application consultations

Camden

It is not easy to track issues that were raised in these early consultations or their influence on the shape of the scheme.[15] However, both Camden council and Argent are clear, from attending meetings, listening to debates and facilitating workshops, that the emerging King's Cross scheme was broadly supported by the majority of the surrounding communities. Camden's officers would have found it difficult to present the scheme to their councillors had there been widespread community opposition.

From Camden council's point of view, the consultations threw up relatively few surprises. The council's dialogue with local communities had evolved over a long period of time, even preceding the Argent scheme and Camden council believed it had a good understanding of the prevailing political conditions in the local area and the needs of the community. The need for affordable housing, open space, recreation, jobs and better education were all central to negotiations from the start. The consultations did, however, help to reinforce Camden's negotiating position, for example by emphasising the degree of support for affordable housing and an accessible public realm. Argent recognised that a broad consensus on certain issues was emerging from the consultations, and that Camden councillors could not ignore the main items. In this respect, the consultation provided an evidence base for the negotiations. Had the scheme ended up at a public inquiry, it is highly likely that this evidence would have formed a significant part of either side's case. The consultation also allowed Camden council to weight the community demands and refine the section 106 agreement to deliver them. A number of items in the scheme, such as the swimming pool and health centre, would not have been provided without clear community demand.

Argent

Argent suggests that in the most general sense, the knowledge and experience that it gained from consultation significantly improved its understanding of the site and its context, and contributed positively to the evolution of the scheme. According to Argent's Robert Evans,[16] the consultations in 2001–02 that led to the Framework document changed the scheme significantly in relation to:

- the townscape and grain of the development south of the Regent's Canal and its relationship with retained historic buildings
- the retention and refurbishment of the listed Great Northern Hotel
- the layout and alignment of new buildings north of the canal
- the relationship between the masterplan and the Channel Tunnel Rail Link (CTRL) embankment and York Way
- the accommodation of a principal park at the centre of the scheme.

Between the Framework document in September 2002 and the first applications in May 2004, feedback from consultees resulted in further changes, such as:

- the decision to commit to a minimum number of residential units
- retention and reuse of the listed gasholders and other the historic buildings north of the Regent's Canal
- provision of community, health, education, cultural facilities, and sports and leisure uses
- preparation of an implementation strategy to address long-term delivery
- preparation of a public realm strategy to respond to aspirations for highest quality public realm.[17]

CONSULTATIONS ON THE ORIGINAL PLANNING APPLICATIONS

Camden council's consultation process on the planning applications was reported in detail in the March 2006 Committee report, and is just briefly summarised here.[18] Consultation on a first set of planning applications, submitted in May 2004, was conducted over 16 weeks during that summer. Once again it involved a wide range of approaches to consultation, each tailored to suit the relevant target audience, with exhibitions, newsletters, leaflets, web pages, conferences, games with local schools,[19] walking tours and workshops.

As well as the statutory consultees,[20] the council contacted all property owners and occupiers within a 1 kilometre radius of the site (approximately 30,000 households and businesses in Camden and Islington), and all non-statutory organisations and local groups. Householders received a consultation leaflet with details of the application schedule and all community groups were offered a council presentation. Printed and online information was also used to target users of public transport,

> **Critically, none of the primary statutory consultees (who might have triggered a public inquiry), raised significant objections to the scheme.**

including commuters. Planning Aid for London (PAL)[21] was commissioned to facilitate outreach and community engagement work with community and resident groups, and to provide specialist independent planning advice. Meetings with 50 individual community groups took place. PAL also trained over 40 members of the King's Cross Community Development Trust (KXCDT) to be facilitators, who were then able to undertake consultation in their own communities. Further consultations were also carried out by Islington council's King's Cross Team, and Camden Primary Care Trust, which ran a health impact assessment for the whole of the King's Cross developments. Camden council then consulted on a number of specific issues in October 2004 through workshops facilitated by PAL, with the newly established citizens panel, Camden Talks, and with a focus group for young people.

Influences of consultations on the original planning application

In response to this community feedback, Argent incorporated a number of revisions in its revised planning application in 2005:[22]

- Changes to landscaping proposals for Station Square and Pancras Square.
- Better pedestrian connectivity between Granary Square and the canal.
- New landscape proposals for Handyside Park, including children's play areas.
- Changes to Cubitt Park to provide a contiguous green space framed by tree planting. Widening the park at north end, to provide larger and more useable space for informal recreational activities and events.
- Reuse of the gasholder No 8 as a new play facility and public open space.

CONSULTATIONS ON THE REVISED PLANNING APPLICATIONS

A further eight-week round of consultations was undertaken following receipt of revised plans and environmental statement reports from Argent in September 2005. This involved re-consulting all respondents from the first round of consultation, again with the support of independent facilitators from PAL; 27,000 consultation letters were sent out to local residents and businesses in both Camden and Islington. A further 237 consultation letters were sent out to local community groups, and Camden council officers attended local meetings on request.

Consultation responses

At the completion of the formal consultation period, the council had received 267 responses from statutory authorities, public organisations and individuals. All responses were categorised into 29 topic areas and entered into a database.

This information was provided to all the councillors in each borough, and to Argent. Camden council's consultations were also monitored by Camden's internal consultation board, a corporate group set up to coordinate consultation activity and promote best practice in the borough.

The report to the March 2006 subcommittee contained 102 pages summarising and analysing the consultation responses to the planning applications. These came from 20 statutory authorities, local councillors, the two local MPs, 10 non-statutory authorities and 71 local groups including resident's groups, faith and cultural groups, conservation bodies, leisure and interest groups, the King's Cross Development Forum, the King's Cross Business Forum, KXRLG and Camden Talks, the council's citizen's panel. It is impossible to document here every point that emerged from the consultations, and the summary below is inevitably partial.

Critically, none of the primary statutory consultees (who might have triggered a public inquiry), raised significant objections to the scheme. Many other consultation responses supported the scheme. For instance, Camden Friend's of the Earth encouraged the two councils to vigorously defend their comprehensive brief for the development. Camden Square Tenants and Residents' Association supported the regeneration plans and the links to surrounding areas. Create King's Cross was very supportive of the values underpinning the proposals, and the King's Cross Business Forum welcomed the proposed development, believing it essential to the future well-being of local business and residential communities.

In contrast, a number of objectors such as The Cally Rail Group and KXRLG objected to a perceived lack of clarity, detail or certainty in the hybrid applications. The main areas of concern from local communities in relation to the final planning application are as follows:

Offices
Several consultees (such as The Cally Rail Group, Camden Civic Society, KXRLG, the Chinese Community and Camden Green Party) objected to the overall balance of the development and wanted a reduction in the amount of office floor space, particularly south of the canal.

Housing
Some respondents (such as KXCDT and The Islington Society) favoured more housing, particularly more affordable housing. The Community Housing Association and the Bangladeshi community argued for an increase in large units for families.

Heritage and conservation
The main critic on heritage grounds was the King's Cross Conservation Area Advisory Committee (KXCAAC). It was concerned that the unique heritage of the site would be severely compromised by the proposals. In particular, it opposed the loss of North Stanley Buildings and the Culross Buildings (see Chapter 5). In relation to other aspects of the historic fabric, it argued that Argent's proposals showed little appreciation of their historical and archaeological value and treated them as objects of incidental decorative interest.[23] KXCAAC argued that the canal and its walls were not part of Argent's site and felt

that the proposal to open up the canal as public space would seriously damage its tranquillity.

Built form
There were concerns (from groups such as Camden Green Party, The Regent's Network and KXCAAC) that the proposed building heights would have a negative affect on the setting of historic buildings and the canal.

Community facilities
There was strong support for the publicly-run sports centre, swimming pool, health facilities, pre-school facilities and primary school. Other consultees sought a museum, community arts space, community theatre, market, cinema, more play areas for young children, space for the various faith groups, and for community meeting space gifted to local groups. Some respondents (such as the Bangladeshi community and KXCDT) also considered that a secondary school should be provided on the site.

Retail
Consultees supported the provision of new shopping activities, particularly convenience shops catering for local needs.

Transport
Most transport comments related to the development's potential impact on local roads and public transport networks. Suggestions from the KXCDT, among others, included improved access to public transport at the northern part of the site through a new Maiden Lane station on the North London Line (now the Overground) to serve the proposed developments, or re-opening the York Road underground station. There were concerns from some groups (such as Camden Square Conservation Area Advisory Committee) that too many car parking spaces were proposed, particularly in a multi-storey building.

Community safety
Many respondents supported a mix of uses both within buildings and across the site, to create 24-hour natural surveillance.

Open space, recreation and biodiversity
Many consultees (such as KXCAAC, the Somers Town People Forum, and the Iraqi, Sudanese and women's workshops) felt that the proposals did not include sufficient green or other forms of public space, or that there were too many hard surfaces on the site. There were concerns from many local groups (such as the London Wildlife Trust) regarding the possible impact of a proposed new pedestrian/cycle bridge on Camley Street Natural Park (CSNP), and of the development generally on the biodiversity of the Regent's Canal.

Environmental sustainability
Camden Friends of the Earth acknowledged that some of its concerns on the environmental standards in the original application had been addressed. Environment groups generally felt that the applicants had not made sufficient firm commitments or firm targets for achieving sustainable development, and did not strive for environmental excellence. There were still demands for Argent to commit to providing 10 per cent of energy needs on site and other measurable initiatives.

The influence of the consultation process on the scheme

In the view of David Partridge, the managing partner of Argent, one of the most important impacts of the consultations was on Argent's internal values.[24] Consultation had allowed Argent to understand not only what people wanted from the scheme, but why they wanted it. Partridge contends that the prolonged relationship with the community impacted directly on Argent's internal culture. The fact that Argent's Robert Evans can still recall comments that he heard from individual consultees perhaps underlines the point.[25] In the strongly contested areas of negotiations, particularly on the levels of affordable housing, section 106 contributions and the provision of facilities such as the swimming pool, it is probable that the consultations tipped discussions in Camden council's favour by making Argent more sympathetic to the communities' interests.

Argent's approach to consultation also gained it considerable political capital. The value of this is not to be underestimated. In future, the development would need multiple consents and amendments, and a positive relationship with the council over the long term was essential.

One difficulty in assessing the degree of opposition to the scheme is that, by and large, only those who do object to some aspect of it will take the trouble to voice their views. That said, it is clear from the above that despite the extensive consultation process, the final scheme did not achieve complete consensus and that some disagreements remained, particularly on the balance between commercial and housing uses. These are picked up below in relation to the concerns of KXRLG.

KING'S CROSS RAILWAY LANDS GROUP

The King's Cross Railway Lands Group (KXRLG) was an umbrella group of some of the resident, business, conservation and transport groups and had been a key opponent of the earlier LRC scheme (see Chapter 3). It provided the most vociferous, focused and enduring opposition to the Argent scheme, culminating in a judicial review of the planning approval in May 2007 (see Chapter 8). It pressed for an assortment of demands, but principally for higher levels of housing, particularly affordable units, and fewer commercial offices. Unfortunately, it was only possible to interview one member of KXRLG for this book. While Michael Edwards was reluctant to be the group's sole source here, he notes that ultimately other members 'were mostly deeply unhappy about taking part. The distrust of Camden officers among local community leaders remains very strong.'[26] It is hoped, therefore, that the views of the wider group are fairly represented here.

> **Consultation had allowed Argent to understand not only what people wanted from the scheme, but why they wanted it.**

The representativeness of KXRLG

Camden council's planning officers did not believe that KXRLG was truly representative of the local community. Apart from a number of businesses, there was no resident community on the site.[27] Had there been a resident community under threat, Camden council's response to the opposition would have been very different. In the absence of one, the council's primary concern was to engage with the wider community, and for this consultation to be inclusive and reflect the area's true diversity.

This does beg the perennial question of who represents the community in planning negotiations. Camden council's reaction to the opposition from KXRLG was shaped by the very nature of council politics. Councillors are democratically elected as the primary representatives of their community. They understand community politics, and those who do the job well act as a channel for local views. Some local ward members had concerns about the development, but these were not allied to those of KXRLG, and officers were never directed by their members to heed KXRLG above other voices. A number of its members were resident in other boroughs (not a reason to ignore their views, but councillors gave those views a different weight to those of voting Camden residents). In consequence, both Camden council and Argent met and consulted KXRLG on many occasions, but gave them no preferential status above other local interest groups.

Camden recognised that KXRLG was a voice in the community, but it was never recognised as *the* voice. Fairly or not, KXRLG was seen by many in the council leadership circle as politically marginal, and consequently it had limited traction with the elected members who controlled policy in the council. This forced KXRLG onto the political margins, forging relationships with smaller groups of councillors, including some on the development control subcommittee. This focused its influence at the decision-making, rather than the policy, end of the council hierarchy.

KXRLG could quite legitimately point to the fact that as an established umbrella group it was one of the most representative single organisations in the area. In 2002, however, the council established the King's Cross Development Forum (KXDF)[28] as an alternative umbrella group that might be more inclusive than KXRLG. By 2004 there were over 350 names on the mailing list for the forum, representing well over 100 organisations from Camden and Islington. Camden council took particular steps to include many of the hard to reach groups representing the Chinese, Somali and Bangladeshi communities, as well as local women's groups. These had not been part of the KXRLG umbrella. Its support to the forum has since been commended in good practice

> **Camden council took particular steps to include many of the hard to reach groups representing the Chinese, Somali and Bangladeshi communities, as well as local women's groups.**

guides.[29] Over 40 forum meetings were held over the course of the negotiations. The two groups were not mutually exclusive; in practice there was a good deal of overlap between their networks. The formation of the KXDF could be viewed as either a cynical attempt to counter KXRLG, or a genuine attempt to engage with local communities.

The reason for giving prominence here to the views of the KXRLG is that it was by far the most vocal group in opposition, and members held fundamentally different views regarding what should happen at King's Cross. As suggested in Chapter 3, its views can be traced back to the campaigns against development in the 1980s and 1990s. At King's Cross in the 2000s, it was employing similar arguments and tactics, but it was no longer campaigning against a disorganised council, or a developer that could be accused of riding roughshod over community views. Argent was intending to consult widely, and from first principles. Allemendinger[30] makes the point that Argent and Camden council were committed to consensus and partnership-based regeneration, while the challenge by KXRLG was based on a more traditional approach to confrontational politics.

Policy constraints on the parameters of the debate

The parameter of the debate is a common problem in planning consultations. The presumption that there would be substantial commercial development on the site, close to the transport interchange at King's Cross, was established before Argent St George had even been appointed. Strategic Planning Guidance for London, Regional Planning Guidance 3 (RPGC),[31] published in 1996, had identified the King's Cross railway lands as a site of national importance and as a major opportunity area for development. It suggested that a mixture of land uses should be accommodated, with the highest densities and most commercial uses closest to the rail termini. Camden council accepted this approach in Chapter 13 of its first Unitary Development Plan (adopted in March 2000). To have any substantial influence over the nature of the scheme, KXRLG would have needed to have influenced the council leadership early on, when discussions on policy for the revised Chapter 13 of the UDP started in 2001. In 2002, the report of the independent planning inspector on the amendments to Chapter 13 deepened the constraints on the debate:

'Firstly I accept that the development proposals cannot ignore the needs and aspirations of local communities. Indeed, in that regard a number of amendments are promoted by the council to ensure meaningful community involvement in the evolution of the development proposals. Having said that it seems to me that in considering the future of the opportunity area it would be a grave mistake for the council to ignore national guidance exhorting the maximum use of land occupying central and highly accessible locations.'[32]

By 2004, RPG3 had been superseded by policy in the mayor's London Plan, which confirmed that King's Cross was one of six opportunity areas in the central London sub-region, having 'the best public transport accessibility in London' and a central location, which offered 'particular scope for high-density business development, as well as housing'.[33]

It could be argued that Camden council was at fault in not having spelt out the limitations of the debate more clearly when the consultations started. In practice, however, it is likely that to attempt to limit the debate in this way would have been provocative, divisive and hard to achieve. To most consultees, policy is highly abstract, and they do not necessarily feel constrained by it.

The political nature of the debate
The debate really concerned the nature of power in planning. While it is difficult to generalise about or to characterise the views of an umbrella group, some members of KXRLG believed that the development of King's Cross should be based not on its potential contribution to London as a global city (through attracting financial services and corporate enterprises), but on its ability to serve local needs.[34] Holgersen and Haarstad argue that the collaborative processes at King's Cross were shaped and limited by institutions with a particular agenda. These institutions represented particular economic interests whose concern was the future of London as a viable business environment. By contrast, KXRLG was concerned about the future of London as a place to live.[35] It was at a severe disadvantage from the outset in terms of its power and potential influence, since it neither set the parameters of the debate nor the process though which it took place.[36] This severely constrained what the participation could achieve. Holgersen and Haarstad argue that such economic relations tend to be downplayed in the focus on consultation and consensus building.

By 2000 the interests of those who were concerned about the future of London as a viable business environment were firmly embedded in government policy. The need to balance local with London-wide and national needs always had to be a key issue for Camden council. The council acknowledged that a common response to their consultations was that 'commercial office space should be reduced as a proportion of the development'.[37] Offices were the obvious candidate for reduction if more space was to be provided for housing, community, leisure and recreation uses, all of which received strong support locally. However, without significant government intervention in the form of large-scale subsidy for public housing, or some form of land expropriation, a predominance of housing on the site was never a realisable proposition. Even if the council had conceded to such demands for a predominance of affordable family housing, it would not have been supported by either national or London planning policies.

Argent itself was constrained by the need to provide a return to the landowners and its board. When land is owned, developed and financed privately and the landowner retains the right under law to enjoy their land, planning can never be an open exercise. The landowners had every right to maximise the value of their land within the confines of planning policy. If there is criticism of major schemes as being foregone conclusions, then this is partly correct. Such demands from local groups cannot be delivered within the present system.

The establishment of a community development trust

The only other way in which the community could have had a wider role in shaping the King's Cross scheme was if some or all of the land had been transferred into community ownership (at the top of Arnstein's ladder – see Table 7.1 on p.148), as had happened in Coin Street.[38] One of the KXRLG's demands was the establishment of a Land Trust or Community Development Trust. As Michael Edwards states:

'Ownership and process issues have been the other main focus of dispute. Ownership is an issue in the sense that there has been no attempt by the authorities to transfer legal or effective ownership of any of the nationally-owned land or buildings to collective or municipal control, using land trusts or other mechanisms such as the Coin Street development at Waterloo (Brindley, 2000).'[39]

Given the way in which the ownership of the King's Cross lands by LCR was tied into the development of Eurostar this was never a possibility. The gift would in any case have been in the hands of central government.

The problem of 'consensus-building' processes in the face of ideological differences

The real question is whether the planning system in general, and consensus building processes specifically, can deal with such fundamental differences in view. Successive governments have proposed partnership and consensus building approaches for the delivery of urban regeneration schemes. However, as Allemendinger argues, consensus on deep ideological differences is impossible to reach, and the present planning system is not a suitable vehicle for handling fundamental differences in ideology.[40] The debate also becomes semantic. If consensus means reaching 'a general agreement', those who disagree will inevitably claim there is no consensus. In these circumstances, the focus on consensus building had no real end point. The objectives of Camden council and KXRLG were very different and the debate was in many ways more about how the system should work than the outcomes. This is not to devalue the role or views of KXRLG, it is just that the system within which Camden council was operating was unable to deliver the outcome that they desired.

KXRLG's criticism of the consultation process
The level of participation

Given the strong views held by KXRLG on the proposed development at King's Cross, it is not surprising that the group was also highly critical of the consultation processes that took place.

Not being part of the process, but observing it from the outside, KXRLG considered that Camden's planning and vision documents seemed to reflect far too closely those of Argent, both in their timing and their content.[41] This observation was, of course, entirely correct. The negotiation process was based on the principle of convergence. It was inevitable, therefore, that the processes were triggered by common milestones and that the emerging documents were coordinated to ensure that they were compatible. To KXRLG, however, it felt as though the council was doing exactly what Argent wanted.[42]

Michael Edwards felt that Argent's consultation process was 'highly manipulative', having been carried out entirely within the constraints of what the developers wanted to see on the site. He likened it to 're-designing deckchairs on the Titanic'.[43] He expands these views in more recent writing: *'More generally, the local communities have felt disenfranchised in the decision process, notwithstanding extensive 'consultation'. Both Argent and Camden have prided themselves upon their extensive and innovative programmes of consultation and have won awards for their efforts. Those who remain dissatisfied are essentially reflecting their lack of influence in the consultation process: they are endlessly listened to but have no detectable power to determine the outcome. And it should be added that these feelings of frustration are shared, not only by low- and middle-income residents but by back-bench local councillors who tend to be marginalised in our "reformed" local councils.'*[44]

Edwards felt it would have been more appropriate if Camden council had undertaken a consultation process that was more along the lines of that carried out in 1990–91 on the LRC scheme. In other words, KXRLG wanted to be active participants or partners rather than consultees.

The arguments about the nature of the consultation process deserve further exploration. Shelly Arnstein's eight levels on a 'ladder of participation' (Table 7.1) are helpful.

Camden council and Argent would probably argue that they were offering a level of participation that lies somewhere between consultation and involvement, and that they did their upmost to ensure that this was as comprehensive and inclusive as possible. As explained in Chapter 4, they were extremely careful to ensure that they were the only two parties at the negotiating table; this is one reason why 'partnership' on Arnstein's ladder of participation was never on offer. They wished to retain tight control over what would be a difficult process, and one that could easily have become bogged down in debates on fundamental differences in the vision, or legitimate but unachievable community objectives.

Table 7.1: Arnstein's 'ladder of participation'

Ladder of participation	Characteristics
Stakeholder community control	Full devolution of all decision-making and action, community management.
Delegated power	Some delegated power to stakeholders/communities.
Partnership	Stakeholders/communities are enabled to negotiate and engage in trade-offs with traditional decision-makers.
Involvement	Stakeholder/community views have some influence, but traditional power holders still make all decisions.
Consultation	Stakeholder communities are given a voice but have no power to ensure that their views will be heeded.
Information	Stakeholder communities are told what is going to happen or asked for their views on a single proposal.
Education	Stakeholder communities are informed as to why a course of action is being adopted, but given no opportunity to give their views on the action.
Manipulation	The information supplied to stakeholder communities is only partial or inaccurate.

Source: Sherry R. Shelly Arnstein, 'A Ladder of Citizen Participation', Journal of American Planning Association, vol 35, no 4, July 1969, pp.216–224

Briefing of members of the development control subcommittee

Michael Edwards was also critical of the inadequacy of members' briefings on such a major planning application and the way it was considered in committee.[45] He is entirely correct here. Councillors clearly need sufficient time and knowledge to be able to consider a complex application in stages from basic principles to detail, and this is normal practice. The reasons for, and near catastrophic effects of, the lack of briefings for members of the development control subcommittee on the King's Cross scheme are explained in depth in Chapter 8. Essentially the chair of the subcommittee refused any briefing, apparently believing that it could prejudice the independence of the decision-making process.

Interestingly, Argent's Robert Evans also argues strongly that committee members must be involved earlier and more systematically if they are to reach informed decisions. Argent has even commissioned research in support of this idea.[46] If community involvement is front-loaded, then it is only logical that the decision-makers must be involved early as well, if they are to avoid being put at a disadvantage. This view was supported by the 2006 Barker review of planning.[47]

CONCLUSIONS

Both Camden council and Argent put considerable time and resources into public consultation. The exercises were extensive, prolonged and systematic, and Camden council's efforts to engage with hard to reach groups still equate to best practice. Given the extent and duration of the consultations, it is perhaps not surprising that there were complaints of consultation fatigue at King's Cross. Camden council and Argent were talking to the same groups about the same things for almost six years. Recent guidance suggests that there could be merit in local planning authorities and developers consulting together to reduce the danger of fatigue.[48] This would certainly be more cost efficient and might be a logical next step in the process of partnership working. However, it would undoubtedly cause further distrust among those with a deep ideological mistrust of developers, and would certainly strengthen any perceptions that the relationships between local planners and developers are becoming far too cosy.

The consultations contributed significantly to the knowledge base that underpinned and shaped the scheme, and in this sense did have a fundamental influence on it. It may have resulted in some major changes, and tangibly shifted the agendas of both parties, strengthening Camden council's hand in the negotiations. Had there

> **❝❝ The consultations contributed significantly to the knowledge base that underpinned and shaped the scheme, and in this sense did have a fundamental influence on it. ❞❞**

been widespread and deep-seated opposition to the scheme, Camden council would not have been able to ignore it and a refusal would have been inevitable. The evidence from the consultations would then have been a major weapon in fighting Argent at appeal.

While public consultation helped to improve the scheme, in the view of Argent's Robert Evans[49] it did not avoid unnecessary objections being made at a later stage, nor did it save any time – the government's two main arguments for pre-application consultations by developers.[50]

The applications were still greeted by some vociferous objections, notably from KXRLG. And it still took nearly two years for the final application on the main site to receive planning permission. The judicial review that KXRLG sought on Camden council's decision to grant planning approval for the main site occupied a further six months, and was followed by a public inquiry on Islington council's last minute decision to refuse planning permission for the 'Triangle' site (see Chapter 8). The public inquiry and judicial review cost over £4 million.[51] The entire process following submission of the applications took four years and two months. Commenting on the process somewhat wryly, Evans felt that it was Argent's own lengthy process of consultation that gave the opponents the opportunity to gear up. The inevitable conclusion is that community consultation cannot build consensus when deep ideological differences mean that the nature of the debate is highly polarised.

8. THE DECISION

By the autumn of 2005, negotiations between Camden council and Argent on the masterplan, the quantum of uses and the elements of the section 106 agreement were complete. In May 2004, Camden council received the planning applications for the King's Cross site and these were subject to extensive public consultation. Following this, Argent reviewed its scheme and submitted revised applications in September 2005. After a further period of public consultation in October and November, Camden council was ready to determine the scheme.

Planning officers started to prepare a report and recommendation for the development control subcommittee meeting scheduled for two evenings on 8 and 9 March 2006. The report had to cover everything from housing numbers and tenure mix to cycle parking, archaeology, noise attenuation and the phasing of development. It also had to include a summary of all the feedback from the council's consultation processes. It had to be exhaustive in order to demonstrate that every conceivable aspect of the scheme had been assessed and weighed against public comments and alternative options, so there could be no justification for a legal challenge or call-in by the mayor or central government. The final report amounted to just under 600 pages of text, in 19 chapters, and with 30 recommendations and 68 conditions. A separate report on the section 106 agreement was over 250 pages long. Both documents had been checked and double-checked, both by Camden council's legal department and by external legal consultants.

The King's Cross development was finally approved by just two votes. This chapter charts the way in which the slender majority in Camden council was achieved. It examines the problems that officers faced in trying to brief councillors on the development control subcommittee, considers the party political issues that influenced the voting, and the delicate balance in the roles of officers and councillors.

CAMDEN'S OFFICER-COUNCILLOR INTERFACE

Under Jane Roberts, Camden council had built a strong collegiate corporate culture that was largely devoid of the officer/councillor mistrust that plagued many other councils at the time.

TABLE 8.1: Key councillors

Labour · Liberal Democrat · Conservative

Councillor Jane Roberts	Leader of Camden Council 2000–05
Councillor Raj Chadhen	Leader of Camden Council 2005–06
Councillor John Thane	Executive member for Environment (including planning)
Councillor Theo Blackwell	Executive member for Regeneration
Councillor Brian Woodrow	Chair of Development Control subcommittee 1998–2005
Councillor Heather Johnson	Chair of Development Control subcommittee 2005–06
Councillor Sue Vincent	Vice Chair of Development Control subcommittee 2002–06
Councillor Keith Moffet	Leader of Camden Council 2006–10
Councillor Andrew Marshal	Deputy Leader of Camden Council 2008–10
Councillor Mike Greene	Executive member for Environment 2006–10

There was an open process of debate on major issues through a series of regular officer/member corporate policy and advisory bodies (Chapter 4). The council leadership was briefed regularly and broadly supported the Argent scheme. The key councillors in relation to the King's Cross application are shown in Table 8.1.

Camden council was a stable and well-run authority during the negotiation period (2000–06), with a Labour administration that appeared (falsely as it turned out) to be secure from challenge from the Conservative and Liberal Democrat opposition. Many of the councillors had been in office for long periods, but most had mellowed from the days of their radical youth. The leadership group under Jane Roberts while not exactly New Labour Blairites, were certainly in the political centre. The dynamics of a political party are however a complex mesh of personalities, histories and agendas.

While planning decisions (see the textbox below) may appear to be technical, in practice they are inherently political, and planning officers in the public sector are inevitably drawn into the political process. This is particularly true for senior personnel. A substantial part of the role of senior officers in a local authority is to manage the interface between the politicians and their particular department. That said, senior officers, as with government civil servants, are politically neutral and their posts should not be subject to the fortunes of a particular political administration.[1]

Senior officers walk a delicate tightrope in their relationship with councillors. To be effective, close working relationships have to be established with the senior councillors of the prevailing political party. Failure to do so can result in exclusion from key policy debates and may even lead to accusations of being obstructive. To be seen as too close, however, can raise suspicion from opposition councillors (in Camden's case, the Conservatives and Liberal Democrats) of political bias. On the other hand, to oppose councillors openly or covertly can be career threatening. Although there are clear rules to safeguard against the politicisation of local government, the looser controls at local level can be open to interpretation and roles can become blurred.[2] Senior officers must

---

DECISION-MAKING ON PLANNING APPLICATIONS

The UK planning system is described in Chapter 2. On major or controversial applications, decisions are made by a subcommittee of the council (usually called the development control subcommittee) comprising elected councillors, with the ruling party usually having a majority. That said, a development control subcommittee is quasi-judicial and should make decisions on the facts presented to them rather than along party lines. It is usual for the subcommittee to receive an officer report and recommendations on a development scheme in advance, and for this to be presented by the case officer. It may then hear representations from the applicant and any other interested groups or individuals before coming to a decision. It need not agree with the officer recommendation but should have sound (planning) grounds should it wish to go against it.

take a clear political steer on issues but cannot overstep the line of professional neutrality. However, the line can become very indistinct where political priorities are unclear or where there is disagreement within the ruling party.

THE DEVELOPMENT CONTROL SUBCOMMITTEE

Camden's development control subcommittee (the subcommittee) had a reputation for independence that sometimes bordered on the maverick. The problem had been going on for several years and both the borough solicitor and previous heads of planning had experienced difficult working relationships with the subcommittee. Anne Doherty, the head of planning, described it as the most legalistic committee she had ever come across. It viewed Camden council's own planning staff with deep suspicion, and sought its own independent advice on several occasions. Officers were routinely accused of 'expressing views' by making recommendations about a scheme, and the subcommittee had, on occasion, overturned officer recommendations with no clear policy justification.[3] Jane Roberts had concerns about the workings of the subcommittee. She wanted it to be proactive, less conservative and to focus on design quality rather than simply exercising a regulatory function. It was chaired by councillor Brian Woodrow, a veteran of battles to save Covent Garden and to stop the British Museum's plans in the 1970s to demolish historic streets in Bloomsbury for a new British Library (see Chapter 4). Woodrow's relationship with officers was far from easy. The problem was compounded by the fact that he had not spoken to Peter Bishop, his chief officer, for four years after Bishop's refusal to recommend that Camden take enforcement action against the British Museum for using the wrong stone in the refurbishment of the Great Court.[4]

The problem of briefing the subcommittee

Councillor briefings are absolutely crucial for a development as substantial and complex as King's Cross. While the leadership was regularly kept informed and was broadly in favour of the King's Cross development (subject to a satisfactory deal being negotiated), councillor Woodrow seemed at best ambivalent. He refused to allow the subcommittee to be briefed, or to give any direction on negotiations during the entire six-year process. His grounds were that this would constitute bias and be contrary to the committee's duty of independent decision-making. This view was not supported by the borough solicitor, the director or the head of planning. However, councillor Woodrow could not be dissuaded and refused all attempts by officers to brief the subcommittee.

The reality was in stark contrast to the way it was portrayed by the KXRLG's Michael Edwards, writing in the Camden New Journal in 2007:
'This [planning permission] all took place against the background of Camden's over-zealous insulation of its committee members from anything which might influence them. On such a complex scheme, councillors could have been informed by regular officer briefings on the negotiations with developers and exposed to debates between developers and residents. In fact, they were protected from these influences

and reached the point of decision-making without enough preparation. In March 2006 they had about ten days to digest a 900-page [sic] report and then a meeting over just two days to decide everything.

No wonder some councillors feel they have been unable to do the proper job which democracy requires of them. And those who did interact with their constituents were warned that they could be reported to the standards board.'[5]

While Edwards was entirely correct in advocating that councillors clearly need sufficient time and knowledge to be able to consider a complex application,[6] he was apparently unaware that the chair of the subcommittee had refused any briefing. Interestingly, Argent's Robert Evans also argues strongly that committee members must be involved earlier and more systematically if they are to reach informed decisions. Argent has even commissioned research in support of this idea.[7] If community involvement is 'front-loaded', then it is only logical that the decision-makers must be involved early as well, if they are to avoid being put at a disadvantage. This view was supported by the 2006 Barker Review of Planning.[8]

The accepted practice in major planning applications is that policy direction is given by the leadership, and within this context, the subcommittee is briefed at regular intervals.

Standards of conduct in public life were examined by the Nolan Report[9] and informed provisions in the White Paper Modern Local Government in Touch with Local People,[10] which in turn informed the Local Government Act of 2000. The Nolan Report accepted that the planning process put elected councillors into the position of taking decisions within a legal framework. However, it rejected the idea that councillors have to behave under the same quasi-judicial constraints as judges or planning inspectors. The Barker Review also accepted the potential benefits of early member briefing:

'Research also suggests that it is beneficial to involve council members at this early stage. Although care needs to be taken that this involvement is not prejudicial to the independence of the decision-making.'

Following a series of judicial review cases, guidance was issued in 2007 that supports the proposition that councillors should be kept well informed of emerging proposals and should meet applicants for briefing to establish the facts behind a scheme.[11] This extends from the pre-application to the post-application period. The proviso is that councillor involvement should operate in a fair and transparent way.[12]

The problem with the subcommittee was well-known to the leadership, but was never

> **Following a series of judicial review cases, guidance was issued in 2007 that supports the proposition that councillors should be kept well informed of emerging proposals and should meet applicants for briefing to establish the facts behind a scheme.**

aired within the Labour group.[13] Councillor Woodrow was well entrenched in the party, and was respected by many on the council.[14] No other councillor had expressed a desire to chair the subcommittee, and there were fears that any attempt to remove him would end in internal conflict and negative publicity in the local paper, the Camden New Journal.[15] The leadership saw the subcommittee and its chair as an irritant, but one to be put up with rather than resolved.

Despite representations from their officers, there was no mechanism whereby Camden's leadership could break the isolation that councillor Woodrow was imposing on his subcommittee.[16] This created difficulties in the negotiations. First, the Camden planning team had in effect been negotiating blind for six years and had little idea of the opinions or voting intentions of at least half the committee. This made the final decision something of a lottery. The second problem was that Argent was well aware of this, and it undermined the position of Camden council's negotiating team. After all, why spend time and resources on negotiation when the Camden team had no brief from, or influence over, their own decision-makers? Why not go straight to appeal?

It is unclear why councillor Woodrow refused to be briefed on King's Cross, although there is little doubt that he viewed Camden's planners with a deep mistrust, believing them to be too close to Argent.[17] He also believed that the correct vehicle for the planning decision was a public inquiry. In his view, Camden council wished to control the permission for the King's Cross development because more 'planning gain' would be won that way, and he viewed such negotiated benefits with cynicism. He had also expressed concerns over the acceptability of the 'hybrid' application. The isolation that he imposed on himself led to a suspicion among officers that he was in fact being briefed independently by opponents to the scheme. The suspicion, based on hearsay, was only circumstantial, but there were similarities between Woodrow's views and those of some opponents. If these rumours were true, it meant that far from being independent, he was likely to oppose the scheme, and would attempt to have it refused when it eventually came to the subcommittee.

In the absence of any formal briefings, members of the subcommittee were having to rely on information from other sources, including informal conversations with their constituents and community groups supporting or opposing the scheme. In such an environment there was certainly a great deal of misinformation circulating.[18] Regardless of Woodrow's insistence on absolute neutrality, members were forming views. When Sue Vincent, vice chair of the subcommittee since 2002, became a member of the council's executive board in 2004, she was shocked and angry at the extent of information that she had not been party to. For her, this confirmed that the scheme was a 'done deal' and it was the beginning of her concern that due process was not being applied and that the wider community was being excluded.[19] This exposed the tensions between the council executive and the subcommittee.

8: THE DECISION

The interview in the Architects' Journal

Matters came to a head in September 2004 when the Architects' Journal (AJ) published an interview with Woodrow in which he condemned the scheme:

'A lot of the bulk and style of the buildings proposed are not the sort of thing that we are interested in for this kind of site [...].

A large part of the southern area of this scheme falls within a conservation area and there is no way that we should have to make a decision based on just an outline application.

What we don't want is for it to come to us for a final decision in its current form because we would probably turn it down [...]. But what is true is that if they choose to stick to a scheme of this size, then we will have to leave it to the secretary of state to decide.' [20]

This statement was particularly worrying since Woodrow had refused any briefing on the scheme, and was presumably relying on his own sources of information. This was ironic, given the highly principled but erroneous stance he had taken regarding bias and impartiality. To emphasise the point that Camden council was now opposed to the scheme, the Architects'

Figure 8.1: Hellman cartoon from the Architects' Journal.

> **The Architects' Journal published a cartoon in the same edition characterising Camden council as an ancient steam train blocking the path of an express train entering King's Cross.**

Journal published a cartoon in the same edition characterising Camden council as an ancient steam train blocking the path of an express train entering King's Cross (Figure 8.1).

Meetings took place between the borough solicitor, chief executive, senior planners and leader. The leader viewed the matter as very serious, damaging and posing a reputational risk to the council. The nature of Camden's internal politics, however, meant that it was virtually impossible at this stage to challenge Woodrow's chairing of the subcommittee.[21] Instead, the leader sought to reduce the potential risk to the council and asked Woodrow to retract his comments. In September 2004, the borough solicitor wrote to Woodrow asking him to publicly 'correct' his statements.[22] Woodrow responded in a non-conciliatory manner: 'The view I expressed in the AJ article indicated no predetermined view of the applications [...]. I see no reason to withdraw from the determination of the King's Cross application and I do not intend to do so.' He went on to suggest that the AJ was not 'a journal of record and that its reliability, accuracy and credibility must be questioned'.[23]

It is unclear why Woodrow refused to retract his comments. It is possible that he suspected intervention by officers in the political workings of the council, a state of affairs that he would not accept.[24] It is also possible that he believed the Labour group would back him if it came to a showdown with the leader. Given the strong views of both officers and some councillors, the leader took independent legal advice that confirmed Roberts' concerns about the risks to the council.[25] In the face of Woodrow's refusal to back down, the borough solicitor reported Woodrow to the Standards Board for England, in September 2004, as being in breach of his duties of impartiality as a councillor.[26]

Councillor Woodrow's removal from the decision-making process

It is difficult to assess just how damaging Woodrow's comments were. They certainly undermined Camden's credibility in the negotiations. There was also a chance that if the subcommittee refused the scheme on Woodrow's casting vote, the council could be legally liable should Argent decide to take them to court. Although the risk might be low, the damages could be very high.

The matter might have ended there, with the political leadership unwilling to pursue the matter further, but Argent, initially relatively sanguine about the article, did expect Camden council to act on it. When it became clear that this would not happen, Argent wrote to Camden's chief executive:

'We are very concerned, however, that the stance apparently being taken by the Chair of Camden's development control committee, Councillor Brian Woodrow, could undermine our efforts

and inhibit the fair and proper determination of our applications [...]. This is not the first time, however, that reporters have approached Argent St George, seeking a comment on an alleged negative "briefing" by Mr Woodrow. I, and other representatives of Argent St George, have been asked to respond to such comments attributed to Mr Woodrow on several occasions over the last 2–3 years. In our view, it would be difficult to dismiss all of this as simply bad journalism.

We have been advised by our lawyers to register our concerns before any determination of our applications is made. However, our purpose is not to make waves within the council or pursue a point against Mr Woodrow. Rather, we wish to stress the importance of putting in place a process of determination that is fair, impartial and professional.'[27]

Argent's letter meant that the council had to respond. The matter was brought to a meeting between senior officers and the executive in January 2005, with a recommendation that Woodrow should either step down as chair or absent himself from the subcommittee meeting.

Figure 8.2: CGI of scheme submitted for planning.

It was referred back to officers to resolve; the leader reasoned that it was an issue that should rightly be pursued by the borough solicitor as the monitoring officer.[28] The borough solicitor had no alternative but to pursue the matter. An internal inquiry was conducted with external legal advice. This concluded that Woodrow's comments, and his refusal to withdraw them, were clear indication of bias and that he should take no part in the decision-making process. While the matter was before the National Standards Board, Woodrow was strongly advised not to take further part in the King's Cross decision-making.[29]

Several factors contributed to the officers' decision to pursue the case, although as noted above, the borough solicitor had little choice. Both Argent and Camden council had been meticulous in avoiding any risk of external challenge, and were acutely aware of the risks posed by taking the scheme to an unbriefed and finely balanced subcommittee with a potentially compromised chair. Given the complexity of the issues, an experienced and capable chair such as Woodrow could have drawn out the debate until the subcommittee ran out of time. This would have had knock-on effects since the timing of the subcommittee was critical. With a local election coming up in Camden council in May 2006, the March subcommittee was the last opportunity to decide the scheme under the present council administration. A new council, with new councillors and new political priorities might have unravelled the entire negotiation process. Furthermore, a new council would be unlikely to hear the case before the autumn, adding to Argent's doubts about whether Camden council would approve the scheme. Such uncertainty might have persuaded Argent to take the scheme to appeal for non-determination. This was not an outcome that Camden wanted.

THE DECISION

Jane Roberts stepped down as leader in May 2006. At the elections for committee chairs, councillor Heather Johnson, a long-serving Labour member of the development subcommittee, stood against Woodrow and was duly elected to replace him (although he remained on the committee). Recognising the continuing risk of a divided and potentially hostile committee, Roberts also joined the development control subcommittee for 2005/06, the year in which the scheme would come up for decision. This added her influence and her vote, but it was perceived by some as part of a deliberate strategy to 'pack the committee'.[30]

Officers now had to consider how to present the scheme (Figure 8.2 shows a CGI). The report amounted to just under 600 pages of text, in 19 chapters, and with 30 recommendations and 68 conditions. Although there had been no formal briefing of the subcommittee beforehand, it is not true to say that all the members were approaching this application without any prior knowledge. The new chair of the subcommittee, Heather Johnson, was briefed extensively on the background to the scheme as the date for the committee approached. Members of the Labour executive who sat on the subcommittee (councillors Thane, Roberts and Blackwell) had been fully involved throughout. Their support was clear.

However, as the date for the subcommittee approached, it was difficult to gauge how other councillors would vote. It would not be a simple matter of voting along party lines, although it was expected that the Conservative members (with local elections just a couple of months away) might oppose it, simply to score political points through embarrassing Labour. The Liberal Democrat position was unclear. It was felt that several longstanding subcommittee members who were close allies of councillor Woodrow would oppose the scheme. Either way, the likely vote two months before the meeting looked to be on a knife edge:

	For	Against
Labour	6	4
Conservative	0	3
Liberal Democrat	1	2
Total	7	9

Pre-application lobbying
The Camden New Journal was openly campaigning against the scheme. The edition in the week before the subcommittee, stated: 'We have to stop this vile, vulgar vision of the future', quoting members of the KXRLG, and claiming that the scheme was widely opposed by local residents.[31] The council's leadership therefore decided that it was too close to leave it to chance.

Councillor John Thane (executive member for Environment) and councillor Theo Blackwell (deputy leader and executive member for regeneration), both members of the development control subcommittee, recognised the importance of the King's Cross scheme and were prepared to champion it. With an election coming up, they were reluctant to hand over the decision to another administration, fearing that the affordable housing element could be watered down. Their reading of the subcommittee was that the Labour councillors were divided between those who viewed almost all large development with suspicion, and those who saw benefits in growth, especially in affordable housing for those in the greatest need.[32]

Councillor Thane had championed the scheme throughout and had worked to build broad support through the Labour administration. Councillor Blackwell also agreed to speak to some of the wavering members of the subcommittee, under the auspices of his role as cabinet member for regeneration. Between them, the key issues were re-framed in a number of ways, emphasising 'now is the time' for both short- and long-term reasons. First, King's Cross's notorious drug and vice problems had long blighted the borough and were perceived as fuelling new drug markets to the north in Camden Town. The council was leading in the use of new community safety powers (anti-social behaviour orders – ASBOs) to tackle such problems.[33] Physical regeneration had to follow, a message that newer members, for whom crime was the number one priority, readily grasped. Secondly, King's Cross was no Canary Wharf, then considered a by-word for commercial-only development and displaced communities. The right balance between affordable housing and commercial development would create the right conditions for future growth and would help to cut Camden council's growing housing waiting lists at a time when the council relied solely on development to do so. The development would ultimately drive up value, potentially enabling regeneration in the longer term of the huge council housing estates surrounding the site on all sides. As the date of the subcommittee approached, the estimated balance of voting began to change:

	For	Against	Abstentions/ Absent	Unable to Vote[34]
Labour	6	2		1
Conservative	0	3	0	
Lib Dem	1	2		
Total	7	7	1	1

This would still be very tight, and the entire strategy could be derailed on the night by a particularly impassioned speech or representation.

The subcommittee meeting
The paperwork presented to the subcommittee was daunting. To address the lack of prior briefing, it was agreed to hold a special meeting of the development control subcommittee spanning two consecutive evenings on 8 and 9 March 2006. The first meeting would hear representations for and against the development and allow councillors to question the various delegations on points of detail. On the second evening, Camden council planners would present the report and councillors would have an opportunity to ask questions before debating the scheme. The committee adjourned at 22.45 on Wednesday and reconvened again at 18.00 on Thursday. On the Thursday morning, the front page of the Camden New Journal condemned the scheme and urged the subcommittee to reject it.[35]

The decision was always in the balance, and at 22.30 on the second evening, with only 30 minutes to go before the vote, Stephen Ashworth, Camden's external lawyer, called Peter Bishop out of the committee room. He had calculated that the committee was going to vote against the scheme and urged Bishop to seek an adjournment. Bishop, meanwhile, had calculated that the committee was probably going to pass it by a single vote, and his view was to continue to a decision.

The key moment came towards the end of the debate. John Thane, who had remained silent throughout, spoke in favour of the scheme, setting out his previous reservations and explaining why he now whole-heartedly supported the development. At this point the wavering Labour members resolved to follow his lead and spoke in favour of the scheme. The outcome had been uncertain right to the end, but ultimately the King's Cross scheme was approved by two votes:

	For	Against	Abstentions/ Absent	Unable to Vote
Labour	7	2		1
Conservative	0	2	1	
Lib Dem	1	2		
Total	8	6	1	1

The Conservative councillor, Mike Greene, who was not present had given no reason for his absence. Councillor Greene had been a diligent member of the committee and a strong voice on the council. He also respected Brian Woodrow,

> **The right balance between affordable housing and commercial development would create the right conditions for future growth and would help to cut Camden council's growing housing waiting lists at a time when the council relied solely on development to do so.**

whom he described as, 'a politician wanting to do his best for the borough rather than himself',[36] and Camden council officers had expected him to vote against the scheme. In interview, however, Greene stated that his non-attendance was due to a combination of a personal dilemma and specific circumstances. He personally believed that the regeneration scheme was essentially one that he supported. However, before the subcommittee took place there had in fact been a meeting of the Conservative party political group where King's Cross had been debated. The Conservative leader gave a strong steer that his members should vote against the scheme. This was not because the Conservatives necessarily opposed the scheme, but with a local election coming up in May, King's Cross had become a party political issue. It was a simple piece of political opportunism. With his leader asking him to reject an application that he would have wanted to support, and election campaigning meaning he would not have sufficient time to read the papers thoroughly enough to participate fully in the debate, the easiest solution was not to attend at all.[37] Had one Conservative councillor not been absent, and had councillor Woodrow still been chair and voted against, the result would have been a tie. In such a tie, the subcommittee chair has a casting vote.

A last minute amendment

One final unexpected event had serious implications for the scheme. At the last minute during the voting, councillor Stewart proposed an unexpected amendment to a standard recommendation that, following approval, council officers would have delegated authority to sign-off the details of the section 106 agreement. No formal approval of the planning application could be issued without this sign-off. The amendment was that the section 106 agreement should come back to the subcommittee for formal approval. This effectively deferred a final decision until after the local election in May 2006. The councillors were probably unaware of the full implications of the amendment, but officers were dismayed. In retrospect though, Heather Johnson, chairing the meeting, was clear that this amendment was possibly necessary to persuade any wavering members to vote for the scheme.[38]

Such was the confusion in the final minutes of the meeting that even Argent was unsure of the final outcome. When Peter Bishop went to congratulate the Argent team, Roger Madelin swore vividly, before Robert Evans confirmed that they did indeed have a consent.

Normally, this amendment would not have caused serious problems. The subcommittee had approved the scheme, and to revoke the decision would have cost considerable sums in compensation. The section 106 agreement could not be used to change this decision, and signing it off should therefore have been routine. However, there would be no opportunity to do this before the local elections in May 2006. What was not foreseen at the time was that Labour would lose the local election, and that the Conservatives and Liberal Democrats (who had largely opposed the development) would take control of the council.[39]

REBUILDING POLITICAL SUPPORT

The whole process of rebuilding alliances to get the scheme through the subcommittee had to start again. Although planning had been granted, approval of the section 106 agreement was still required, before a consent could be issued. Due to the late amendment this now had to go back to the subcommittee, now controlled by the two parties that had in the end opposed the scheme.

The new leadership settled down remarkably quickly. The council deputy leadership passed to Andrew Marshal (Conservative), who also took the regeneration portfolio. Early briefings with him and Mike Greene (Conservative), who took the environment and planning role, established positive working relationships. The briefings emphasised the following points:

- The scheme had approval, and although the section 106 agreement had to return to committee for approval, any attempt to use this to overturn the consent would potentially expose the council to challenge and damages.
- The scheme would bring in high levels of private sector investment that would transform the southern part of the borough. It was all about business and enterprise.
- The political control over implementation of the scheme, and the subsequent development of related projects, would be the legacy of the Conservatives.

In getting the new administration on side, it helped that the project had been seen as officer, rather than member, driven.[40] The new leadership met Argent and they were impressed. They reviewed the terms of the section 106 agreement, and were happy to endorse it. The political line was to proceed, and there was no further debate.

Approval of the section 106 agreement

The project still had to be taken back to committee for section 106 agreement to be signed-off. Greene took on the task of reassembling a cross-party coalition on the subcommittee. The working assumption was that the Conservatives would support investment and development, Labour would support projects that had commenced under its administration, and the Liberal Democrats would vote at random. Although a few councillors wanted to use the section 106 issue to reopen the King's Cross debate, the legal advice was unequivocal. On 25 November 2006 the subcommittee approved the section 106 agreement by a clear margin.

The planning approvals were signed on 23 December 2006, which was, coincidentally Bishop's last day working for Camden council. Following Camden's grant of planning permission, the mayor, satisfied that Transport for London's interests had been accommodated, endorsed Camden's decision within four days and passed it on to the secretary of state. The secretary of state's staff at the Government Office for London (GOL) had received letters asking for a call-in for an inquiry. GOL wavered but accepted that with such a thorough planning report, a call-in would have completely invalidated the principles of the plan-led system and the legitimacy of both local decision-making and the office of the mayor.

Normally, the achievement of planning consent would have cleared the way for construction to begin. The London property market was booming and the King's Cross scheme was ready to start. Throughout the negotiations, however, it was anticipated that KXRLG would seek a judicial review of the planning permission, and the scheme could not start until this had been resolved.

THE JUDICIAL REVIEW

As a judicial review had been considered inevitable, Camden council and Argent's legal teams had laboured hard to ensure that the procedures followed were watertight, and both were confident that the risk of losing was slight. Under regulations then in force, a judicial review had to be made no later than three months after the grounds to make the claim arose.[41] Until the threat had passed, it would have been too risky for lenders to make capital available to start the development. This was frustrating as the London property market was booming. As anticipated, a challenge was made close to the deadline, in February 2007, from the King's Cross Think Again Group (a partnership of several local groups including KXRLG). The court agreed to limit their liability, should they lose, to £10,000.[42] The 'rolled up' hearing was held in May 2007. The presiding judge had a reputation for understanding technical development issues. Argent's legal team, aware of the timetable for hearings had timed matters to coincide with his availability.[43]

Grounds for the judicial review

The application for judicial review was made on two grounds, both of which were dismissed. The first was whether the newly elected council had been wrongly advised by officers and the council's legal consultant that they had no legal grounds to reject the scheme when the section

JUDICIAL REVIEW

Judicial review is used to mount a legal challenge to a planning permission on the grounds that a public body has failed to follow, or has been inconsistent with, its own procedures in reaching its decision. It challenges the way in which a decision has been made, rather than the rights and wrongs of the decision itself. In the absence of third party rights of appeal, it is the activist's weapon of last resort against a development. Although a court can only direct that a decision is reconsidered, judicial review inevitably causes delay and brings additional uncertainty to what is already a long, expensive and risky process. And behind every challenge lurks the spectre of a new campaign to reverse the decision. The standard practice is for the challenge to be made by a named individual who is eligible for legal aid, which will cover costs. A review is therefore a relatively cost-effective method of community opposition.

106 agreement came back to subcommittee for consideration. Given the change in political control, it was argued that members should have had 'full and unfettered discretion to reconsider all or any of the matters of the old committee'.[44] The judgement accepted that Camden council's advice to members was 'both clear and correct', and that as a whole it did not fetter their discretion or 'box them in'.[45]

The second ground was that the planning permission went against policy regarding affordable housing. It was argued that the decision should have taken into account emerging guidance on affordable housing (PPS3).[46] On this, the judgement found that 'there is, in practical terms, no difference whatsoever between the definition of affordable housing in PPS3 and the definition of affordable housing in the section 106 agreement'.[47] The judgement also found that the advice given to the committee on the adequacy of the affordable housing, and whether or not the committee could decide for itself whether the failure to meet the 50 per cent target meant that there was a departure from the development plan, 'was impeccable'.

Commenting on the experience, KXRLG's Michael Edwards had no regrets on seeking the judicial review, and expressed a personal view that such challenges are an important check on the 'autocratic power of the cliques which run "reformed" local government, and on the power of officers, who are far too often in a dangerously cosy "partnership" with developers'.[48] Costs were awarded against the King's Cross Think Again Group. Camden council pursued these but Argent waived them.

Ironically, the relentless opposition by KXRLG may well have saved the King's Cross scheme. By October 2008 the effects of the credit crunch were affecting the entire banking industry. The six-month delay between the grant of planning permission in December 2006 and the judicial review hearing in May 2007 meant that Argent had delayed and then scaled back its borrowing to finance the development. Had Argent not done so, it could have faced severe financial difficulties. This is picked up in Chapter 9.

ISLINGTON'S DECISION ON THE 'TRIANGLE' SITE

The final element in the planning equation was the application for the 'Triangle' site. As this site was partly in Camden and partly in Islington, it had been agreed in early discussions that it would be subject to a separate application. Should Islington council delay or refuse it, this would not affect the main site.

As discussed in Chapter 4, the leadership of Liberal Democrat-controlled Islington supported the development of King's Cross, and had no political association with the groups that were opposing the scheme. In March 2006, when Camden council resolved to grant consent for its part of the 'Triangle', Islington council had raised no objections to this or to the main application. As with Camden, strategic decision-making started with its cabinet, but unlike Camden, development control was devolved to focus neighborhood committees.[49] The one that would deal with the 'Triangle' site was Labour controlled.[50]

Against its officers' advice, Islington council refused permission for the 'Triangle' site in July

2007. Phil Allemendinger suggests that this was due to lobbying of councillors by community activists who opposed the scheme.[51] The stated reason for refusal was the extent of affordable housing. Across the whole scheme, 44 per cent of housing units would be affordable. Within the Islington site (2.5 acres of the 67 acre total), the proportion would be 34 per cent. Islington's own policy was for 35 per cent affordable housing. Over previous negotiations, however, Islington had accepted that the site would be treated as a whole and the council's executive had made no objection to the main planning application, even commending Camden council on the intermediate affordable housing achieved. While its leadership and officers supported the 'Triangle' scheme, it was unable to control the area committee that took the decision. This represented an embarrassment for Islington. In considering Argent's appeal, the planning inspector's report in May 2008 stated:

'In these circumstances it is surprising that Islington's evidence has focused on figures for the triangle site alone, has not referred to the different stance now being adopted, or provided any explanation for it. This is a complete departure from everything that had gone before.

It seems to me that the developers have gone to considerable effort to discuss the appropriate housing mix with the councils and the local communities. While significant differences remain with the latter, I consider that the developers have produced an exemplary range of provision that, especially with regard to the intermediate housing sector, fully reflects the principles advanced in PPS3 and its daughter document Delivering Affordable Housing.'[52]

The secretary of state upheld Argent's appeal and granted permission, and since the inspector approved the application as submitted, Islington lost the changes that it had subsequently negotiated. The appeal and the judicial review, however, had delayed the scheme and cost Argent almost £1 million.

CONCLUSIONS

Planning is a contested and inherently political process. Successive governments have tried to address the central conundrum of the system, namely, how to make it streamlined and efficient while maintaining meaningful democratic debate. Government guidance has also tried to provide a framework for transparency in local political decision-making, since any lack of transparency, real or perceived, undermines trust in the system. Given the degree of flexibility that exists in the UK system, trust is paramount.

The King's Cross planning decision was exposed to political forces and personal agendas, some of which went back a long way and had little to do with the scheme itself. This required political management, at which point the roles of paid employees and elected representatives become blurred. The affair concerning councillor Woodrow is detailed here because it illustrates the tensions both within the council's ruling party and between officers and councillors. The referral to the Standards Board was taken at officer, rather than political, level. This was technically correct, since the monitoring officer has a duty to ensure probity within his or her council. Nevertheless, the problem was essentially one of political

> **In a process as fragile as this, would a public inquiry, as favoured by some councillors and community organisations, have been a better, more rational and more open option?**

management, and in many councils it would have been resolved within the machinery of the political group. The fact that it was not, exposed senior council officers to considerable personal risk. The process of constructing support within the subcommittee was not unusual. Lobbying and persuasion is the stuff of politics. The officer's involvement in this was with the express consent of the council's leadership and was in line with agreed policy.

Much of the difficulty regarding the decision arose from the refusal of certain councillors, against the clear government guidance to entertain any pre-application briefing from their own officers. Circumstances have changed in Camden. Pre-application briefing of development control subcommittee members is now routine, often in open public meetings. It is also quite normal for officers to sound out the chair or cabinet member and receive a political steer on contentious schemes.[53]

The change of political control in Camden council was unexpected, but in the end was less significant than it might have been. The fact that King's Cross was not viewed as a political project associated with the outgoing administration meant that the transition was relatively smooth. Under both administrations the presence of politicians who were prepared to champion the scheme personally eased the process considerably.

Political management is a key skill for both the public and private sector. Even then, unexpected events such as a last minute amendment to a recommendation or a local election can still derail a scheme. In a process as fragile as this, would a public inquiry, as favoured by some councillors and community organisations, have been a better, more rational and more open option? The scheme was compliant with local and regional policy and an inquiry would have undermined the notion of a plan-led system. It would have taken the decision out of local democratic control and placed it into the hands of a government inspector. It would have been costly and time-consuming, and although it is highly unlikely that it would have found any new evidence to add to the debate, the outcome would still have been unpredictable and hard-negotiated benefits could have been lost.

9.
BUILDING KING'S CROSS CENTRAL

This chapter follows the story of King's Cross after the grant of planning permission.[1] It covers the steps that were required in order to trigger the valuation of the site, its transfer to the developer and the difficulties that the global financial crisis from 2008 presented in the early phases of development. It considers the importance of Argent's programme of place-making activities in animating the area and putting it on the map for both investors and visitors, and reviews the success to date of some of the local employment and training initiatives. The scheme is already triggering new investment on adjacent sites and the chapter concludes with a brief summary of these. However, any assessment of the impact of the development on the surrounding areas and their social composition must await dedicated research.

As far as possible the events are covered chronologically, but some are covered thematically in order to simplify the narrative. Key financial data is set out in Appendix 2.

THE LAND VALUATION AND TRANSFER

With the judicial review out of the way, the next step was for London and Continental Railways (LCR) and Argent to value the land so that it could be transferred for development to commence. The valuation process had three triggers:
1 Outline planning consent to be in place for the whole site.
2 LCR to have obtained vacant possession.
3 Detailed planning for phase one of the development to have been agreed.
With the first trigger in place, the next step was to achieve vacant possession and agree phase one of the development.

Achieving vacant possession

Delivering vacant possession[2] met unforeseen difficulties. By the end of the 19th century, King's Cross was one of the largest railway depots in the world, and had been developed by different railway companies. Each company had legal rights to run trains along their respective lines through Acts of Parliament and easements. When the railways were nationalised and brought under a single authority in 1948, these rights transferred to the new authority, British Railways.[3]

While it was still an operational railway, these rights and wayleaves were unimportant and they lay dormant. However, when the land was transferred to LCR, vacant possession required that all previous rights be extinguished. This was not an academic exercise. While these rights existed, it was theoretically possible for someone to run a train through the site. Costly indemnities would have been required to cover potential outstanding liabilities, and these would have had significant implications for institutional borrowing. Over 50 different legal agreements, some dating back to the 1830s, had to be extinguished through a tortuous process of negotiation with Railtrack (successor body to British Railways). While Railtrack did not use these as a ransom to extract payment from the landowners, the process was slow and for Railtrack, at least, a low priority.

It is likely that the problem would have dragged on without the impetus of London's successful bid for the 2012 Olympic Games

9: BUILDING KING'S CROSS CENTRAL

in July 2005. King's Cross was to be the main central London terminus for the games, and the concourse had to be finished before August 2012. In order for this to happen, government funding for the interchange had to be unfrozen and land ownerships had to be resolved. The proposed site for the new station concourse, that had been transferred to LCR in the original contract, now had to be transferred back to Network Rail. This enabled a new concourse to be built, with the design problems resolved through the construction of an elegant lightweight canopy designed by architect John McAslan + Partners (Figures 9.1 and 9.2).[4]

As Figure 9.3 indicates, the area beneath Euston Road and King's Cross station was a mass of underground lines. The works were technically difficult and expensive, and the overlap of landownerships, design approvals, liabilities, construction access, working areas and contracts had to be resolved quickly.

While previous works to the interchange had been loosely coordinated (see Chapter 3), there was now an urgent need to put more robust arrangements in place. The government appointed Michael Hurn from the Department for Communities and Local Government (DCLG) to act as the project sponsor for King's Cross and Thameslink. The Department for Transport (DfT) had inherited three separate projects:

1 The London Underground works, in itself three separate elements – the refurbishment and redesign of the ticket hall following the 1987 fire;[5] the new Western Concourse – part of the Channel Tunnel Rail Link (CTRL) works; and

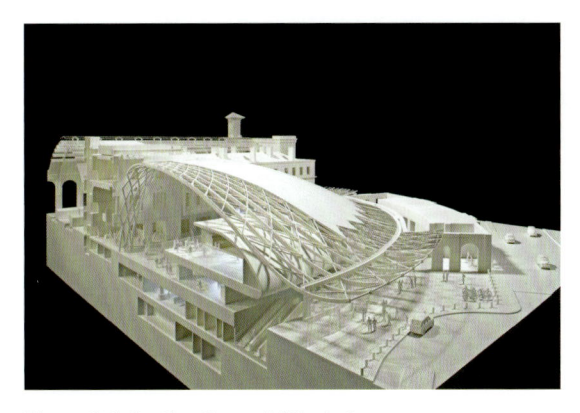

Figure 9.1: Section through King's Cross concourse and underground.

Figure 9.2: Interior of the new King's Cross concourse.

Figure 9.3: King's Cross – a tangle of underground lines.

the new Northern ticket hall to connect with the Midland Main Line services in St Pancras. The DfT was in effect client and funder for these works (Figure 9.4).

2 Network Rail's refurbishment of King's Cross station, the construction of a new concourse to the west of the station and the demolition of the existing concourse to create a new public square.

3 The improvements to Thameslink and the construction of a new station beneath St Pancras.

As the land on which the new concourse was to be built had previously been transferred to LCR and Argent had already incorporated the Great Northern Hotel and taxi/bus interchange into its masterplan (and the Great Northern Hotel had been leased to a boutique hotel operator), all of these commitments had to be incorporated into the wider solution. In response, a tri-partite agreement was made between Network Rail, the DfT/London Underground Ltd (LUL) and LCR/

Figure 9.4: Underground and subway link designed by Allies and Morrison.

9: BUILDING KING'S CROSS CENTRAL

> **The failure of Northern Rock Building Society in September 2007 was a warning of problems on the horizon, but there was no real sense of what was to come.**

Argent. This set out arrangements for major land transactions on top of existing engineering contracts.

Transport consultants Mott Macdonald were brought in and a new programme was drawn up. LUL was paid performance incentives to complete works and clear its working areas by September 2008 so that work on the main concourse could start. By December 2009, the new platforms for the domestic rail services from Kent were complete. After much technical wrangling, the positioning of the escalators to connect the underground and main concourse was agreed and the plans started to fit together. Finally, listed building consents were signed-off for alterations to the Great Northern Hotel. As part of this, Network Rail cleared the wayleaves and other residual land encumbrances in order to provide LCR with vacant possession. Summing up this tortuous process, Michael Hurn, the DfT project sponsor, commented that, 'the technical aspects were less important than the people. It was the individual relationships that eventually made it come together.'[6]

Agreeing phase one of the development

The final trigger for the valuation of the site was agreement of phase one of the development. This included the realignment of Pancras Road, which in turn required the demolition of the northern Stanley Buildings. This project had been delayed by the judicial review, but had to be completed by November 2007, when the Queen was scheduled to open the new CTRL terminus at St Pancras. Argent accelerated the contract to meet this deadline but this involved significant costs. According to Robert Evans, 'the judicial review resulted in this possibly being the most costly piece of road ever built'.[7]

Valuing the land

With the three triggers in place, the parties could now proceed to the valuation of the land. The land transfer contract between the landowners and Argent specified that land value would be determined by the average of three independent valuations (unless one valuation was clearly an 'outlier'). Argent would have the option to 'buy' into 50 per cent of the development by paying 50 per cent, less an incentivised discount related to increases in the overall value of the scheme achieved through planning.

THE FIRST PHASES OF DEVELOPMENT

While the parties had been busy securing the land transfers needed to start work, conditions in the London property market had changed dramatically. The failure of Northern Rock Building Society in September 2007 was a warning of problems on the horizon, but there was no real sense of what was to come. Argent, through its development partnership, King's Cross Central Limited Partnership (KCCP), started to prepare contracts and raise money to begin development.[8] Initially looking to borrow £600 million, it reduced the programme and scaled back preliminary borrowings to £400 million. From August 2008 the world was sliding towards a liquidity crisis as the property bubble, based on easy credit, burst. With the collapse of Lehman Brothers in September 2008, the financial slump intensified and banks began to get into difficulties. By October 2008, the credit crunch was in full swing, the entire banking industry was in crisis and lending came to a virtual halt. With the exception of the Olympic Games site, development in London and elsewhere all but stopped.

KCCP had been ready to sign major contracts, but its programme had been held back partly due to the judicial review. Had it not delayed the process by six months, KCCP would have committed to up-front expenditure prior to the worst property slump in living memory and may well have faced substantial financial difficulties. Ironically, the implacable opposition of the King's Cross Rail Lands Group (KXRLG) may have saved the scheme.

University of the Arts London

Despite increasing uncertainty in the property market, the KCCP took the decision to commence development with the University of the Arts London (UAL) as occupiers of the Granary Building. The introduction to UAL came by chance at a marketing event organised in October 2002 by Pat Brown of the Central London Partnership,[9] and a deal was agreed in principle the same day by Roger Madelin and UAL's head of estates. The university had cash reserves and property to sell in central London. While anchoring a development with a university was unconventional, it did mean that the centre of the site would be activated early, and UAL would bring in over 4,000 staff and students. UAL was also prepared to commit to the site in its early, undeveloped state and to take certain risks on this basis. Without having the full funding for the Granary project in place, KCCP and the university agreed to commit to enabling works, splitting the costs 50:50.

As the global financial situation deteriorated further, there was a time in early October 2008 when UAL was no longer able to continue to pay its share of these costs. The property assets that it had intended to sell to finance the deal remained unsold, and there was little prospect that it would be able to raise additional money to complete the project. While the scheme looked dead, Madelin took a decision (without the full support of the landowners), to continue the works and cover UAL's share of costs. After three fraught weeks and against all the odds, UAL's bank, Lloyds TSB (technically insolvent at the time) extended its overdraft limit, and one of the university's properties sold, albeit well below the original asking price. According to Madelin, if the UAL contract had been stopped at this point the King's Cross development may well have stalled indefinitely.[10]

Work resumed, but the problems were far from over. The £108 million contract only included works to the Granary, a 3-metre strip of land around it, the energy centre and a narrow entrance path to connect it to York Way. As there was no guarantee that the wider development around its new building would be achieved, UAL took a considerable risk. However, the start on site, risky as it was, represented a significant milestone and the lease of the Granary gave KCCP a small capital sum to invest in further enabling works.

Early infrastructure and housing projects

To maintain the momentum, KCCP ploughed back all its receipts to cover the next phase of infrastructure. With the housing market in the doldrums, student housing was one of the few areas that remained commercially viable and a block was brought forward on York Way, which required little up-front infrastructure/expenditure. By March 2009, the mayor and the London Development Agency (LDA) were desperate to help reactivate the housing market and as a consequence the Homes and Community Agency (HCA) pumped additional grant money into affordable housing schemes that were ready to be developed.[11] KCCP re-phased the work, brought forward the sites allocated for affordable housing and with cash from the HCA, continued to develop. After this period, HCA grants reduced considerably.

First office buildings

As the market slowly began to stabilise, KCCP completed deals on two office developments in the southern part of the site (Figure 9.5). In 2010, a substantial plot was sold on a long lease to the real estate company BNP Paribas, and the money ploughed back into completing key infrastructure. Camden council then approached KCCP with a proposal to move its town hall and

Figure 9.5: First office buildings. From left to right, buildings by Allies and Morrison, David Chipperfield and Barton Willmore.

main corporate offices to the King's Cross site. The building selected already incorporated the public swimming pool and gym, and being the closest building to Somers Town, it was a good location for the new town hall. From KCCP's perspective it was probably the least valuable of the commercial buildings. As the market was only just picking up, the deal gave KCCP an additional cash injection when it most needed it. Camden council gained efficient new premises, and subsequently covered its costs by selling other properties on the back of a rising market.

Financing the early stages of the scheme had been hand-to-mouth and involved a great deal of improvisation. During the height of the recession KCCP had committed over

£150 million in up-front investment on infrastructure and site preparations. Much of this investment gave no immediate income. The first phases of the UAL, affordable housing and the renovation of the Great Northern Hotel had achieved enough income to keep the development going, and KCCP ploughed its returns back into the scheme. The first phases of the public realm, the Boulevard and Granary Square had been completed, and a place was emerging with distinctive character and growing activity. The development had survived, but it had been a close call requiring strong nerves. KCCP had not taken on significant debt, but neither had it received any return. In some ways the recession had worked in its favour. It had received HCA money and was well positioned to respond to a recovering office market that was suddenly facing a shortage of supply.

VARIATIONS TO THE PLANNING CONSENT

Since all the individuals who negotiated the planning consents on behalf of Camden council have since left the authority, a comprehensive archive has proved essential in maintaining continuity for the council. Since planning permission was granted in 2006, Camden council has agreed to a series of amendments to the consent, in the form of deeds of variation. Some of these were due to changes in the HCA funding regime for affordable housing, or changes in the market, while some were requested by Camden council. Responsibility for signing off reserved matters and details rests with Camden's major developments team. Argent now funds approximately 2.5 planning posts in the team under a planning performance agreement.[12] The deeds of variation cover:

- Changes in the intermediate housing triggered by changes in HCA grant subsidy (significantly reduced from £120,000 per unit to £30,000). The restructuring was on better terms than the cascade agreement and allowed Camden council to have more one-bed units for the frail elderly, allowing them to free up larger, under-occupied public housing units elsewhere in the borough for re-letting to larger families.
- The provision of an additional tall building on the north of the site for student housing. This is outside the Greater London Authority (GLA)'s viewing corridors and was a change proposed by KCCP in response to early difficulties in getting the scheme underway. For Camden council, additional student housing was desirable as it met a clear demand and took pressure off the existing housing stock.
- The replacement of the pre-school provision with an extension of the primary school to allow the Frank Barnes School for the Deaf to relocate on the site. This was requested by Camden

> **Since planning permission was granted in 2006, Camden council has agreed to a series of amendments to the consent, in the form of deeds of variation.**

9: BUILDING KING'S CROSS CENTRAL

> **During negotiations it was seen as a fundamental guarantee that the area would have a civic and inclusive character.**

council. Twelve affordable units were lost as a result of this variation.

- The walk-in health clinic (but not the local health centre) was removed because the Primary Care Trust declined to take on the management of the facility.
- Minor reductions to building sizes have also been agreed. The cost savings to KCCP have been passed over in bonds and commuted sums to Camden council and have been put towards the provision of a larger sports hall on the site.
- The Construction Training Centre has been increased in size with additional funding provided by the KCCP.
- The size of the cycle storage has been reduced because TfL was unwilling to manage the facility. Cycle storage is now provided privately through a cycle shop.
- Residential car parking provision has been reduced, due to the lack of demand, particularly from occupants of the market housing.

ADOPTION OF THE PUBLIC REALM

By the end of 2015, KCCP had completed over 90 per cent of the public realm and open spaces, but Camden council has not exercised clauses under the section 106 agreement to adopt the main street and pedestrian network. It can still do so until the end of the development period, but its reluctance so far reflects both a desire to save money and KCCP's high maintenance standards and inclusive approach to management. Adoption of the public realm will be an important test of Camden council's resolve. During negotiations it was seen as a fundamental guarantee that the area would have a civic and inclusive character. The ambience of King's Cross could be altered fundamentally by a change in ownership or management approach. Planning has few controls over this. Adoption might be a crude way of exercising long-term control, but it is effective.

PLACE-MAKING AT KING'S CROSS CENTRAL

Attracting the right cafés, bars and shops

Argent understood that the King's Cross brand needed to address all the elements that make up a place, down to the cafés, bars, public art and temporary events. Argent's model was to enter into joint ventures with prospective tenants. One example is the lease arrangement with the restaurant Caravan, which occupies a prime location on Granary Square. Argent had visited its restaurant in nearby Exmouth Market, liked it, and persuaded the owners to open up in King's Cross. Under the joint venture, Caravan pays a peppercorn rent for five years, KCCP pays towards the fit-out costs and in return receives a percentage of the turnover. Within three months of opening, a rent equivalent to that which was anticipated after five years of trading had been

Figure 9.6: The Granary Building, now University of the Arts London, art installation and canalside steps.

exceeded. This joint venture model allows independent firms to come to King's Cross, and this contributes towards creating a more interesting place.

Estate management events
Right from the beginning, Principles for a Human City had set out Argent's objective that King's Cross should be an accessible place with a vibrant mix of uses, a place that engaged and inspired.[13] Active estate management was implicit in this and KCCP has worked hard to establish King's Cross as an attractive location.

The place-making programme is now managed by a dedicated internal team,[14] but originally evolved through a process of trial and error. Understanding how the area works and why has been crucial to its success. The programme is loosely divided into three strands – arts, events and community. All aim to develop links with surrounding communities and broaden involvement in the site.

Arts
Prior to the start of development, the German Gymnasium was the initial venue for the arts programme and hosted a range of photography

and other exhibitions. KCCP soon recognised that it needed more professional input to the programme and set up an Arts Advisory Panel and employed a specialist curator. In 2009, an artist-in-residence programme was established in partnership with the Arts Council. The curators[15] commissioned a series of temporary artworks, including an over-sized illuminated birdcage with a swing,[16] and an installation of geometric aluminium foil across the Victorian buildings (Figure 9.6).[17] A recent project, completed in summer 2015, is an art installation in the form of a 40-metre-long natural bathing pond (Figure 9.7).[18]

Events

The opening of Granary Square with its choreographed fountains (Figure 9.8) has proved to be a major attraction, particularly for local families and attracted 175,000 visitors in 2012 and 2013. It has provided a new venue for events, such as live Wimbledon tennis screenings, a floating cinema, yard sales, sports days, music and poetry performances, battle re-enactments, steam events, festivals and events (Figure 9.9). There is also a regular programme of baseline events and a range of stalls selling street food. Most events are free, but receipts from any commercial events are ploughed back into the events fund.

PLANNING, POLITICS AND CITY MAKING

Community

KCCP has devoted considerable resources to maintaining the conversation with the local communities through an extensive programme of tours for local schools and groups. The visitor centre, set up and funded by KCCP, conducts two formal guided tours a week, and in 2014 it received 11,000 visitors from across the world.

The programme has also included temporary activities and pop-ups such as the Filling Station, a bar and café in an old petrol station on Goodsway (Figure 9.10) and the Skip Garden, a series of portable allotments in construction skips.[19] This was one of the first temporary projects on site and is run by Global Generation, a charity that involves young people.[20] As different areas of the King's Cross scheme are developed, the skips are moved to new locations.[21] In 2015, it moved to a new site next to the outdoor swimming pond, and was rebuilt in partnership with students from the Bartlett School of Architecture (Figure 9.11).

As the development grows, it is increasingly difficult to separate KCCP's place-making programme from its property management role. Some of the property management costs are recovered from the tenants' service charge and tenants are involved through an events forum. This work was initially funded through the section 106 package (£1.75 million for public art), but is now funded directly by KCCP. The use of site hoardings for art and site interpretation (Figures 9.12 and 9.13), and the production of numerous publications and leaflets have all

Figure 9.7: Natural bathing pool.

Figure 9.8 (above): Granary Square fountains.
Figure 9.9 (top): An event at Granary Square.

helped to create a buzz, attracting potential new investors and occupants. The £1 million social fund has yet to be allocated pending agreement by Camden and Islington councils of its spending criteria.

At the time of writing (February 2016), approximately 50 per cent of the development was complete, but a new community was emerging with a mixture of different housing types, a primary school and new areas of public space (Figures 9.14 and 9.15).

EMPLOYMENT AND TRAINING[22]

King's Cross Recruit (KXR), a skills and recruitment centre, was funded by Argent through the section 106 agreement and opened in January 2014. Essentially KXR acts as a placement or referral agency between those wanting a job at King's Cross and those offering such jobs. It handles vacancies in any sector, though in practice these are largely in the retail and hospitality sectors. Jobs in construction are handled by the Construction Skills Centre, with training delivered by Carillion. The centre offers training, apprenticeships, employment advice and job opportunities to local people looking to work in construction. To date, over 450 people have gained a qualification through its work.

The remit of KXR is explicitly employer-focused; it aims to find the best candidate for the job. Ideally, these will be from local communities in Islington and Camden, but also further afield where necessary. Local employers provide details of vacancies which are posted on the KXR website and social media. KXR then works with local authorities, schools, colleges, skills and training agencies, social enterprises, charities and others to encourage referrals of suitable candidates. It interviews, screens and filters these before passing a shortlist on to employers.

KXR has placed over 380 people in local jobs since the beginning of 2014, and 80 per cent of these have come from either Camden or Islington. However, the task is less straightforward than originally envisaged when the section 106 agreement was outlined. The programme was designed to level the playing field and tackle high levels of disadvantage and unemployment by ensuring that local residents have better access to local jobs. However, many of the harder-to-place unemployed have been out of work for a long time; some have disabilities, many are young people who left school disillusioned, some with few qualifications. Many also have little concept of the working environment, of the expectations of employers or the basic communication skills required to deal with customers. KXR has formed clear views on the kind of training needed, but at present has no remit or budget to provide training itself. Instead it must rely on local training providers, but finds that the training on offer is sometimes inappropriate or of poor quality. KXR can only help those who are work-ready.

NORTH CENTRAL ONE

The new piece of London emerging at King's Cross now has its own postcode: NC1. When completed in 2020, the scheme will comprise 23 office buildings (316,000 square metres), 46,400 square metres of retail and leisure space, and close to 2,000 homes. An estimated 45,000 people a day will work in or visit King's Cross overall. One-quarter of the scheme is dedicated to art, culture and leisure uses and more than 20 historic buildings will have been refurbished. Within the scheme will be 10.5 hectares of parks and other public space, including ten new public squares and 20 new streets. In the centre of the scheme is the new University of the Arts London with 4,000 students and staff. Argent did not set out to attract any particular sector or tenant, but wanted the mix to reflect London in all of its diversity. In some respects, by attracting the creative sector to the area, Argent has been able to broaden the site's appeal beyond the financial services sector (from which demand is now limited). In January 2013 Google announced that King's Cross would be its headquarters for several thousand staff and has bought a long lease for a 93,000 square metre building to the east of King's Boulevard.

There will be 13 different residential developments in a mix of tenures on the scheme, including a 27-storey tower for 650 students.[23] Most of the homes on site will be single family units (1,309), and over one-fifth have been developed and already sold. Predicted values for the first residential units were around £700 per square foot. Today, the blended average is around £1,400 per square foot and is still increasing.[24] One Housing Group is the partner

Figure 9.10: The Filling Station, temporary bar and café in a disused petrol station.

Figure 9.11: Skip Garden and temporary pavilions designed by students from the Bartlett School of Architecture.

Figure 9.12: Hoarding as art.

Figure 9.13: Hoarding as viewpoints.

for the first phase of affordable housing – 250 affordable homes for rent in three separate buildings.

THE NEW KING'S CROSS STATION SQUARE

Once the decision had been taken to fund the new concourse for King's Cross station, the opportunity arose to remove the existing temporary concourse and create a new public space.[25] Initially Network Rail was inclined to retain it for the retail income, but this was rejected by Camden council. Network Rail proposed extending the contract for the concourse and commissioning John McAslan + Partners for the redesign. Camden council held McAslan in high regard, but argued for an open competition for what was, after all, the largest new public space to be carved out of the fabric of London since Trafalgar Square. Camden council wanted to canvas new ideas as widely as possible and Network Rail agreed to a competition through the Royal Institute of British Architects (RIBA).

The site presented considerable challenges. The underground concourse had been built with no consideration for any public space above it. It was like designing landscape on the lid of a tin. Moreover, the position of stairways, entrances, vent shafts and emergency escape points were all predetermined. Sandwiched between a mainline station and Euston Road, it was hardly going to be a 'piazza'. It has three main functions. First, it is a place of transit, between different modes of transport. Second, it is an external waiting room for the station. Finally, it provides a setting for the grand south façade of

Figure 9.14 (above): Mixed tenure housing and primary school.

Figure 9.15 (top): Gasometer Park.

King's Cross station.

The competition was won by Stanton Williams - architects for the Granary Building refurbishment. The scheme started immediately after the 2012 London Olympic Games and was completed in early 2014. By and large, it has successfully dealt with the complexities of the brief and has revealed the grandeur of the front of King's Cross. It is a far busier space than envisaged, and provides a popular external space, with a kiosks and temporary stalls selling food. The detailing is simple and the operational structures that intrude into the space have been elegantly incorporated into the design (Figure 9.16). The only disappointments are the intrusive ring of security bollards, the inconsistency of the paving between the Euston Road and the concourse, and the poor detailing of the canopy over the station exit. These elements, all outside the architect's remit, should have been resolved by Camden council and Network Rail.

IMPACT ON THE SURROUNDING AREAS

One of Camden council's original objectives was that the King's Cross development should bring about regeneration of the wider area. While it is difficult to separate the impact of the development from that of the CTRL and the refurbishment of St Pancras, new investment is apparent.[26] The King's Place scheme by Parabola Land Ltd was the first development on a site close to King's Cross.[27] Housing development is taking place along the canal at Jubilee Wharf (the Shaw Corporation), and the Health Authority is now considering the options for the redevelopment of the nearby St Pancras Hospital. To the rear of the British Library, the Crick Institute (a major cancer research centre developed under a partnership between University College Hospital, University College London and the Wellcome Trust), is nearing completion. Planning applications have been submitted for two commercial blocks immediately opposite King's Cross station. Finally, Camden council's old offices, next to the Town Hall, have been sold for redevelopment as a boutique hotel.

Camden council has once again become a housing developer, and is carrying out estate restructuring in the immediate area, retaining the social housing but building additional private and mixed tenure units to cross-subsidise the development. The Maiden Lane Estate, to the north of King's Cross, and parts of Somers Town are being transformed. To the east, in Islington, investment in the Bemerton estate has improved the immediate area without radically changing

Figure 9.16: King's Cross station square.

> **Today, Camden council planners are generally very positive about the thoroughness of the planning process, the documentation and the scheme. The balance of certainty versus flexibility has worked.**

its social composition. The southern end of Caledonian Road in Islington is, however, gentrifying rapidly and this is likely to continue. In the absence of dedicated and detailed research, it is not possible to assess the impact of the development on displacement and gentrification or on the social composition of the wider area. The authors hope to assess this in due course.

CONCLUSIONS

The achievement of a planning consent was just the start of the process for Argent. The complexities of coordinating the interchange, removing easements and dealing with other statutory bodies have only been touched upon in this chapter and could be areas of study in their own right. On top of all of this, the development still had to be built.

The scheme had been designed to be sufficiently robust to cope with at least two business cycles, with the flexibility to adapt to changing technological requirements and market conditions. It passed both tests, but by the skin of its teeth. The flexibility afforded by the hybrid planning permission allowed works to be re-phased to deal with very difficult market conditions. Elements such as the university and the affordable and student housing made the scheme more robust by picking up alternative funding streams. The scheme is likely to be extremely profitable in the longer run, but at the beginning was right on the margin. This underlines the virtual impossibility of judging the right amount of affordable housing or the size of the section 106 benefits package in such a scheme. KCCP's use of hoardings, art installations, events and temporary uses has animated King's Cross and created an identifiable location during a period when it is still a substantial building site.

Today, Camden council planners are generally very positive about the thoroughness of the planning process, the documentation and the development. The balance of certainty versus flexibility has worked. There have been teething difficulties, including the definition of what constitutes a unit of student housing and the over-provision of car parking, but these are probably inevitable given the complexity of the scheme. So, too, are the relatively minor changes to the scheme. The flexibility built into the consents and into aspects of the section 106 agreement has allowed it to be built, and there is no evidence that the KCCP has abused this latitude.[28] The scheme always depended on openness and trust, and this has been maintained by both sides.

10. CONCLUSIONS

This book has explored the political forces and other dynamics that drive urban change, through reference to the development of King's Cross. These dynamics are complex, often irrational and unpredictable, and are difficult to accommodate within the strictures of urban planning systems. Yet despite the apparent chaos, the planning system did manage to shape a scheme that is actually being built and is largely in accordance with the original planning consent, in defiance of turbulent economic conditions.

This chapter has a number of aims. First, it seeks to assess whether and to what extent the emerging scheme is successful. In the absence of alternative criteria, it reviews international interest in the scheme and the relatively little market analysis that exists. It also assesses the scheme's success against Camden council's original objectives and those of the developer, Argent. Second (to the extent that it can be viewed as successful), it seeks to identify those factors of the planning and development process that contributed to its success and any lessons that might be taken from these. Finally, it reviews some of the recent changes that have occurred in the UK planning system and associated government programmes in order to evaluate whether such a scheme would be possible under current conditions.

EVALUATING THE SUCCESS OF THE KING'S CROSS DEVELOPMENT

It is only possible to make a tentative assessment of the success of the King's Cross scheme while it is still under construction.[1] However, in August 2015 Jones Lang LaSalle carried out an assessment for British Land of how various sectors of the property industry viewed major regeneration schemes happening in London. King's Cross came top overall in terms of transport connectivity, attractiveness and atmosphere. Against all criteria the industry viewed it as London's best new office location.[2] The 'wordle' from the report illustrating perceptions is shown in Figure 10.1. While quantifying the success of the scheme may be difficult, there are certain criteria against which it can be judged. These are Camden's policy objectives, Argent's development objectives and how the industry views the scheme, both nationally and internationally. By examining how the King's Cross development measures up to these criteria, we can gauge a tentative measure of its success.

Camden's policy objectives

Camden council had clear objectives for the scheme to address the imbalance of opportunity in the immediate neighbourhood of King's Cross. The council wanted affordable housing,

Figure 10.1: Occupier and property agent's perceptions of King's Cross as illustrated in a 'wordle'.

local facilities, employment opportunities and a place that seamlessly merged with its surroundings. Both Camden and English Heritage wanted to see the historic fabric of the site retained and embedded sensitively in a new neighbourhood. This has been largely achieved. On a more basic level, councillors wanted a development that had the wide support of the local communities and one that they could personally be proud of.

Many of these objectives have been achieved and in interviews, councillors and officers working in the council today were positive. There is a sense that Argent has delivered on its promises and that a genuine partnership exists between the council and the King's Cross Central Limited Partnership. Aspects of the scheme, such as the University of the Arts London, were not part of the original objectives, but it is seen as making a major contribution to the life of the area. Despite the failure to overcome the physical barriers around the site, there is evidence that King's Cross is not viewed as a hostile corporate no-go area. It is becoming 'another piece of London' faster than comparable developments elsewhere.

There is also little doubt that King's Cross has been a commercial success (which was always part of Camden council's objectives), but it is too early to assess whether it has really addressed the needs of local people. It would be an interesting case study to track the long-term impact of the development on the life chances of members of the local community in terms of health, education and employment against any displacement impacts due to rising land values.

Argent's development objectives
From Argent's perspectives, the scheme is proving a phenomenal success. Despite incorporating a higher percentage of affordable housing than was anticipated in its initial business plan, commercial rents are considerably higher than anticipated and businesses are eager to locate there. This is no accident, but the result of a well thought out strategy that includes the management of the site and the selection of tenants. As a company, Argent is justifiably proud of what it has achieved and King's Cross has proved to be a very convincing calling card to attract other major development contracts.

National and international interest
Alongside the Olympic Park, King's Cross is now on the standard London tour for students and city and government delegations, especially from other European cities and Asia. The World Bank has identified four main aspects of the King's Cross scheme that have wider applicability:[3]

1 Well connected transport hubs, when combined with high quality public space can generate major market value.
2 Public/private partnerships are an effective instrument for funding such infrastructure and property developments which require a wide range of skills and the ability to secure long-term funding.
3 Genuine community engagement and consultation can achieve better results and ensure that there is local buy-in to proposals.
4 Development proposals of this nature require a long-term commitment and sufficient flexibility to be able to respond to changing market conditions and requirements.

Is it a success so far?

The King's Cross scheme is genuinely mixed use in a way that earlier London commercial developments such as Broadgate and Canary Wharf were not (Figure 10.2). The market clearly views it positively; rents are rising steadily (Figure 10.3) and buildings are being let. The strategy of up-front investment in key infrastructure and the public realm has established a clear, identifiable (and marketable) place and brand. The early occupation of the Granary Building by the University of the Arts London has established an active public centre in the site, and this has been supported by early provision of restaurants and bars, and an arts and events programme. As a consequence, headline rents are over double those that were predicted when planning approval was granted, despite the intervening property crash.

Judging by the largely complimentary reports in newspapers, property and architecture magazines, and by the number of visitors to the site, the emerging development is becoming a popular destination. It is still too early to assess the public reaction, but from observation, people from surrounding neighbourhoods are using the site. The canal steps are popular and children are playing in the fountains (Figure 10.4).

Figure 10.2: King's Cross mixed uses in comparison to other developments.

Figure 10.3: Comparative office values in Central London.

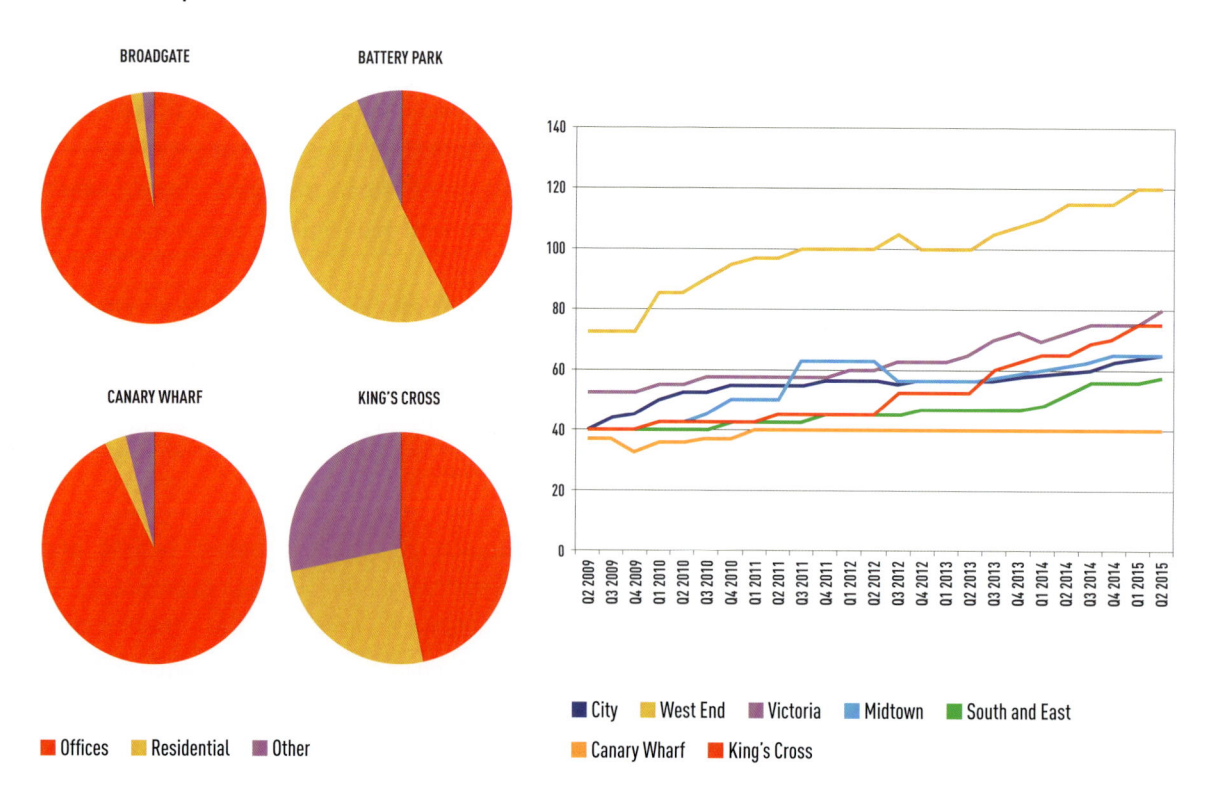

> **While aspects of the planning and development process could inform schemes elsewhere, the circumstances could not be replicated and it would be impossible to turn the King's Cross process into a manual, design code or quality system for other schemes.**

The management regime is encouraging rather than controlling this.

Changes in the London economy towards creative industries, and the relocation of the University of the Arts London, mean that King's Cross is probably a more varied, vibrant and interesting place than was envisaged at the start of the process. Inevitably, the development will deviate from the original plan in response to market conditions, and small-scale changes will occur to buildings and spaces as dictated by innovations in technology, social taste, transport and environmental considerations. By the 2030s it will require a certain amount of retrofitting, renewal and adaptation. In time, parts will be redeveloped and renewed. The real test will be whether it adapts, consolidates, maintains value and achieves long-term success similar to London's 'great estates'.

LESSONS FROM THE KING'S CROSS DEVELOPMENT

If the planning system can work given the right conditions, what are these conditions and are they replicable in other developments in the UK and beyond? It does need to be said from the start that King's Cross was a bespoke development scheme, and very much a product of a particular period in London's development. While aspects of the planning and development process could inform schemes elsewhere, the circumstances could not be replicated and it would be impossible to turn the King's Cross process into a manual, design code or quality system for other schemes. Each new development scheme needs to find its own pathway. There are some lessons, though, that might be adapted and used in other complex development schemes.

The role of central government

Various government administrations played key roles behind the scenes in relation to King's Cross.

- Without the earlier government decision to retain the non-operational land holdings of British Railways on privatisation (in contrast to the privatisation of the Post Office), and the subsequent decision to put these into the public/private partnership, a very different scheme might have emerged. The government also held its nerve and decided not to sell the railway lands when the Channel Tunnel Rail Link (CTRL) deficit emerged.

- When London's successful Olympic Games bid created pressing deadlines for the completion of the various rail infrastructure projects at King's Cross, the government stepped in, provided the funding and appointed a project sponsor and drew up the tripartite agreement to coordinate works.

However, none of the investment plans for the underground station at King's Cross St Pancras had considered the detailed design implications for development over the station. In retrospect, therefore, the new King's Cross concourse is a triumph of architectural ingenuity rather than central coordination. Infrastructure decisions had also been made without a detailed consideration of their impact on the future development of the railway lands. The construction of a high-level embankment into St Pancras (rather than a viaduct with through routes) limited options for connecting the site to its adjacent communities, particularly Somers Town to the west.

The financial model
The approach taken by the landowners set many of the conditions that enabled King's Cross to succeed:

■ The decision not to seek outright financial bids for the site meant that the landowners were able to give more weight to criteria around deliverability.

■ The use of a formula to value the land in the future meant that neither the landowners nor the developer were left chasing unrealistic expectations set by too high a land price. Government procurement practice is becoming increasingly complex and risk averse, with too much emphasis on financial considerations. Had the King's Cross site been tendered today by a government agency where financial criteria dominate the selection process, it is highly unlikely that Argent would have won.

■ The model of creating an entire mixed-use estate under long-term ownership rather than 'develop and dispose' building by building, set the conditions to produce a place of high and lasting quality. For the long-term owner of an estate, the provision of high quality open space is as important as it is to the public. A long-term commitment to own and manage a site also reduces the risk profile. The developer is not tied into a strategy of hitting the market near its peak, but can benefit from long-term appreciation in values. This leads to the important, but counter-intuitive conclusion that large-scale multi-phased regeneration schemes can actually be less risky than a series of ready-to-go buildings.[4] A long-term model requires long-term thinking. Had the development been carried out by a publicly limited company, the board would probably have put the short term interests of its shareholders first.

■ As a single estate rather than a collection of individual developments, control over its build out has never been relinquished.

■ Finally, the decision to seek a development partner for the whole site and to set up a joint delivery vehicle also played to the strengths of both parties. The landowners might alternatively have sought planning consent for all or part of the site before disposing of parcels of land for development. This model is being applied on the site of the London Olympics. Here a public development corporation has commissioned a masterplan and is bringing forward development on individual plots. As a rule, public development bodies do not have sufficient commercial expertise to understand the key relationship between a masterplan and the optimisation of land values. It will be interesting to see which model ultimately produces the best piece of city and the best financial return.

Local politics

The way in which the planning system operated in Camden was a product of its political history. Every borough has political agendas that go back a long way, are parochial, not always logical, and are often hidden. Early campaigns against insensitive development proposals had left a legacy of suspicion among some Camden councillors and community activists. This created tensions within council politics and it was always uncertain whether decision-makers in committee would follow the policies set by the leadership. The King's Cross experience challenges any notion that planning can be divorced from the political process.

- Investing time in researching the local political context can pay dividends. Public relations agencies are no substitute for personal commitment from the landowner and developer.
- As the majority of Camden councillors had relatively little interest in King's Cross at the start of negotiations, support had to be built and the complex planning issues had to be reinterpreted in terms relevant to politicians. This demonstrates the value, in an overtly political context, of reframing technical problems into more compelling, everyday propositions. While plans are necessary, narratives can be more effective in establishing buy in to ideas and concepts. The propositions that were used to frame the development gained the attention of councillors and established broad objectives that were then translated into Camden council's policy agenda. The process of convergence allowed time for the concepts to mature and become embedded within the organisation.
- The work by London and Continental Railways (LCR), before Argent's appointment, provided an invaluable foundation for cooperation with the Council and other stakeholders such as English Heritage. It established significant political capital and goodwill that facilitated the planning negotiations.
- Complex projects also need individuals, often politicians, who are willing to act as their champion and to take responsibility for managing the political interface. Without their intervention at King's Cross, the scheme is unlikely to have received planning consent.
- Having set a policy direction, the council leadership gave officers considerable freedom to ensure it was implemented. This is rare in councils. This empowerment was essential to the credibility of Camden's council's team at the negotiating table. It also allowed negotiations to proceed in a structured manner without being deflected by short-term political agendas. It enabled lateral thinking and problem-solving at critical times. An unexpected outcome of the independence granted to Camden officers was that when the council changed political control, the King's Cross scheme was not tainted as a politically driven project.
- Both negotiating teams recognised the inherently political nature of planning, and were politically astute. Argent understood that Camden council had to deliver on key agendas,

especially affordable housing, and that the interests of external stakeholders had to be respected.

- Internal political management was essential in taking the scheme through Camden's decision-making process. This had the approval of the leadership and was supported by key champions among the politicians.

There are areas where the political process within Camden council broke down and this could have undermined the entire process. The council leadership was reluctant to address problems within its development control subcommittee and this put officers dangerously close to the fine line between implementing council policy and interfering in the political process. To negotiate with any credibility, officers need to be sure that their committee will support their recommendations, and must adapt their approach to shifts in political direction. The refusal of members of the development control subcommittee to accept any pre-application briefing or debate on the development was potentially disastrous. Times have moved on since then. Government guidance and accepted practice mean that such bizarre circumstances will be increasingly rare.

The negotiation process

The negotiation process built towards agreement rather than away from an initial proposal. Its rules were: discuss, propose, consult, evaluate, agree, abide by agreements and move on. While the negotiating teams had not been schooled in the theory, they had the benefit of long experience, and it helped that both wanted to reach an agreement as long as this did not undermine their basic starting principles.

> **A key feature of the negotiations was the ability of each side to generate creative solutions to resolve deadlock.**

- By consulting from first principles, each side could learn, and shift positions towards compromise without retrenching.
- The negotiating teams were similarly structured, with strategic and technical strengths, and they had a similar style of operation. They avoiding haggling, brinksmanship and bluffing.
- Considerable store was placed on reasonable behaviour and rational argument.
- A key feature of the negotiations was the ability of each side to generate creative solutions to resolve deadlock, and to trust each other sufficiently to explore alternative options without prejudice.
- The mutual desire to avoid a public inquiry provided a keen focus in moments of deadlock.
- By adopting a process-driven, rather than an adversarial, approach to negotiations, the conditions for a genuine partnership were built at King's Cross. The negotiation process was based on partnership at many levels. Partnership working is a state of mind, about a willingness to find shared goals, and to be prepared to explore shared approaches that might result in richer outcomes. Like any relationship, a partnership has to be built and nurtured, which requires trust and shared values.

Both sides engaged, consulted, listened and where possible acted to represent others' interests, but they followed deliberate strategies to limit the direct involvement of other stakeholders at the negotiating table. While this may not follow best practice in negotiation, it was effective. The tactic to lock Islington into Camden's approach and position removed a major external uncertainty. Argent's early resolution to work constructively with English Heritage allowed a considered debate to take place regarding the preservation of the site's historic buildings. The management of all these relationships effectively minimised risk in the planning process.

The planning process
That the King's Cross development would be commercial, dense, and mixed use was implicit in the CTRL funding, and in the parameters already set by national and regional policy. Camden council had no scope to propose alternative development scenarios, nor was there the political desire to do so. There was a simple choice: work to get the best possible scheme within these constraints, or face quixotic opposition.

- Even in the year 2001, few councils could have resourced the negotiations as Camden did. Its chief executive recognised that up-front investment in the planning team would result in a better development that would bring significant long-term investment into the borough.[5]
- Argent's decision to separate the planning application for the Islington 'Triangle' site removed a major external uncertainty.
- The process of negotiating from principles rather than hard-set plans meant that the adversarial nature of the planning system was largely bypassed. The planners were free to engage in a more constructive debate and were thereby liberated to some extent from their traditional reactive role.
- The hybrid application developed for King's Cross shows that there is latitude in the planning system despite its apparent inflexibility. This solution provided the flexibility Argent needed to respond to changes in the property cycles and it gave Camden council the degree of certainty that it required. It was legal and practicable, and has since provided a useful template for similar developments elsewhere.
- Camden council went to great lengths to ensure that its policy framework, particularly the requirement on affordable housing, was aligned with its emerging objectives for the scheme. The alignment of the Camden Unitary Development Plan to the emerging London Plan removed any policy grounds for mayoral intervention. This minimised the risk of an appeal and subsequent decision by a public inquiry.
- The judicial review had been anticipated and its risks were controlled successfully through meticulous legal checks on documents and procedures.

Ultimately, however, planning can control but cannot mandate, and it is ill equipped to move outside its role in allocating land uses. For instance, it cannot dictate the day-to-day management of place, and the long debate over Camden council's right to adopt the public realm reflects the inability of planning to really make places. Nor can planning ever be a fair process. Argent's Robert Evans admits there is some truth in community criticism that it can be 'a one way cheque that binds the council, but not the developer, who can always come back with amendments and changes'.[6] The ability of planners to negotiate effectively on such complex development schemes also remains severely constrained by their lack of expertise in property and construction finance. Camden was always at a disadvantage in this respect. Current changes to local government finance and the planning system mean that far from levelling the 'playing field' for such negotiations, planners face an ever-steeper uphill struggle.

Masterplanning
The masterplan provided a framework for discussion on obtaining the legal consents; it determined the quantum of development (rather than any preconceived, fixed or unrealistic figure), and through the masterplan, tensions and anomalies in the social, commercial and financial agendas could be brought together and resolved.

■ Flexibility was built into the masterplan in terms of the street network and the arrangement of building plots. It was capable of being built in different configurations and sequences. This allowed Argent to be opportunistic and creative during a very depressed period in the market. If inflexible geometries or excessive building or plot sizes had underpinned the masterplan and required single-phase implementation, it is unlikely that the scheme would have been built.

■ Commissioning two masterplanners and a landscape practice avoided stylistic bias and generated healthy creative tension.

■ Robust masterplans with lasting social and economic value cannot be produced quickly. The time that was allowed for challenge and debate led to a better masterplan. Even two years into its design, the framework was still evolving in response to a deeper understanding of the site and its context.

Historic buildings
The importance of city-building that incorporates the historic fabric is gaining acceptance beyond the UK and Europe in other parts of the world, including China. Historic buildings can be seen as a barrier to development but in fact they act as a creative challenge to designers and developers to produce richer and more complex pieces of city.

■ Although there was a presumption to retain the heritage at King's Cross, it was the decision to embed and reuse it that was significant. The heritage buildings are the basic building blocks of the scheme; they not only provide the unique character of King's Cross, but were integral to the strategy of creating commercial value.

■ English Heritage brought both a scholarly approach and technical expertise to the debate. Its officers understood the development constraints and could relate these to difficult questions over the preservation and reuse of historic buildings. English Heritage was pragmatic enough to support significant change while ensuring that it did not damage the intrinsic character of the area and its buildings.

Architecture
One of Argent's guiding principles was never to relinquish control over the appointment of architects. Within the framework provided by

the masterplan, they commissioned a range of good architectural practices to design individual buildings. The result was never meant to be radical architecture but to build an enduring piece of city, London's next 'great estate'. In support of this approach, Rowan Moore, architecture critic of the Observer, suggests that extravagant new architecture would have been inappropriate in the presence of powerful historic structures like the stations and the Granary, and that prioritising the design of open spaces that set off these historic structures, rather than individual buildings, was the right approach.[7]

Consultations

The community consultation processes were extensive and in many respects exemplary.

- They contributed significantly to the knowledge base for the scheme, and did lead to specific changes in the development, albeit on the margins.
- They strengthened Camden council's negotiating hand by providing a clear rationale for the debate on local issues.
- They changed Argent's internal culture, a factor that influenced the community benefits package and had a subtle influence on the company's approach to estate management in the long term.

That said, it is clear that the consultation process (when related to Arnstein's Ladder, see Chapter 7), lay somewhere between consultation and involvement rather than a genuine partnership where stakeholders are enabled to negotiate and engage in trade-offs with the decision-makers. Within the fluid world of fragmented governance, rapid changes in political priorities and single-issue politics, stakeholder management is key to minimising risk. The ideal of genuine consensus-building through multi-party negotiation is unachievable in the face of deep ideological differences where the policy framework (and the underlying power structures) have already constrained the parameters of the debate. Sometimes conflicting objectives cannot be reconciled and political choices have to be made. Ultimately, the pre-application consultations did nothing to speed up the planning process. Ironically, they gave opposition groups the time to gather force.

Trust

A key lesson from this case study is that individuals make places through engaging in a political process. Personal relationships do not necessarily fit comfortably within academic research, but they are the building blocks of city-making. The subject of trust comes up constantly in the narrative: trust between officers and councillors, between the landowners, and between the negotiating teams.

- This trust, or social capital, allowed informal off-the-record problem-solving at crucial junctures.
- It also allowed deals to be made, from that agreed between LCR and Exel on the value of the land, to the signing-off of each step in the negotiation process.
- The process allowed sufficient time for trust to be built. It was not blind trust, but it was the product of considerable up-front investment in time and effort.

> **The King's Cross development is a product of its time and outcomes would have been very different had economic conditions and political priorities been different.**

Timing and luck

At times the process also involved a considerable amount of luck.

- London's successful Olympic Games bid unlocked the finance to restart the transport infrastructure.
- The judicial review delayed the scheme, but also meant that Argent was not dangerously exposed financially or contractually at the height of the financial crisis.
- The University of the Arts London managed, against the odds, to extend its borrowing.
- Having survived the financial crisis, Argent's first commercial buildings met a rising market.

Argent made its own luck by taking sizeable risks and seizing opportunities when they arose. As Roger Madelin commented, 'in the past, commentators in the property sector used to say that the three important factors in successful property development were, "location, location and location". The reality is more "timing, timing and timing".'[8]

IMPLICATIONS OF RECENT CHANGES TO PLANNING AND FUNDING REGIMES

The King's Cross development is a product of its time and outcomes would have been very different had economic conditions and political priorities been different. The period between 2000 and 2007 was also one of sustained boom and optimism in the London economy. In such conditions it is far easier to take a more enlightened approach to the creation of mixed communities, the provision of affordable housing and the design of high quality buildings and public spaces. To the extent that the scheme was driven by key individuals who came together at a unique juncture, it is clearly not replicable. Those involved entered into what was in many ways a unique partnership that was driven by a shared vision, a desire to make the scheme happen and a willingness to work in an open and trusting way.

A number of recent and proposed changes by the present government affecting housing and planning policies, and the funding arrangements for affordable housing, would make the construction of a truly mixed community with high levels of affordable housing such as King's Cross almost impossible today. The government housing grant for Resident Social Landlords to build affordable homes has been steadily eroded. The current four-year settlement is worth £4.5 billion, and represents a 60 per cent reduction on the previous allocation (2008–11). The grant works out on average at just £20,000 per home or 14 per cent of its cost. The spending review in June 2015 announced further reductions in housing association funding. As well as cutting the level of investment, the type of home funded was also changed in 2010

10: CONCLUSIONS

with the ending of capital subsidy for forms of housing with lower rents (social rent) which cost more in up-front subsidy.[9]

On top of this, the government has pledged to scrap the rules that require property developers to build affordable homes for rent, instead favouring the provision of affordable homes for purchase. In 2011 the new National Planning Framework scrapped the threshold that forced private developments of 15 properties or more to contain some affordable rental housing.[10]

Existing planning agreements to provide affordable housing for rent are also being steadily eroded. The Growth and Infrastructure Act 2013 introduced a new appeal procedure for the review of planning obligations on planning permissions that relate to the provision of affordable housing.[11] The changes require a council to assess the viability arguments, and renegotiate previously agreed affordable housing levels in a section 106 agreement or face an appeal. Developers now have the ability to fast-track a challenge against a section 106 agreement if it can show that building the low-cost homes makes a scheme unviable. It is estimated that in over five years more than 2,300 affordable homes have been lost from housing schemes across the UK.[12]

The Housing and Planning Bill[13] aims to extend the right to buy to housing association properties. This means housing association properties can be bought at a discount by their tenants.[14] The discount will be financed by the forced sale by local authorities of their most valuable properties. Both moves will reduce the amount of affordable housing for rent, and in Central London will accelerate the displacement of those on the lowest incomes. It is anticipated that many housing associations will increasingly build for open market sale and rent.

The Housing and Planning Bill also sets out plans to order councils to deal with planning applications much more quickly. The Bill provides greater powers to the mayor of London on the types of planning applications that can be called in for the mayor's determination, or where the mayor can direct a local authority to refuse a scheme. The balance in London has shifted significantly away from boroughs to the Greater London Authority (GLA). It is unlikely that Camden council would have been allowed the same freedom on the King's Cross scheme in today's context. In addition, the housing targets that are now allocated by the GLA to opportunity areas have not only increased density exponentially, but have moved the focus of local planning away from the creation of sustainable places towards hitting housing targets.

The section 106 agreement has largely been superseded by the Community Infrastructure Levy (CIL). If this had been in place at the time of the King's Cross planning application, it is quite possible that the scheme would not have been viable. CIL is paid in advance and is calculated on a simple formula against the floor space of the scheme. Under current arrangements the CIL would have been approximately £80 million.[15] On this basis there would have been little scope for the affordable housing or community benefits that contribute towards making the scheme a sustainable community and a real piece of city. It makes little sense to marry a highly discretionary planning system with fixed development tariffs that export the community benefits away from the site in question. CIL is, in this respect, a form of taxation.

POSTSCRIPT

In early 2016, two significant events occurred that may have a bearing on the future of King's Cross. First, the government sold its 36.5 per cent stake (held by LCR, a state-owned company) for £371 million to an Australian pension fund, AustralianSuper.[16] This represents the end of LCR's 20-year involvement in the project. The second was the announcement that Roger Madelin was stepping down as Argent's chief executive to join British Land and take control of its Canada Water development, a major mixed-use scheme in south-east London. Coming together, these announcements represent the end of a particular era in the history of King's Cross.

The question now is whether the particular approach that LCR and Argent, under Madelin, brought to King's Cross will continue. Is the culture of the scheme so well established that it will endure, or is King's Cross destined to become just another development? These are questions over which the planning system will have little influence.

Figure 10.4: Granary Square – children playing in fountains.

11.
APPENDICES

APPENDIX 1: SUMMARY OF THE SECTION 106 AGREEMENT

Planning obligations may be used to secure the provision of, or contributions towards, a number of social and regenerative benefits that are in accordance with Circular 1/97 and the councils' Unitary Development Plan, and are:
- necessary
- relevant to planning
- directly relate to the proposed development
- fairly, and reasonably relate in scale and kind to the proposed development
- reasonable in all other respects.

The King's Cross section 106 agreement[1] was over 250 pages long and contained detailed clauses on payment schedules, lease arrangements, conditional requirements and operational requirements for uses, services and facilities. This Appendix therefore represents a highly simplified summary of the main provisions.

Employment and training
- Provision and operation of a construction training centre
- Provision of a skills and recruitment centre, plus operating costs
- Support to a community enterprise credit union and community development finance initiatives offered to communities
- Provision of a range of space suitable for small businesses and voluntary organisations (unsubsidised)
- Local business support and a local purchasing strategy
- Establishment of a business volunteering scheme

Community facilities
- Establishment of a social and community fund – grants or loans to projects which would mitigate the effects of the development and/or enhance its benefits
- Provision of community meeting facilities
- Implementing community safety measures including CCTV

Education
- Secondary education – payment to assist with the council's programme of expansion and or upgrading of local secondary schools
- Provision of a pre-school children's centre
- Provision of a two-form entry primary school
- Establishment of an exploratory centre – a temporary centre for visitors to explore issues of education, sustainability and building, to facilitate links between schools, higher education and employers
- Provision of a floating classroom

Leisure
- Provision of a public indoor sports facility
- Provision of high quality local area for play
- Provision of a public health and fitness facility

Health
- Provision of a primary healthcare centre
- Provision of a primary healthcare walk-in centre

APPENDIX 1: SUMMARY OF THE SECTION 106 AGREEMENT

Public realm areas and development estate realm areas
- Agreement of the principles for adoption, delivery, maintenance and management of public realm
- Funding of adjacent street improvements
- Funding of improvements to adjacent/local open spaces
- Funding of a programme of public art within the public realm areas
- Financial support to Camley Street natural park
- Provision of a pedestrian bridge – Wharfdale Road to the Boulevard
- Funding for canal enhancements

Support for implementation panels

Access and inclusivity clauses

Environmental sustainability requirements

Gasholder guide frames
- Requirements for dismantling, refurbishment and re-erection

Code of construction practice

Transport
- Financial contributions to establishment of controlled parking zones in Camden and Islington
- Establishment of various incentives for sustainable travel
- Provision of a bicycle storage facility
- Payments for improvements to bus services
- Financial contribution to reopening Maiden Lane station

Land use details on nightclubs and casinos, retail, nursing homes, housing and affordable housing, estate management charges, etc

APPENDIX 2: DEVELOPMENT DATA AND FINANCIAL INFORMATION

Table 1: Land uses (% of site) at King's Cross Central[1]	
Buildings	53%
Streets/surface parking	15%
Landscaping/open space	32%
Total	100%

Table 2: Land uses (sq ft) at King's Cross Central[2]	
Office	3.4 million sq ft (316,000 sq m)
Retail	500,000 sq ft (46,451 sq m)
Hotel (Great Northern Hotel)	91 rooms (30,000 sq ft / 2,787 sq m)
Residential	2,000 units
	13 residential developments
	1,309 single-family units
	391 three- to four-bedroom units
	250 affordable homes for rent
Open space	26 acres (10.52 hectares)
Parking	865 spaces (800 in a car park, 65 on the street)
Total gross building area planned	6 million sq ft (557,418 sq m)
Total site area	67 acres (27 hectares)

Table 3: Comparative plot ratios – King's Cross and other developments[3]			
Development	Site area	Gross external floor area (sq m)	Plot ratio
Broadgate	8.6	359,200	4.2
Canary Wharf	34.8	1,626,800	4.7
Brindleyplace	6.9	146,600	2.1
Potsdamer Platz	10.4	357,400	3.4
Battery Park City	37.0	1,814,300	4.9
Euralille	30.5	268,500	0.9
Covent Garden	8.0	199,500	2.5
Mayfair	33.5	824,900	2.5
KX South	6.5	272,300	4.2
KX Heritage	7.7	105,700	1.4
KX North	11.5	415,300	3.6
KX Overall	25.7	793,300	3.1

APPENDIX 2: DEVELOPMENT DATA AND FINANCIAL INFORMATION

Table 4: Comparative site coverage and building heights – King's Cross and other developments[4]

Development	Site area	Footprint of building	Site coverage	Mean number of storeys
Broadgate	8.6	5.1	60%	8.6
Canary Wharf	34.8	12.1	35%	19.0
Brindleyplace	6.9	3.5	51%	5.9
Potsdamer Platz	10.4	5.2	50%	11.3
Battery Park City	37.0	14.3	39%	16.5
Euralille	30.5	12.1	40%	4.2
Covent Garden	8.0	5.3	67%	4.6
Mayfair	33.5	14.1	42%	5.7
KX South	6.5	2.8	43%	9.1
KX Heritage	7.7	3.3	43%	2.7
KX North	11.5	5.4	47%	12.1
KX Overall	25.7	11.5	45%	8.9

Table 5: Comparative uses – King's Cross and other developments[5]

Development	Offices	Education	Residential	Hotels	Retail	Leisure/Other
Broadgate	97%	0%	0%	0%	2%	2%
Canary Wharf	93%	0%	3%	1%	2%	1%
Brindleyplace	70%	0%	9%	5%	5%	11%
Potsdamer Platz	50%	0%	19%	8%	11%	12%
Battery Park City	42%	3%	51%	1%	2%	1%
Euralille	26%	4%	16%	4%	34%	15%
Covent Garden	55%	0%	7%	0%	18%	20%
Mayfair	49%	0%	32%	14%	4%	1%
KX South	81%	1%	1%	2%	5%	10%
KX Heritage	10%	44%	16%	0%	25%	5%
KX North	34%	7%	44%	2%	3%	11%
KX Overall	47%	10%	25%	2%	7%	10%

Table 6: Financial information	
Ownership %	
Argent LLP	50.0%
LCR	36.5%
DHL (Excel)	13.5%
Senior debt package for initial phases	
Barclays Bank	Revolving credit and term facility of £75 million
Hypothekenbank Frankfurt AG	Investment loan
Deutsche Postbank and HSBC	Development loan facilities totalling £104 million
Public funding for initial phases	
U.K. Homes and Communities Agency	£42 million
Investment partner: Hermes Real Estate on behalf of BT Pension Scheme	
Infrastructure investment 2009–14	£250 million
Construction contract University of the Arts London	£100 million
Granary Building development costs	£200 million
Total development cost expected at completion	£3 billion

NOTES

1: Introduction

1   Dark Matter (noun): a hypothetical form of matter invisible to electromagnetic radiation postulated to account for gravitational forces observed in the universe. http://dictionary.reference.com/browse/dark-matter (accessed 8 October 2015).

2   Planck Mission Full Results Confirm Canonical Cosmology Model   http://darkmatterdarkenergy.com/2015/03/07/planck-mission-full-results-confirm-canonical-cosmology-model/ (accessed 28 October 2015).

2: The planning and development process

1   Design for London (2006–2013) was the mayor of London's architecture studio. The diagram was produced for the exhibition 'London Open City', Somerset House, 20 June–20 July 2008.

2   Town and Country Planning Act, 1947.

3   Department for Communities and Local Government, Plain English Guide to the Planning System, January 2015. https://www.gov.uk/government/uploads/system/uploads/attachment_data/file/391694/Plain_English_guide_to_the_planning_system.pdf

4   Since 2011 the mayor also has powers to direct approval.

5   The main legislation that sets out the process for the preparation of local plans can be found in Part 2 of the Planning and Compulsory Purchase Act 2004 as amended and The Town and Country Planning (Local Planning) (England) Regulations 2012 as amended.

6   David Hickey, 'Cameron labels planning official "enemies of enterprise"', Planning, 7 March 2011. http://www.planningresource.co.uk/article/1058481/cameron-labels-planning-officials-enemies-enterprise (accessed 8 October 2015).

7   Community Infrastructure Levy. http://www.planningportal.gov.uk/planning/applications/howtoapply/whattosubmit/cil (accessed 12 November 2015).

8   The deregulation of the financial markets in 1986.

9   Through its workplace programme, Newham council has placed 30,000 local residents into jobs as part of the large scale regeneration happening in the borough. Interview with Sir Robin Wales, 18 February 2016.

10   Acronym 'not in my back yard'.

11   Interview with Alison Lowton, 9 February 2015.

3: History and development context

1   John Rocque, An Exact Survey of the Citys of London, Westminster, ye Borough of Southwark, and the Country near Ten Miles round, 1769. http://www.bl.uk/onlinegallery/onlineex/crace/a/007zzz000000019u00018000.html.() (accessed 8 October 2015).

2   Charles Booth Online Archive, Maps Descriptive of London Poverty. http://booth.lse.ac.uk/static/a/4.html (accessed 1 October 2015).

3   John R. Kellett, The Impact of the Railways on the Victorian City (London and Henley: Routledge and Kegan Paul 1979), pp244–262.

4   Urban Initiatives, 'Regent Quarter, King's Cross, London' rudi.net. http://www.rudi.net/node/21006() (accessed 8 October 2015).

5   Stock Conversion's holdings around Balfe Street were subsequently acquired by P&O Developments, and their first plan in 2000 involved the demolition of many buildings. Again it attracted intense opposition from local residents and community groups as well as English Heritage, and in February 2001 the plans were rejected by Islington council. P&O, shocked at the strength of local opposition to its piecemeal approach, went back to the drawing board. The new scheme was considerably more sympathetic. It retained the historic buildings alongside modern structures of a similar scale built around a series of internal courtyards. The scheme, Regent Quarter, received planning permission in December 2001.

6   Letter from LRC to director of British Rail property board, 28 September 1987.

7   For further information on these campaigns see: Angela Inglis, King's Cross: A Sense of Place (Matador Publishing Ltd, September 2012); and Michael Edwards, 'King's Cross: Renaissance for Whom?' in Urban Design, and the British Urban Renaissance, ed. J. Punter (London: Routledge, 2009), pp189–205.

8   It is interesting to compare this to present policies in the London Plan, which expect 650–1100 hra, or up to 10 times this density.

9   Letter from LRC to director of British Rail property board, 28 September 1987.

10   Letter from LRC to director of British Rail property board, 28 September 1987.

11   See: http://coinstreet.org/

12   London Borough of Camden, King's Cross Central, Officer's Report, 2006, paras 1.5.2–1.5.16. The decision was finally confirmed in January 1994 by transport minister, John

MacGregor, in a statement to Parliament.

13 Roger Madelin, interview, 27 September 2015.

14 Michael Parkes, King's Cross Railway Lands: Towards a People's Plan (London: KXRLG, 1991); Michael Parkes, 'Community Participation and Urban Regeneration: King's Cross and the Elephant and Castle', in The Contested Metropolis: Six Cities at the Beginning of the 21st Century, ed. Raffaele Paloscia (Basel: Birkhäuser Verlag, 2004).

15 Edwards,'King's Cross', pp189–205. Reproduced by permission of Taylor & Francis Books UK.

16 Additional planning contributions would have been required, which would have had a direct impact on land values. Moreover, the land was substantially owned by the government, which had funded the improvements in the first place. There was therefore no direct windfall to the eventual developers of the site.

17 The Railways Act 1993 provided for the restructuring of the British Railways board (BRB), the public corporation that owned and operated the national railway system and allowed separated parts of the railway to be transferred to the private sector.

18 Given the huge sums required for the engineering works, property receipts were never a key element in the funding package. The site was valued at current use value (about £50 million for land at both King's Cross and Stratford), and LCR's government grant was reduced by that amount. Effectively, this meant that a significant percentage of the uplift in value from any development would accrue to LCR. The development lands overage gave LCR a 20 per cent profit with the remainder then being split 50:50 with the government.

19 LCR was a consortium of various companies including Warburg (now UBS), Virgin (who left early), National Express Group, SNCF, Systra, Halcrow, Arups, Bectel and later London Electricity. Virgin and National Express were to run Eurostar, with Bectel and Halcrow overseeing the railway design and construction.

20 This had design implications for the development of the railway lands. The high-level embankment further isolated the site from its immediate surroundings, in particular the communities to the west in Somers Town.

21 In January 2016, the government announced the sale of its stake in King's Cross to AustralianSuper for £371 million. Financial Times, 28 January 2016.

22 This funding remained blocked until London won the Olympics bid in July 2005 and completion of the station became essential in order to service the Olympics site at Stratford (see Chapter 9). Interviews with Stephen Jordan, June 2015, and Roger Madelin, December 2014.

23 Interview, Stephen Jordan, June 2015.

24 Interviews Stephen Jordan, 24 June 2015, and Roger Mann, January 2015.

25 Interview with Stephen Jordan, June 2015.

26 Two of the firms, Allies and Morrison and Porphyrios Associates, were to be employed subsequently as the King's Cross masterplanners.

27 Interview with Roger Madelin, 28 September 2015.

28 Until 2004, Argent St George is used to refer to the joint company, but where Argent was leading the negotiations, the company is referred to just as Argent.

29 London Communications Agency, press release, Argent St George, 31 March 2000.

30 The Channel Tunnel Rail Link Act was eventually enacted in 1996.

31 Interview with Sir Stuart Lipton, 25 November 2015.

4: Establishing the framework for negotiations

1 The 26.1-hectare development site (figure taken from the planning submission on 28 April 2004) was not exactly a blank sheet of paper. Apart from the canal, gasholders and a set of historic 19th-century buildings, the site contained a number of later buildings and structures. At the time of Argent St George's appointment, it was also occupied by CTRL and LUL construction compounds, a gas company depot, a golf driving range, a go-kart circuit, car storage areas and nightclubs. There were also a number of small businesses operating on short-term licenses agreed with the landowners. Although the Culross and Stanley Buildings had been squatted, these were now empty and there were no people living on the site. (Interview with Roger Madelin, 20 October 2015.)

2 The London Government Act 1963.

3 Nick Wates, The Battle for Tolmers Square (Routledge & Kegan Paul, 1976).

4 Interview with Dr Jane Roberts DBE, Leader of Camden Council (2000–05), 21 September 2015.

5 The official measure of multiple deprivation, which compromises 37 different indicators.

6 'Local Demographic Context', Camden Local Implementation Plan 2005/06 to 2010/1. https://www.camden.gov.uk/ccm/cms-service/stream/asset/?asset_id=572104 (accessed 18 January 2016).

7 Camden Childcare Sufficiency Assessment April 2011 Annexe 1 Camden Demographics. http://www.camden.gov.uk/ccm/content/education/pre-school/camden-childcare-sufficiency-assessment-/ (accessed 13 AprilOctober 2016)

8 LB Camden, Social Inclusion Strategy, August 2003. http://www.camden.gov.uk/ccm/cms-service/stream/asset/?asset_id=630419 (accessed 6 October 2014).

9 Camden Neighbourhood Renewal Strategy Part 1. The Strategy January 2003. www.camden.gov.uk/ccm/cms.../Part%201%20Jan%202003.pdf?asset... (accessed 18 January 2016).

10 ibid.

11 ibid.

12 London Borough of Camden, Our Camden Our Future.

13 ibid.

14 Camden Council's Borough wide Tenancy Strategy, January 2013.

15 Greater London Authority, London Divided, Income Inequality and Poverty in the Capital, November 2002.

16 London Borough of Camden, Our Camden Our Future.

17 Camden Neighbourhood Regeneration Strategy, Part 1, Analysis, January 2003.

18 ibid.

19 ibid.

20 ibid.

21 Letter from Jane Roberts to Steve Bundred, 18 May 2000.

22 Letter from Jane Roberts to Steve Bundred, 17 September 2000.

23 Interview with Theo Blackwell, 2 October 2015. A similar trip was organised to Bilbao in the autumn of 2006 between the same officers and councillor Mike Greene, the executive member for planning under the new Conservative administration. The result was very similar, garnering good working relationships and new political aspirations. On both trips officers and councillors paid their own expenses.

24 See Chapter 6 for definitions of affordable housing.

25 Interview with Roger Madelin, 28 September 2015.

26 Interview with Roger Madelin, 6 November 2015.

27 Argent St George, Principles for a Human City, July 2001.

28 London Borough of Camden, King's Cross – Towards an Integrated City, October 2001.

29 London Borough of Camden, King's Cross – Camden's Vision, June 2002.

30 A planning authority can refuse a development purely on the grounds of architectural design but this is rarely done. It is considered by many planners to be beyond their remit or expertise to argue a case on design grounds.

31 A subsidiary of LCR.

32 See also Rebecca Allison, 'Residents fight to block 24-hour work on Channel link', The Guardian, Monday 12 January 2004. http://www.theguardian.com/uk/2004/jan/12/london.transport (accessed 23 January 2016).

33 Section 2 of the Local Government Act 2000, includes a power to 'do anything' which a local authority considers likely to achieve 'the promotion or improvement of the economic well-being of their area, of the social well-being of their area, or of the environmental well-being of their area'. http://www.legislation.gov.uk/ukpga/2000/22/section/2 (accessed 13 April 2016).

34 Inspectors report, February 2004.

35 In theory the Environmental Agency could also force an inquiry, but in practice its remit over the site was too limited.

36 Interview with Steve Hitchins, 26 January 2016.

37 Interview with Jane Roberts, leader of Camden council 2000–05, 21 September and interview with Roger Madelin, 28 September 2015.

38 Interview with Peter Bishop, 29 September 2015.

39 At the time the mayor's powers were limited to directing that a local planning authority should refuse a planning application, although subsequent powers allow the mayor to intervene and grant planning consent.

40 Interview with Colin Wilson, then principal planning and design officer, now strategic planning manager at the GLA, 17 November 2015.

41 Regional Planning Guidance for the South East, March 2001.

42 Stale Holgersen and Havard Haarstad, 'Class, Community and Communicative Planning: Urban Redevelopment at King's Cross, London,' Antipode vol 41, No 2. (2009):348.

43 KXRLG, 2006, Letter to John Prescott, 29 March. King's Cross Railway Lands Group, p4.

44 Confidential memorandum from Peter Freeman to the Argent St George development team, 28 June 2000.

45 Confidential memorandum from Peter Freeman to the Argent St George development team, 28 June 2000.

46 Interview with Roger Madelin, 5 November 2015.

5: The masterplan

1 Interview with Demetri Porphyrios, 19 January 2015. 'classicism is not a style' (London: Academy Editions, 1982).

2 Camley Street Natural Park, http://www.wildlondon.org.uk/reserves/camley-street-natural-park

3 David Partridge, Introduction to King's Cross Development Seminar, 28 February 2001.

4 Design Charette notes, 28 February/9 March, 2001.

5 ibid.

6 Giambattista Nolli's 1748 plan for Rome uses a figureground representation of buildings and depicts the interior of religious and civic buildings as publicly accessible spaces.

7 Design Charette notes, 28 February/9th March, 2001.

8 ibid.

9 Interview with David Partridge, 2 November 2015.

10 The principle of development on a 'human scale' had been set out in Principles for a Human City. It has also been championed by the Urban Task Force. Towards an Urban Renaissance, chaired by Richard Rogers, June 1999.

11 Meeting between Camden council, Argent St George and the mayor, 28 September 2001.

12 CABE, letter to Argent St George, March 2002.

13 English Heritage, letter to Argent St George, April 2002.

14 Early in 2004 Argent St George presented its outline scheme to the Victorian Society, stressing the sensitivity of its treatment and expressing its view that it hoped that the Victorians would appreciate its proposals. Apparently, a senior member of the Victorian Society retorted with, 'no they wouldn't, the Victorians would have had the balls to tear the whole lot down – that is what made them so great!' Interview with Roger Madelin, 22 October 2015.

15 Interview with Graham Morrison, 13 February 2015.

16 King's Cross Conservation Area Advisory Committee, Respecting the Railwaylands, November 2005.

17 Using the criteria of Planning Policy Guidance 15: Planning and the Historic Environment (1990 to 2010) that their loss was outweighed by the significant benefits of the scheme.

18 This is now a single building occupied by Google.

19 This was in response to Camden council representatives to the meeting.

20 Letter from CABE to Argent St George, August 2002.

21 Now part of AECOM.

22 Interview with David Partridge, 2 November 2015.

23 Tim Clarke, 'Exclusive AJ Interview: Hadid and Schumacher', Architects Journal, 18 September 2014.

24 Rowan Moore, 'All Hail the New King's Cross', The Observer, The New Review, 19 October 2014, p28.

6: The middle game

1 Interview with Bob West 6 June 2015.

2 Interview with Roger Madelin, 5 October 2015.

3 Ibid.

4 Interview with Richard Kirby, King's Cross Principal Planning Case Officer, 22 October 2015.

5 London Borough of Camden, Leader's Briefing Paper, 6 June 2005.

6 Government Office for London (1996) RPG3: Strategic Guidance for London Planning Authorities.

7 It should be noted that the current trend in London under the London Plan is to allocate (extremely high) housing targets to opportunity areas in the expectation that masterplans will have to accommodate them. The impact of this policy on the London skyline and the quality of some of the new neighbourhoods under construction, such as Battersea, Stratford and Blackfriars, is causing growing concern.

8 The idea that socially mixed neighbourhoods are desirable originated in the writings of Jane Jacobs and others. Jane Jacobs, The Death and Life of Great American Cities (New York: Random House, 1961); Colomb, C, 'Urban regeneration and policies of "social mixing" in British cities: a critical assessment', Architecture, City & Environment / Arquitectura, Ciudad y Entorno (17) 223–244, 2011.

9 Planning Policy Guidance 3: Housing (1992-2006), March 2000, since superseded by Department of Communities and Local Government, Delivering Affordable Housing, November 2006.

10 Under models of shared ownership a tenant rents a part share in a property from an RSL and owns the remainder.

11 Interview with Roger Madelin, 6 November 2015.

12 L Cousins, K Dunmore, M Oxley and A Golland, Affordable

Housing in London (London: Greater London Authority, 2001). Commissioned by the Greater London Authority (GLA) from consultants Three Dragons, the report concluded that, assuming the ongoing availability of public subsidy, a 50 per cent affordable housing target was achievable in most 33 London boroughs.

13 In practice, the 50 per cent target has rarely been achieved on the grounds of 'market viability'.

14 London Borough of Camden, Camden Unitary Development Plan, Deposit Draft, Ch. 13, November 2001.

15 In 2004, the Office of the Deputy Prime Minister estimated that Camden had 5,000 overcrowded households. Affordability and the Supply of Housing, Session 2005–06: Select Committee ODPM: Housing, Planning, Local Government and the Regions, memorandum by the London Borough of Camden (AH 93) House of Commons. http://www.publications.parliament.uk/pa/cm200506/cmselect/cmodpm/703/703we110.htm (accessed 18 November 2015).

16 The Joseph Rowntree Foundation is an independent charity working to inspire social change through research, policy and practice. https://www.jrf.org.uk/?gclid=CNyTyreFi8kCFSgXwwodXDgDtA (accessed 11 November 2015).

17 Average child densities in Camden at the time were 35%. Janet Sutherland, Camden Housing, interview 10 November 2015.

18 Interview with Roger Madelin, 6 November 2015.

19 Standard housing letting policy will not allocate a house to a tenant with rent arrears.

20 Interviews with Roger Madelin and Robert Evans, 6 November 2015.

21 The 'hoodie test' was applied to all the streets and spaces in the masterplan. Should a security guard object to an individual's appearance of behaviour, they would need to walk less than 20 metres to be on a Camden adopted street. In so doing they would be outside of the control of the estate. It was argued that this would make any over-zealous estate management pointless.

22 At the time of writing (December 2015), Camden council had not exercised its right to adopt the street network. The authors consider this to be a serious omission of responsibility on the part of the council. The option will expire once the development is completed.

23 In fact, the Green Party did take this seat in the May 2006 local elections, but it is unlikely that this was linked to the King's Cross scheme.

24 Camden development control subcommittee report, Para 14.3.30, March 2006.

25 Camden development control subcommittee report, Para 14.3.31, March 2006.

26 Interview with Andre Gibbs, 4 November 2015.

27 Small rooftop turbines, solar thermal, ground source heat pumps and use of biofuel boilers were also part of the package. Camden development control subcommittee report, Para 14.3.32, March 2006.

28 It should be said that TfL has now matured into an effective transport authority.

29 Interview with David Lunts, GLA, 10 November 2015 and interview with Camilla Ween, 24 November 2015. The tram went to the wire with last minute meetings between Argent and TfL lawyers. Before agreeing not to direct refusal to the scheme, Livingstone asked the question as to whether TfL was happy with the compromise arrangements.

30 In 2008, when Argent went back to TfL to agree the operational details, TfL decided it did not want to pursue the offer. Interview with Camilla Ween, 24 November 2015.

31 The provision in the scheme was 0.47 spaces per house. Since the consent was granted the demand for residential parking in central London has dropped dramatically. As a result, Argent has built far less parking – an average of 0.25–0.3 spaces per house.

32 Introduced in 1998, this government-funded programme was aimed at giving children in poor neighbourhoods a better start in life in terms of education, healthcare and family support programmes.

33 N Glass, 'Sure Start: The Development of an Early Intervention Programme for Young Children in the United Kingdom', Children and Society, Vol 13, 1999.

34 To emphasise this point, Madelin claims that Argent saw no tangible sign of the £750,000 that they contributed to Islington council for the upgrading of York Way and Copenhagen Street. Interview with Roger Madelin, 5 October 2015.

35 Westminster and Kingsway College provides vocational training for 16–18-year-olds and adults.

36 Interview with Robert Evans, Argent, 6 November 2015.

37 Interview with Robert Evans, Argent, 6 November 2015.

38 Interview with Roger Madelin, 20 October 2015.

39 Now Cushman and Wakefield DTZ.

40 Interview with Robert Evans, Argent, 6 November 2015.

41 Interview with Roger Madelin, 20 October 2015. The main areas where Argent felt it benefited was Camden council's agreement to fit-out the school and leisure centre. In strict negotiating terms Argent would probably have accepted these costs but there was no planning justification for it to do so.

42 Roger Fisher and William Ury, Getting to Yes (Random House Business Books, 3rd edition, May 2011) and Roger Fisher and Danny Ertel, Getting Ready to Negotiate (Penguin Random House, August 1995).

43 Tanya Alfredson and Azeta Cungu, 'Negotiation Theory and Practice: A Review of the Literature', FAO Policy Learning Programme 7, EASYPol Module 17,9 Food and Agriculture Organization of the United Nations, FAO, January 2008. http://www.fao.org/docs/up/easypol/550/4-5_nogtiation_background_paper_179en.pdf (5 October 2015).

44 Ibid.

45 Leonard Susskind, Robert H Mnookin, Lukasz Rozdeiczer and Boyd Fuller. 'What we have learned about teaching multi-party negotiation', Negotiation Journal 21(3), 2005: 395-408.

46 Interview with Robert Evans, Argent, 6 November 2015.

7: Community consultation

1 The SCI is a statutory document that is part of the local development plan, and was introduced in the Planning and Compulsory Purchase Act 2004. Local authorities must explain in their SCI how the public will be involved in the preparation of local development plan documents. (PPS 12) Camden's first SCI was adopted in 2006. A revised document was published in July 2011. http://www.camden.gov.uk/ccm/content/environment/planning-and-built-environment/two/planning-policy/local-development-framework/revised-statement-of-community-involvement-2015/ (accessed 27 January 2016).

2 'Community Involvement in Planning: The Government's Objectives' (2004), para 3.18, p15.

3 Argent, 'Statement of Community Involvement', Document 1 – The Story of Argent St George's Community Consultation on King's Cross, January 2004, p9.

4 London borough of Camden, King's Cross Opportunity Area Planning and Development Brief, December, 2004, section 1.5.2 and 1.5.3.

5 London borough of Camden, Key Issues UDP Consultation Paper, July 2001.

6 Argent, Principles for a Human City, July 2001.

7 Argent, Parameters for Regeneration, December 2001.

8 London borough of Camden, King's Cross Camden's Vision, June 2002.

9 Argent, A Framework for Regeneration, August 2002.

10 Argent, Framework Findings – an interim report on the consultation response to A Framework for Regeneration (June 2003).

11 London Borough of Camden, Draft Planning and Development Brief for the King's Cross Opportunity Area, September 2003.

12 London Borough of Camden, Executive Report on King's Cross Opportunity Area Draft Planning Brief, 3 September 2003.

13 London Borough of Camden, King's Cross Central, Officer Report, 2004, Paras 3.2.16–3.2.21.

14 Argent, Statement of Community Involvement, Document 1 – The Story of Argent St George's Community Consultation on King's Cross, January 2004, p9.

15 Camden council did not archive the consultation reports when it moved to its new offices in 2014.

16 Robert Evans, 'Planning and the People Problem', Journal of Planning Law, Issue 13, 2008, p92, and interview with Robert Evans, 20 November 2015.

17 Top in the analysis of consultations by Fluid were 'safe' and 'clean' new spaces.

18 London Borough of Camden, King's Cross Central, Officer Report, 2004, Paras 3.2.25–3.2.61.

19 Local schools were engaged through a consultation game, Urban Carpet, developed by architectural agency Leitwerk Ltd.

20 Statutory consultees for planning applications are: British Waterways, Commission for Architecture and the Built Environment, Civil Aviation Authority, Department for Transport, Environment Agency, English Heritage, Garden History Society, Health and Safety Executive, Highways Agency, Greater London Authority and Transport for London, Natural England, National Amenity Societies (including Ancient Monuments Society, the Council for British Archaeology, the Georgian Group, the Society for the Protection of Ancient Buildings, the Victorian Society and Twentieth Century Society), National Air Control Transport Services and Operators of Officially Safeguarded Civil Aerodromes, Rail Network Operators, Sport England and Theatres Trust.

21 Planning Aid for London is an independent service which offers an advice and information service using volunteers – qualified planners and legal specialists.

22 Argent (King's Cross) Ltd, Revised Development Specification, Annex F, Main Site Revised Development Specification, Summary of Scheme Revisions and Refinements, September 2005. https://www.kingscross.co.uk/media/Main_Site_Rev_Develop_Spec.pdf (accessed 28 November 2015).

23 KXCAAC, Respecting the Railwaylands, King's Cross Conservation Area Advisory Committee, November 2005.

24 Interview with David Partridge, managing partner of Argent, 2 November 2015.

25 Robert Evans, 'Planning and the People Problem', Journal of Planning Law, Issue 13, 2008, p92.

26 Email correspondence with Michael Edwards, 5 May 2015.

27 Squatters occupying the Stanley and Culross Buildings had vacated the site prior to Argent's appointment in 2000. Interview with Roger Madelin, 20 October 2015.

28 See https://kxdf.wordpress.com/category/purpose-/

29 KXRLG 'King's Cross Development Forum,' Network, Summer 2005, p3.

30 Phil Allemendinger, New Labour and Planning: From New Right to New Left (London: Routledge, 2011, pp70–76 and 85–89.

31 Government Office for London, Strategic Guidance for London Planning Authorities, Regional Planning Guidance (RPG3), May 1996.

32 Planning Inspectorate, Inspector's Report, Chapter 13 – King's Cross Opportunity Area.

33 Mayor of London, The London Plan, 2004, Para 5.37.

34 Interview with Michael Edwards (Bartlett School, University College and Member of KXRLG), 19 March 2015.

35 M Edwards, K MacDonald, P Newman and A Thornley, 'A vision for London,' The Crisis of London, ed. A Thornley (London: Routledge, 1992, pp185–201).

36 Stale Holgersen and Havard Haarstad, 'Class, Community and Communicative Planning: Urban Redevelopment at King's Cross, London', Antipode Vol 41, No 2, 2009, pp348–370.

37 London Borough of Camden, King's Cross Central Development – Initial Survey of Consultation Results (London: London Borough of Camden, 2005) p9.

38 At Coin Street, land had been vested with a community-owned development trust (Coin Street Community Builders) by the Greater London Council in 1986.

39 T Brindley, Community Roles in Urban Regeneration: New Partnerships on London's South Bank, City 4(3), 2000, pp363-377, Cited in: Michael Edwards, 'King's Cross: renaissance for whom?', in Urban Design, Urban Renaissance and British Cities, ed. John Punter, London: Routledge, Chapter 11. Reproduced by permission of Taylor & Francis Books UK.

40 Phil Allemendinger, New Labour and Planning: From New Right to New Left, Routledge, London, 2011, pp70–76 and 85–89.

41 Interview with Michael Edwards (Bartlett School, University College and Member of KXRLG), 19 March 2015.

42 ibid.

43 ibid.

44 Michael Edwards, 'King's Cross: renaissance for whom?', in Urban Design, Urban Renaissance and British Cities, ed. John Punter, London: Routledge, 2009, Chapter 11. Reproduced by permission of Taylor & Francis Books UK.

45 Interview with Michael Edwards (Bartlett School, University College and Member of KXRLG), 19 March 2015.

46 Government Office for London, London Councils and London First (supported by Argent, British Land and London Communications Agency), Connecting Councillors with Strategic Planning Applications: A Good Practice Guide for London, November 2007.

47 Barker Review of Land Use Planning Final Report, December 2006, para 5.16. This aimed to achieve an improved framework for the delivery of major infrastructure projects, a simpler national policy framework and decision-making processes focused on outcomes. https://www.gov.uk/government/uploads/system/uploads/attachment_data/file/228605/0118404857.pdf (accessed 28 January 2016).

48 Local Spatial Planning, Planning Policy Statement 12, June 2008, advocates local planning authorities and others working together in this way.

49 Robert Evans, 'Planning and the People Problem', Journal of Planning Law, Issue 13, 2008, p95.

50 Community Involvement in Planning: The Government's Objectives (2004).

51 Phil Allemendinger, New Labour and Planning: From New Right to New Left, London: Routledge, 2011, pp70–76 and 85–89.

8: The decision

1 The practice is less clearcut. There have been many cases of councils where a new council political administration has had a clear-out of its senior officers. The checks and balances that exist at central government level are weaker at local level.

2 The Widdecombe Report, The Conduct of Local Authority Business, London: HMSO, 1986.

3 Interview with Anne Doherty, head of planning at Camden council (2002–11), 5 November 2015.

4 The problem had surfaced when it was discovered that the south portico had been rebuilt in the wrong limestone. Although clearly noticeable, the question was whether it would be in the public interest for Camden to take enforcement action to try to have it demolished and rebuilt. This action would have closed the Great Court for a lengthy period and would have cost the museum a considerable amount of money. As it was, legal advice confirmed that the precise wording of the planning consent was not precise enough to guarantee that Camden council would have won the case.

5   Michael Edwards, 'We need a rethink over KX', Camden New Journal, 22 February 2007, p24.

6   Interview with Michael Edwards (Bartlett School, University College and Member of KXRLG), 19 March 2015.

7   GOL, London Councils and London First, supported by Argent, British Land and London Communications Agency, Connecting Councillors with Strategic Planning Applications: A Good Practice Guide for London, November 2007.

8   Barker Review of Land Use Planning, final report, December 2006, para 5.16.

9   Nolan Report, Third Report of the Committee on Standards in Public Life, July 1997.

10   White Paper Modern Local Government in Touch with Local People, July 1998.

11   GOL, London Councils and London First, Connecting Councillors with Strategic Planning Applications: A Good Practice Guide for London, November 2007.

12   Robert Evans, 'Planning and the People Problem', Journal of Planning Law, Issue 13, 2008.

13   The Camden Labour Party, separate from the council.

14   Interview with Dr Jane Roberts DBE, 21 September 2015.

15   The Camden New Journal was a source of many critical articles about the council. Its coverage on King's Cross was initially relatively neutral but later became hostile.

16   Since this period, successive chairs of the subcommittee have taken a completely different line. The committee, at the time of writing (2015) chaired by councillor Heather Johnson, is well-informed of current major applications through: briefings with developers, often in open public meetings; pre-meeting briefings of the committee, with developer presentations and plans; quarterly officer briefing on all major 'live' applications; regular email updates on specific high-profile schemes; telephone and other informal conversations between the chair and officers as required.

17   It was not possible to interview Brian Woodrow for this book, as he died in May 2015.

18   In an interview with councillor Sue Vincent, 26 October 2015, she recalled a rumour (untrue) that was circulating at the time that senior planning officers had been on holiday with Argent staff. This deliberately scurrilous rumour was intended to undermine the integrity of senior council officers.

19   Interview with Sue Vincent, 26 October 2015.

20   Ed Dorrell, 'King's Cross future under threat', Architects' Journal, 2 September 2004, p4.

21   '[...] other Labour groups in London would not have tolerated this behavior and would have removed him from the subcommittee', interview with Jane Roberts, 21 September 2015.

22   All the dates and quotes are taken from the decision letter of the Adjudication Panel for England, 20 December 2006.

23   The Adjudication Panel for England, Decision Report, Case Ref: APE 0352 Hearing Date: 25, 26 October and 12, 13 December 2006.

24   Interview with Sue Vincent, 26 October 2015.

25   Interview with Dr Jane Roberts DBE, 21 September 2015.

26   On 22 September 2004.

27   Letter from Roger Madelin to Moira Gibbs, chief executive of Camden, 12 November 2004.

28   The council's monitoring officer, usually the borough solicitor, has specific powers to intervene, irrespective of any political mandate, in the event of wrongdoing or inappropriate behaviour.

29   Councillor Woodrow's case was eventually heard by the Standards Board in October and December 2006. Its decision letter of the 20 December concluded that, 'the breach is at the low end of seriousness [...] taking into account that he concedes with the benefit of hindsight that he would not again behave in the way he did'. The tribunal decided to impose no sanction, but since the planning decision had been taken eight months earlier, this was no longer of relevance.

30   Interview with Sue Vincent, 26 October 2015.

31   Camden New Journal, 2 March 2006.

32   Interview with Theo Blackwell, 2 October 2015.

33   The anti-social behaviour order was introduced in the Crime and Disorder Act 1998. It was a civil order made against a person who had been shown to have engaged in anti-social behaviour, and was designed to correct minor incidents that would not ordinarily warrant criminal prosecution, through restricting behaviour, eg by prohibiting a return to a certain area.

34   An internal inquiry had concluded that councillor Woodrow

NOTES

should take no part in the decision-making process.

35 'SOKX! (Save our King's Cross)', Camden New Journal, 9 March 2006.

36 Interview with Mike Greene, 22 October 2015.

37 ibid.

38 Interview with Heather Johnson, 25 September 2015.

39 This was largely due to the political fallout from the Iraq war and a focused, and a not entirely accurate Liberal Democrat campaign to save Kentish Town Baths from closure (Labour never planned to close the Baths!). Labour lost six local seats to the Liberal Democrats, who were able to form a coalition with the Conservatives.

40 It was seen as Bishop's personal project. After the borough solicitor, Bishop was apparently 'second on the Conservative's list of officers to remove', but the briefing convinced the Conservatives that they could work with him. Interview with Mike Greene, 22 October 2015.

41 Under the The Civil Procedure (Amendment No 4) rules, 2013, which came into force in July 2013, the time limit for filing a claim has been reduced from three months to six weeks. http://www.out-law.com/en/articles/2013/june/reforms-to-cut-the-judicial-review-period-will-come-into-force-next-month/ (accessed 25 October 2015).

42 Richard Osley, 'Round one to King's Cross Refuseniks', Camden New Journal, 29 March 2007. http://www.thecnj.com/camden/032907/news032907_09.html (accessed 25 October 2015).

43 Interview with Robert Evans, Argent, 6 November 2015.

44 Richard Osley, 'High Court to Test King's Cross Plan', Camden New Journal, 15 February 2007, p2.

45 R (on the application of AFP King's Cross Railway Lands Group) v London Borough of Camden Administrative Court (Sullivan J), judgement by Mr Justice Sullivan in the High Court of Justice Queen's Bench Division, Administrative Court, EWHC 1515 (Admin), 25 May 2007.

46 Planning Policy Statement 3: Housing, PPS3 replaced previous government policy guidance in DETR Circular 6 of 98: Planning and Affordable Housing, and Planning Policy Guidance 3: Housing (PPG3), November 2006.

47 Judgement by Mr Justice Sullivan in the High Court of Justice Queen's Bench Division, Administrative Court, EWHC 1515 (Admin), 25 May 2007.

48 Michael Edwards, 'Think Again on King's Cross? No Chance!' Network, KXRLG October 2008, p6. http://www.kxrlg.org.uk/group/Network.Oct2008.pdf (accessed 6 July 2015).

49 The only exception to this was the Arsenal development that went to full council.

50 Interview with Steve Hitchins, 26 January 2016.

51 Phil Allemendinger, New Labour and Planning: From New Right to New Left (London: Routledge, 2011), pp70–76 and 85-89.

52 'Planning Inspectorate Report on Triangle Site', 16 May 2008, case APP/X5210/A/07/2051898, paragraph 7.2. http://www.kxrlg.org.uk/inquiry/08-07-22InspectorReport.pdf (accessed 14 November 2015).

53 Interview with Heather Johnson, chair of Camden development control subcommittee, 25 September 2015.

9: Building King's Cross Central

1 Peter Bishop left Camden council in 2007, therefore the narrative in Chapter 9 relies on interviews with Camden's current planning officers and with the developer.

2 Vacant possession is the right of a purchaser to exclusive use of a property on completion of the sale, any previous occupant having moved out.

3 The Transport Act, 1947.

4 Architect John McAslan + Partners' canopy took its geometry from the Great Northern Hotel and its structural support from a single piling point by the station. An arcade was constructed on the ground floor of the hotel to address a pinch point next to the taxi rank and allow a public thoroughfare when the station was closed. English Heritage approved the scheme (see Chapter 5).

5 And in accordance with the recommendations of The Fennell Report, Secretary of State for Transport, November 1988.

6 Interview with Michael Hurn, 23 October 2015.

7 Interview with Robert Evans, Argent, 21 October 2015.

8 The scheme is being developed by the King's Cross Central Limited Partnership (KCCP). This comprises: Argent (owning 50 per cent through Argent King's Cross Limited Partnership), London and Continental Railways Limited (LCR), with a 36.5 per cent interest; and DHL Supply Chain (formerly Exel), with a 13.5 per cent stake. In January 2016, LCR sold its stake to an Australian pension fund.

9 The Central London Partnership was a non-profit organisation that acted as a facilitator bringing the public and private sectors together to improve central London.

10 Interview with Roger Madelin, 6 November 2015.

11 The Homes and Communities Agency (HCA) is an executive non-departmental public body sponsored by the government's

Department for Communities and Local Government. It regulates social housing providers and helps create successful communities by making more homes and business premises available. https://www.gov.uk/government/organisations/homes-and-communities-agency (accessed 14 November 2015).

12 Planning performance agreements, now common practice, are agreed voluntarily between an applicant and the local planning authority prior to the application being submitted. They can be a useful focus of pre-application discussions, and for agreeing timetables. A charge can be made by the local planning authority on the developer to cover staff cost. www.planningportal.gov.uk (accessed 25 October 2015).

13 Argent St George, Principles for a Human City, July 2001.

14 This section is based on an interview with Anna Strongman, Argent, 30 October 2015.

15 Michael Pinsky and Stephanie Delcroix. http://delcroixpinsky.com/projects/relay/ (accessed 31 October 2015).

16 Identified Flying Object by Jacques Rival. http://delcroixpinsky.com/projects/relay/jacques-rival/ (accessed 31 October 2015).

17 Across the Buildings. http://delcroixpinsky.com/projects/relay/felicevarini/ (accessed 31 October 2015).

18 Of Soil and Water: King's Cross Pond Club, designed by architects Ooze (Eva Pfannes and Sylvain Hartenberg) and artist Marjetica Potrč. http://delcroixpinsky.com/projects/relay/marjetica-potrc-ooze/ (accessed 31 October 2015).

19 Skip Garden. https://www.kingscross.co.uk/skip-garden (accessed 31 October 2015).

20 It is part-funded by the Big Lottery Fund, and the site and materials have been provided by KCCP, BAM Nuttall, Carillion and Kier.

21 Skip Garden Kitchen. https://www.kingscross.co.uk/skip-garden-kitchen (accessed 31 October 2015).

22 This section is based on an interview with Anne Hughes, centre director, King's Cross Recruit, 18 November 2015.

23 This was a later amendment to the planning permission (2010) and is located outside the St Paul's Viewing Corridor.

24 Urban Land Institute Case Study: King's Cross – London, United Kingdom, July 2014. http://uli.org/case-study/uli-case-study-kings-cross-london-united-kingdom/

25 The planning permission had in fact expired in 2003 and in theory Camden council could have taken enforcement action to have had it demolished. In advance of its replacement this would not have been popular with rail passengers.

26 Estate agents in Islington are now referring to properties in up-market Barnsbury as 'King's Cross borders', a proximity that they would have denied vehemently less than five years previously.

27 King's Place includes two new concert halls, two art galleries, a bar, café and restaurant, and seven floors of office space currently occupied by The Guardian newspaper.

28 Interview with Frances Wheat, assistant director regeneration and planning for Camden council, 23 October 2015.

10: Conclusions

1 The KCCP is expending around £1.25 million a day in King's Cross and is likely to continue at this rate for the next three years. Interview with David Partridge, 2 November 2015.

2 Jones Lang LaSalle, Occupier Survey, August 2015.

3 World Bank, IBRD, IDA, King's Cross Regeneration Program, London, United Kingdom – Relevance to the Chinese Railway Sector. Hiroaki Suzuki, Jin Murakami, Yu-Hung Hong and Beth Tamayose, Financing Transit-Oriented Development with Land Values, World Bank Group, Urban Development Series 93686, 2015, pp147–157. http://www-wds.worldbank.org/external/default/WDSContentServer/IW3P/IB/2015/01/14/000406484_20150114091425/Rendered/PDF/936860PUB00ISB0TransportDevLV0final.pdf (accessed 25 November 2015).

4 Interview with Peter Freeman, 20 November 2015.

5 This is impossible to calculate with any accuracy but over the six years probably amounted to over £3 million.

6 Interview with Robert Evans, Argent, 20 November 2015.

7 Rowan Moore, 'All Hail the New King's Cross', The Observer, The New Review, 19 October 2014, pp28 and 29.

8 Roger Madelin, email, 23 November 2015.

9 Pete Jefferys, 'The Affordable Homes Programme 2015-2020: Policy Briefing Note', Shelter. https://england.shelter.org.uk/professional_resources/policy_and_research/policy_library/policy_library_folder/policy_brief_affordable_homes_programme (accessed 30 November 2015).

10 Mayor of London, 'Can housing associations afford affordable housing?' 18 November 2015. https://www.london.gov.uk/media/assembly-press-releases/2015/11/can-housing-associations-afford-affordable-housing (accessed 30 November 2015).

11 The Growth and Infrastructure Act (26 April 2013) – Affordable Housing Modification (clause 7). http://www.legislation.gov.uk/ukpga/2013/27/contents/enacted (accessed 30 November 2015).

12 Nick Mathiason, Will Fitzgibbon, George Turner, 'The Housing Crisis Thousands of affordable homes axed', The Bureau of Investigative Journalism. https://www.thebureauinvestigates.com/2013/09/18/thousands-of-affordable-homes-axed// (accessed 30 November 2015).

13 Housing and Planning Bill, Second Reading, 2 November 2015.

14 Danielle Aumord, 'How has England fared in building affordable homes for rent?' The Guardian, 5 November 2015. http://www.theguardian.com/housing-network/2015/nov/05/england-building-affordable-homes-rent-section-106 (accessed 30 November 2015).

15 Interview with Robert Evans, Argent, 20 November 2015 – calculation based on 8 million square feet gross floor space at £10 per square foot.

16 Judith Evans, 'King's Cross Redevelopment Stake Sold by Government to Pension Fund for £371m', Financial Times, 16 January 2016.

Appendix 1

1 London Borough of Camden, King's Cross section 106 agreement, final version, 2006.

Appendix 2

1 Urban Land Institute Case Study: King's Cross – London, United Kingdom, July 2014. http://uli.org/case-study/uli-case-study-kings-cross-london-united-kingdom/ (accessed 1 February 2016).

2 Ibid.

3 David Partridge, Making Cities – Examples of Urban Development, 2015.

4 Ibid.

5 Ibid.

LIST OF ACRONYMS

BR	British Railways
BWB	British Waterways Board
CABE	Commission on Architecture and the Built Environment
CHP	Combined Heat and Power
CIL	Community Infrastructure Levy
CTRL	Channel Tunnel Rail Link
DCLG	Department for Communities and Local Government
DfT	Department for Transport
EIA	Environmental Impact Assessment
HCA	Homes and Community Agency
GLA	Greater London Authority
GNH	Great Northern Hotel
KCCP	King's Cross Central Limited Partnership
KCP	King's Cross Partnership
KXCAAC	King's Cross Conservation Area Advisory Committee
KXCD	King's Cross Community Development Trust
KCIG	King's Cross Impact Group
KXDF	King's Cross Development Forum
KXRLG	King's Cross Railways Lands Group
LCA	London Communications Agency
LCR	London and Continental Railways
LDA	London Development Agency
LUL	London Underground Limited
NFC	National Freight Corporation
PAL	Planning Aid for London
RSL	Registered Social Landlord
SCI	Statement of Community Involvement
SPG	Supplementary Planning Guidance
SRB	Single Regeneration Budget
TfL	Transport for London
UDP	Unitary Development Plan
UNESCO	United Nations Educational, Scientific and Cultural Organization

INDEX

Note: page numbers in italics refer to figures; page numbers in bold refer to tables.

acronyms 221
adoption of the public realm 116–17, 177
affordable housing 107–15
    cascade agreement 111, 176
    completion *113*, 185
    construction 175
    council nomination rights 112–13
    definitions 109–10
    government policy change 201
    grant funding 111
    historical perspective 108
    judicial review regarding 166
    opportunity cost 115
    percentage of 110–12, 128
    quantum **114**
    requirement for 63, 64, 65, 67
    sustainable lettings policy 114
    'Triangle' site 167
    types of 110
    variations to the planning consent 177
Allies and Morrison 54, 73, 86, *172*
AMEC 40
ancillary uses **68**, 69
'another piece of London' 54, *55*, 79
anti-development campaigns 44–5
Architects' Journal (AJ) 157–8
architecture 198–9
area of special character 66
Argent 39–41
    breakup of partnership with St George 106–7
    development objectives 191
    initial business plan **68**, 69
    Principles for a Human City 55, 116, 137, 178
Argent St George 40–1, 42, **51**, 52, 58, 106–7
artist-in-residence 179
Arts Advisory Panel 179
Arts Council 179
arts venue 178–9
artworks *178–9*, 179, *180–1*, 185
Arup 33, 92, 96
AustralianSuper 202

Balfe Street 25, 26
Bangladeshi community 141, 142, 144
Barker Review 155
Barnsbury 45
Bartlett School of Architecture 181, *184*
bathing pool *180–1*
Battery Park *192*
Bemerton estate 45, 97, 187–8
Berkeley Homes 40, 106
Berlin 50
biodiversity 142
BNP Paribas 175

Boulevard 79, *80*, 82, *88*, 89, *91*, 92–3, 176
Brindleyplace 39, 40, 53, 54, 73
British Land 190
British Rail 29, 42
British Railways (BR) 25, 170
British Telecom Pension Fund 40, 41
Broadgate 26, 29, *192*
building heights 67, 69, 84, 142, **208**
built form 142
bus depot 122
business plan **68**, 69
business start ups 125, 127

cafés, bars and shops 177–8, 181, *184*
Caledonian Road 97, 188
Caledonian ward 45
Cally Rail Group 141
Camden 44–7, **46**
Camden Civic Society 141
Camden council
    change of political control 164, 168
    Community Planning Brief 26
    construction oversight 49
    consultation strategy 136–7
    councillor engagement 47–50
    decision-making structure 46–7, 196
    development control subcommittee 47, 50, 149, 152, 154–64
    Draft Planning and Development Brief 137
    as housing developer 187
    housing strategy 108
    key councillors **152**
    King's Cross – Camden's Vision 56, 60, 137
    King's Cross – Towards an Integrated City 137
    negotiating tactics 58–9
    negotiating team 50, 51
    new town hall 175
    objectives for the site 56, 67, 190–1
    officer-councillor interface 152–3
    policy framework 63–5
    policy objectives 195
    political management 168, 196
    politicians and officers **51**
    sale of old offices 187
    success at planning appeals 57
    sustainable lettings policy 114
Camden Friends of the Earth 141, 142
Camden Green Party 141, 142
Camden New Journal 161, 162
Camden Primary Care Trust 140
Camden Square Conservation Area Advisory Committee 142
Camden Square Tenants and Residents' Association 141
Camden Talks 140
Camley Street Natural Park (CSNP) 74, 142
Canary Wharf 26, 54, 79, 97, 116, *192*
car parking 122–3, 177, **207**
Caravan 177
Carillion 182

central government role 193–4
central spine 78, 79–80 (see also Boulevard)
Channel Tunnel Rail Link (CTRL) 26, 30, 32, 33, 35, 171
child density 112
Chinese community 141, 144
City Thameslink see Thameslink
coal and fish offices 62, 74
Coin Street Community Builders 29, 147
commercial floor space **68**, 107, 108, 141
Commission for Architecture and the Built Environment (CABE) 84, 86, 93
'community chest' 127
community consultation 134–50
　consultation processes 137–8, 139–40
　consultation responses 140–2
　consultation strategy 136–7
　influence of 138–9, 140, 143
　lessons learnt 199
　participation 'ladder' **148**, 199
　policy constraints 145–6
　political considerations 146
　requirement for 15–16
community development trust 147
community facilities 142, 205 (see also leisure facilities)
Community Housing Association 141
Community Infrastructure Levy (CIL) 11, 201
community opposition 25, 26, 29, 144, 145
Community Planning Brief 26
community programme 181–2
community safety 142
comparative data **207–8**
connectivity to the wider area 80, 94–101
consensus building 58–9, 77, 147, 199
conservation see historic buildings
conservation areas 61, 62, 65, 74
construction 173–6
Construction Training Centre 125–6, 177, 182
consultation processes 137, 147–8, 199
Copenhagen Street 80, 96–7
Create King's Cross 141
Crick Institute 187
Cross River Tram 119–22
Cubitt Park 140
Culross Buildings 22, 62, 69, 74, 89–92, 103, 141
Culross Hall 74
cycle parking/storage 122, 177

Department for Communities and Local Government (DCLG) 57, 171
Department for Transport (DfT) 171–2
Design for London 8
design parameters 77
design review 84, 86, 93
design standards 67–8
development parcels 79, 80, 86
development partner selection 39–41
development sector 14–15
district heating scheme 118
DTZ 128

Eastern Coal Drops 22, 74, 75
EDAW 77, 97
education 48, **68**, 124, 205 (see also primary school)
employment 48, 49, 124–7, 182–3, 205
energy centre 118
energy performance 118
English Heritage 61, 69, 86, 87, 92, 191, 198
environmental performance 117–18
environmental sustainability 142
estate management events 178–82
Eurostar terminal 26, 30, 33, 36, 41
Euston Road 88
evaluation 190–3
events 179
Exel 25, 38, 40, 107

family units 112, 183
Filling Station 181, *184*
financial crisis (2008) 174
financial data **209**
financial model 194–5
financing considerations 33, 35, 39, 40, 41, 175–6
Fish and Coal 62, 74
floor space 67, **68**, 107, 108, 141
Fluid 137
Foster, Norman 26, 28, 33, 36, 42
Framework Findings 137
A Framework for Regeneration 137, 139
Frank Barnes School for the Deaf 176
Friends of the Earth 141, 142

gasholders 22, 61, 74, *88*, 140, 205
Gasometer Park *186*
German Gymnasium 22, 74, 178
Global Generation 181
Goodsway 92, 94, 99, 181
Google offices 183
Government Office for London (GOL) 31, 165
government role 193–4
grain 79, 86
Granary Building 22, 74, 80, 92, 174–5, 178
Granary Park 97
Granary Square 92, 93, 94, 96, 98, 99, 101
　completion 176, 179, *182*, 202
Great Northern Hotel 87–9
　collonading 119
　history *21*, 74
　lease to boutique hotel 172
　listed building consents 173
　proposed demolition 80, 86
Great Northern Railway (GNR) 19
Greater London Authority (GLA) 61, 63, 110, 111, 117, 122, 201 (see also mayor of London)
green chain and corridor *66*
Green Party 141, 142
green spaces 78, *101* (see also parks)
ground floor land uses 93, *100*
Growth and Infrastructure Act 2013 201

INDEX

Handyside Park 140
health centre 124, 205
health clinic 177
health impact assessment 140
heritage see historic buildings
Hermes 40, 41
historic buildings 74–6, *75*
    consultation responses 141–2
    lessons learnt 198
    refurbishment 61, 89–90, 103, 183
historical perspective 18–25
hoardings as art *185*
'Homebuy' 111
Homes and Community Agency (HCA) 175, 176
'hoodie' test 116
housing (*see also* affordable housing; student housing)
    consultation responses 141, 146
    density 108, 201, **207**
    family units and child density 112, 183
    historical perspective 22
    quantum **68**, 107–8, 183, **207**
    requirement for 67
Housing and Planning Bill 201
housing associations 201
housing grants 110, 111, 175, 176, 200–1
Hyperion 25, 26, 38

information provision 137
intermediate housing 110, *113*, 167, 176
international interest 191
Islington 45, 46, 49
    connectivity with 77, 80, 94, 96–7
    conservation areas *62*
    regeneration 187–8
    'Triangle' site 59, *60*, **110**, **114**, 150, 166–7
Islington council 59–60, 140, 166–7
Islington Society 141

joint ventures 26, 39, 40, 177–8
Jones Lang LaSalle 39, 190
Joseph Rowntree Foundation 130
Jubilee Wharf 187
judicial review 150, 165, 173

key worker housing **110**, 112
King's Cross – Camden's Vision 56, 60, 137
King's Cross – Towards an Integrated City 137
King's Cross Business 141
King's Cross Central
    boundary 62, *66*, 75
    location map *3*
King's Cross Central Limited Partnership (KCCP) 2, 174–88, 191
King's Cross Community Development Trust (KXCDT) 140, 141, 142
King's Cross conservation area 61, 62
King's Cross Conservation Area Advisory Committee (KXCAAC) 90, 141, 142
King's Cross Development Forum (KVDF) 136, 137, 144–5

King's Cross Impact Group (KCIG) 49
King's Cross Partnership (KCP) 31, 125, 129
King's Cross Railway Lands Group (KXRLG) 4–5, 26, 31, 67, 131, 141, 143–8, 154–5, 165–6
King's Cross Recruit (KXR) 127, 182–3
King's Cross station
    history 19–20
    new curved concourse roof 88, 171
    new station concourse 29, *30*, 88, 171, 172, 194
    refurbishment 172
    site context 74
    station box beneath 29
    station concourse area 90
    station square 185–7
King's Cross Think Again Group 165, 166
King's Cross underground concourses 33, *34*, 49
King's Cross ward 63–4
King's Place 187

land ownership 25, 38, 193
land rights and wayleaves 170, 173
land transfers 170–3
land uses **207**
land valuation 29, 38, 41, 173, 194
landscape strategy 93
legibility 102
leisure facilities 99, 124, 142, 205 (*see also* recreational facilities)
Lend Lease 40, 41
lessons learnt 193–200
listed buildings 61, 65, 69, 74, *75* (*see also* historic buildings)
Local Development Framework 9, 135
Local Development Plan 10
local employment 48, 49, 124–7, 182–3, 205
Local Planning Authorities (LPAs) 10
London and Continental Railways (LCR) 31, 35, 36, 37, 38–9
    bus depot 122
    lessons learnt 195
    obtaining vacant possession 170
    sale of government stake in 202
    Stratford development 114–15
London Communications Agency (LCA) 41
London Development Agency (LDA) 175
London mayor see mayor of London
London Olympics 35, 38, 170–1, 193, 194
London Plan
    alignment of UDP to 10, 63, 65, 197
    car parking 122–3
    energy assessments 118
    housing targets 108, 110, 111
    King's Cross as opportunity area 145–6
London Regeneration Consortium (LRC) 26–31, 40, 41–2, 125
London Underground *see* underground concourses
London Underground Limited (LUL) 57, 172, 173
London Wildlife Trust 74, 142

Maiden Lane Estate 187
Manhattan Loft Corporation 37
    masterplan 72–103

role of 72–3, 198
Skidmore, Owings and Merrill (SOM) 27, 29, 42
Norman Foster's 28, 29, *30*, 42
first version 77–81
final version *100*, *101*, 102–3
masterplanning team 73
mayor of London 61, 63, 121–2, 164–5, 201 (see also Greater London Authority (GLA))
McAslan + Partners 88, 171
medical facilities 124, 177, 205
Metropolitan Railway 20
Metropolitan Walk 66
Midland Grand Hotel 20, 21
Midland Main Line *32*, 172
Midland Railway 20
mid-tenure housing 110, 111
minority groups 136
mixed community 115
mixed tenure **110**, 111, *186*
mixed use development 68, 69, 145, 183, 192, 194, **208**
Mott Macdonald 173

National Freight Corporation (NFC) 25
national interest 191
National Planning Policy Framework (NPPF) 10, 201
natural bathing pool *180–1*
negotiating process 52–6, 129–31, 196–7
negotiating tactics 56–63
negotiating teams 51–2, 196
Neighbourhood Renewal Strategy 45
neighbourhoods 109 (see also place making)
Network Rail 92, 171, 172, 173
night time economy 93, *100*
Nolan Report 155
Nolli plan 77
North Central One (NC1) 182, 185
North London Line 33
Northern ticket hall *34*, 172

office buildings 175–6, 183
office floor space **68**, 107, 108, 141, **207**
office values in Central London *192*
Olympics see London Olympics
open space see public open space

Pancras Road 173
Parabola Land Ltd 187
Parameters for Regeneration 137
parks 67, 80, 82, 101, 140, 183
participation 'ladder' **148**
partnership working 39, 52, 58, 106–7, 126, 196
personal relationships 199
perspectives 82, *85*
physical connections 94, 96–7
place making 177–82
planners' role 11–12
Planning Aid for London (PAL) 140
planning appeals 57, 58
planning application 152 (see also section 106 agreement)
approval of section 106 agreement 163–5
community consultation 139–43
decision 153, 160–4
development control subcommittee 154–64
hybrid application 65, 67, 188, 197
variations to the planning consent 176–7
planning constraints 145–6, 197
planning process 8–16, *134–5*, 197–8
planning system 9–11
implications of recent changes to 200
Plimsoll Viaduct 62
plot ratios **207**
policy constraints 145–6, 197
policy framework 63–5
policy objectives 49–50, 56, 67
political considerations
anti-development campaigns 44–5
community consultation 146
councillor engagement 47–50
decision-making structure 46–7
effect of 195–6
planning decisions 153, 161–4, 167–8
planning inquiries 58–9
political management 168, 196
social equality agenda 45–6
stakeholder management 131, 199
politicians' role 12–14
Porphyrios Associates 73, 76–7, 80, 86, 92
portable allotments 181, *184*
pre-application consultations 134–9
pre-school provision 176
primary school 124, 176, *186*
Principles for a Human City 55, 116, 137, 178
privately managed space 116, 177
project coordination 38
psychological connections 97, 99
public consultation see community consultation
public information 137
public inquiry 57, 150
public open space *66*, 78, 80, *88*, 92–3, 101
consultation responses 142
management and maintenance 116–17, 177
quantum **68**, **207**
public realm 67, 93, 115–17, 177, 205
public-private finance initiative (PFI) 33, 42

rail infrastructure 33, 36–8
Railtrack 31, 170
recreational facilities 99, 124, 142
recruitment centre 182
regeneration 26–31, 127, 161–2, 187–8, 190
Regeneration House 62, 74
Regent's Canal *66*, 74
canalside steps 93, *98*, 179
conservation area *62*
consultation responses 141–2
history 19, *22*
Regent's Network 142
Regional Policy Guidance (RPG) 108, 145

INDEX

Registered Social Landlords (RSLs) 108, 110
renewable energy 117
Resident Social Landlords 200
residential accommodation *see* housing
restaurants 177
retail **68**, 142, 177–8, 179, 183, **207**
Right to Buy 111, 201
Rosehaugh Stanhope 26, 30
Rowntree Foundation 112
Royal Institute of British Architects (RIBA) 185

schedule of accommodation 67
schools 124 (*see also* education; primary school)
section 106 agreement 11 (*see also* affordable housing)
    approval by development subcommittee 162–5
    calculating the value of 127–9, 131
    other planning benefits 123–7
    policy changes affecting 201
    summary 205–6
shared ownership/equity **110**, 111
Shaw Corporation 187
Single Regeneration Budget (SRB) 31, 125
site assembly 38–9
site context 74–6
site coverage and uses **208**
Skidmore, Owings and Merrill (SOM) 26, *27*, 29, 42
skills and recruitment centre 182
Skip Garden 181, *184*
social community fund *123*
social equality agenda 45–6, 127
social housing *see* affordable housing
social mix 109, 110–11, 112
social sustainability 109
Somali community 144
Somers Town 45, 57
    connecting with 94
    historical perspective 22
    regeneration 63–4, 187
Somers Town People Forum 142
squares *see* public open space
St George 40 (*see also* Argent St George)
St Pancras Chambers 36–7, 42, 74, **114**
St Pancras Hospital 187
St Pancras Square 92, 101
St Pancras station 33, 45, 74
    Barlow canopy *21*
    history 19, 20
    redesign 33, 36
St Pancras ward 45
stakeholders *8*, 49
    management of 58, 131, 199
Stanley Buildings 22, 74, 89, 92, 103, 141, 173
Stanton Williams 186
Statement of Community Involvement (SCI) 135
statistical data **46**, **68**, 183, **207**–**8**
statutory consultees 131, 139, 141
Stock Conversion and Investment Trust 25
strategic views *66*, 84, 176
street blocks *87*, 88

street grids 81, *82*, 84, 93
street scales *99*
student housing *113*, 114, **114**, 175, 176, 183
Supplementary Planning Guidance (SPG) 63
sustainability 109, 142
sustainable lettings policy 114
swimming pool and gym 99, 124

tall buildings 84, *89* (*see also* building heights)
Thameslink 35, 37–8, 96, 172
Three Dragons Report 110
tours of site 181
Towards an Integrated City 56
Townshend Landscape Architects 73, 93
training 182–3, 205
    for construction 125, 177, 182
tramway proposal 119–22
transport 119–23, 142, 205
Transport for London (TfL) 63, 87, 88, 119, 120–2, *122*
transport interchange 119
'Triangle' site 59, *60*, **110**, **114**, 150, 166–7
trust 199

underground and subway link *172*
underground concourses 33, *34*, 49, 88, 171
Union Railways 57
Unitary Development Plan (UDP) 63, 137
    alignment to London Plan 10, 63, 65, 197
    housing targets 64, 67, 108, 110
University of the Arts London (UAL) 174, 183
urban planning 76, 77

vacant possession 170
viewing corridors *66*, 84, 176
vision 54–6
visitor centre 181

walking times 120
West Paddington Partnership 126
Western Coal Drops 22, 62
Western ticket hall *34*
'The Wheel' 123, 126, 127
workshops (public consultation) 137
workspace 125
World Bank 191

York Way 29, 80, 84, 126

IMAGE CREDITS

Allies and Morrison   3, 22, 36, 37, 44, 60, 81, 82, 85, 88–90, 96, 98–100 (all), 115, 120, 121

Allies and Morrison/A–Z   55

Allies and Morrison, based on work by Design for London   8

Anderson-Terzic Partnership   **Front cover, 94–95 (top)**

Architect's Journal/Hellman   157

Argent   126, 134–135, 192 (both)

Argent/EDAW   32, 34, 62, 64, 66, 75, 91

Peter Bishop and Lesley Williams   viii–xi, 21 (bottom), 113, 118, 125, 136, 172 (both), 175, 186 (bottom), 187

Peter Bishop and Lesley Williams/Allies and Morrison   123

Foster + Partners   28, 30

Reproduced by permission of Historic England   20, 21 (top left), 25

JLL Research   190

John McAslan + Partners   171 (both)

London School of Economics   23

Miller Hare Limited   159

Ordnance Survey   18, 19, 24

Demetri Porphyrios   74, 80, 83, 87, 94–95 (bottom), 97

Demetri Porphyrios/Allies & Morrison   78, 79

Skidmore, Owings and Merrill LLP   27

John Sturrock   21 (top right), 53, 178–182 (all), 184 (both), 185 (both), 186 (top), 202

Robert Townsend   101